The Love Of Dangerous Men

A Secret History in Letters

Tony Nicholson

With best wishes
from
Tony

Published by Cavernwood Press

ISBN: 978-1-5272-1636-5

In memory of Grace and Colin

CONTENTS

ILLUSTRATIONS

Note on the Text

All words, phrases or sentences taken from Annie's letters are italicized.

This is a true story, based on extensive research. I have not included references here, but you can see them on my website:-
http://tonynicholsonbooks.com

The website also contains extra illustrations and sources, as well as a section on the story's enduring mysteries.

PROLOGUE

c/o Mr Burnett
No 1 Kings Cross Rd.
W.C.

My dear wife
My reason for not writing to you is that I did not think you would
care to hear from me.

For sixty years the letter had died its own kind of lingering death, decomposing and curling in the darkness, developing that dingy tan that only comes from decay. Yet as I fished it out from the surrounding rubbish I could see that it was stained by deeper things; soiled by human longing; a weary patina of rented rooms, yellowing wallpaper, drawn curtains and loneliness.

'Why do you never write?'

My reason for not writing to you is that I did not think you would
care to hear from me.

He squeezed her. 'Would it be asking too much', he hissed from behind the tight-lipped firmness of that first sentence, 'for you to try and control yourself and keep your voice down, so that we might at least conduct this conversation in private?'

As to my reasons for leaving you as I did I think we had better leave that to be discussed at some future time.

A file somewhere was closing. He was moving on.

I am very pleased to hear that you are getting well and strong & sincerely trust that you will soon be your old self again.

The tension began to ease as he stepped clear. Her illness had been a terrible bore but she was evidently on the mend and he might cast her off. He talked of a job in London and began edging towards *the needful*, the point in every letter when he tickled her for money and clothes.

Now if you really wish the past to be of the past, and feel disposed to assist me to get what is absolutely necessary to take a position that will be worth £2 a week to me, I will endeavour to be all that you may wish in the future.

The same old promises.

Should you feel disposed to assist me in this case (in spite of what has happened) it will be for a mutual benefit, and as soon as I am settled I will look for a suitable place for you to come to - in the meantime will consider what is best to be done re. furniture etc.

That final transformation: his petty cadging turning itself into a business proposition. *Should you feel disposed to assist me in this case* was nothing less than a rare opportunity, her final chance to back a winner.

Should you fail me in this case I shall go out East with <u>no intention</u> whatever of returning

I am
Your husband
Gus Bowen

Chapter 1: Attic

'I think you'd better come and look at this.'

We were lifting carpets and staring at the bruised face of floorboards.

'Dry rot?' I asked, prodding away at the timber and scratching my head.

'I think you'd better come and look at this.'

The voice again, this time louder and echoing down from the attic. I climbed the stairs and tried to prepare myself. He was standing beside a door leading into the roof eaves where a fierce December wind was slicing through the slates and making the little door seem anxious and agitated. I inched closer, he stretched out his hand, gave me a metal torch, and then smiled, 'See for yourself,' he said.

I knelt down, he held the door steady, and I fumbled with the torch. Finally, I forced myself into the darkness.

I had grown up with this house. It had been there in the corner of my eye when I ran to school and had imprinted itself on my childhood memory, so when I opened my first box of crayons and was asked to draw a house, I drew a doll's house with a door at the centre, a window either side, three windows above, and two wisps of smoke rising up in the languid air. And above it, the sky. Always

1

the blue sky. For what is a Georgian house if not a doll's house? It was there when I came back from college in the early 1970s and took a job as a postman.

The House

I walked up the drive, a clutch of letters in my hand, the early morning sun shimmering through the beech trees. At the side of the house, a door was wide open and I stared into a cool whitewashed passage running to the back where a second door gave views of the garden beyond. Splashes of red and yellow. Edna called it her 'tulip time'. And that was the moment I fell in love. Another twenty years and we were sinking everything we had after Jim and Edna decided to sell.

It seemed as though the two of them had spent a happy retirement camped out in the garden. There were photographs to prove it. Before we took possession of the house, I think it's safe to say that the photographs took possession of us. Jim and Edna dug out their family album and we gazed longingly at the images; strings of onions hanging glossy and plump in the old washhouse; Jim in a white collarless shirt glimpsed through the branches of an apple tree, mowing the lawn on a summer afternoon; Edna wrapped in a white sheet, doing an impish impression of a Greek statue. And every time we talked of buying and selling, they walked us into the garden. Nothing else was needed. The garden did its work.

We met Jim and Edna on the last day as they loaded up their belongings.

'Don't forget', Jim said as he ran his fingers through his hair and looked over our heads to the house, 'you're just stewards. One day you'll hand it on.' Part of me loved him for that, but then as the removal van veered round the corner, the house sank into a glum silence, like an abandoned dog, and I began to have doubts.

I flicked on the torch and crawled into the darkness. As the wind blew through the roof slates, I could feel the attic door fretting against me. The last golden eagle to fly across an English sky and think it could get away with it was shot down in the summer of 1917. Or so they say. I'm not entirely convinced. I think the old bird somehow dodged the shot and struggled north, taking refuge in our roof. How else could I explain it? Here, in the crumpled darkness between the partition wall and the chattering slates, it must have nursed its wounds and lived in brutal squalor. The size of the nest was unbelievable; straw and feathers scattered everywhere and mixed in amongst the carnage, mummified birds in different states of decomposition. Caught in the torch beam, the scene was monstrous. I moved the light from side to side, trying to find something reassuring, but all I could see was death and decay. Everything covered in an uncanny dust, silky in texture and strangely scented - part soot, part cobwebs, part something else.

'All of it,' he said, pointing to the darkness, 'all of it needs clearing before our lads start tomorrow.' The firm was scheduled to start treatment of the woodwork the next morning. 'Shouldn't take more than an hour.'

Overalls, thick balaclavas, plastic goggles, wet handkerchiefs, pink rubber gloves - we put on anything that might protect us. Finally, we took a deep breath and crawled into that little hole of ungodliness. No room for shovels or spades or anything like that, so everything had to be lifted by hand. Dead birds, broken glass, rotting paper, stained cloth, all feeling strangely alive through the rubber gloves. Handful by handful, we lifted the debris and pushed it through the door where it lay in heaps, waiting to be bagged. And all the while, we kept tightening the handkerchiefs across our faces, thinking they would protect us, but they never did. There was no protection from this. We finished after midnight and dumped the bags into an unloved corner of the garage.

The soft ticking of time.

Sunlight in the garden, daffodils blooming, the old hawthorn hedge growing fat and green. Somehow or other we had weathered the first winter, the winter that nearly broke us; the winter when the house fell vacant and looked bruised. Everything needed to be damp-proofed, so the interior plaster on the ground floor had to be hammered away to a height of three feet. Whenever we drove home on those winter nights and stepped through the door, the place looked forlorn. We gritted our teeth. Now that the walls were ruined, we may as well set about rewiring the place, and whilst we were at it, a new central heating system seemed a sensible option. So floorboards came out and holes gaped and the house sagged.

But somehow it never quite fell. We had come through. The central heating was working, the house warm, Nat King Cole was playing on the radio, sunlight was streaming through the windows, the world seemed to be blossoming again. Standing in a makeshift bedroom on that Spring morning, looking out through dusty glass, I saw the air swelling with leaves.

'I wonder what's in those bags?'

'What bags?' Gill asked.

'In the garage. The ones from the attic.'

'I thought you threw them out?'

I stared blankly at the trees. Why had the bags come back to haunt me on this Spring morning?

Gill climbed out of bed and looked at her husband. 'Have some breakfast first.'

'Just a quick look.'

Once inside the garage, I grabbed the nearest bag and dragged it into the sunshine. Sharp slivers of glass were cutting through its sides and spewing out the contents. Circling the heap, I began lifting torn flaps and squinting inside. Everything as I remembered it: an ugly mix of crumpled paper and stained cloth, broken glass and crockery, and every time I poked a finger into the squalor, I seemed to find a dead bird, its soiled feathers matted to the bone. So in truth, I don't know what drew me to the edge.

I reached down and fished it out. A Victorian photograph. A quick wipe across my sleeve and two ghosts appeared. The first stood before me in a three-quarter coat with a light waistcoat and watch chain hung across his belly. A bearded man, balding and probably in his forties, wearing light-coloured trousers with a stripe down the sides, and radiating a faint air of male menace. One arm was bent against a thickening waist and he presented himself to the world as a man who was not to be trifled with. The woman sat on a chair, wrapped in her own melancholy. A dark air of resignation enveloped her. I noticed how her jet-black hair was parted down the middle and brushed back with a glossy kind of severity.

The soft ticking of time. In the filth and squalor, dust and droppings, I had found something, and it was only then that I remembered what I had seen on that grim December night, but not seen at all; poignant faces staring out at me from mid-Victorian photographs; fat envelopes ripe with words; cheap Edwardian postcards covered in pencilled messages; neatly-folded newspaper cuttings . . . handbills . . . concert programmes . . .

When I came to my senses, there were faces everywhere, rising up from every level of the rubbish, all beseeching me. I spent the morning saving them, pulling them out like survivors, lining them up in neat rows on a hastily-improvised dustsheet draped across the lawn. And there I sat in the midst of this new kingdom like an astonished god. And when there were no more photographs to pluck, I went deeper, and then I found it.

It was filthy and crumpled, almost unreadable and pockmarked with dead insects; a grubby inconsequential piece of paper that would change my life. I held it against the soft afternoon light and saw for the first time that it was a letter. Brushing aside the last of the cobwebs and flicking off the dead insects, I started to read. *Dear Mrs. Bowen, Your kind grateful letter received last evening too late to answer.* The normal pleasantries about health and weather were dropped like coats to the floor and the writer rushed to the point, grabbing her reader by the shoulders. *Well dear friend I note all you said about Mr. Bowen and that vile woman.*

I steadied myself. *I am truly surprised at Mr. Bowen lowering himself in such a manner and making so little of his lawful wife . . .* More dirt had to be brushed away before the next bit could be read *. . . but there are some women that would tempt the best men born with their fascinating ways . . .* Two wood pigeons sat in the bay tree above my head cooing like lovers. *. . . . but you may depend, he will tire of her before long, the vile drunken hag.*

And so it started; the unplanned journey. Soon, there were more letters and more still. Incredibly, so much had survived. Like the tiny envelope I came across a few days later addressed to:

Miss Annie Johnson
North Road
Gainford
Near Darlington
England

I blew off the dust and the envelope fell open. Inside there was an invitation:

> *Mr. and Mrs. BOWEN present their*
>
> *Compliments to*
>
> M̲ r̲s̲ ̲ ̲J̲o̲h̲n̲s̲o̲n̲ .... ,
>
> *and request the pleasure of* ....
>
> *Company to a*
>
> # MOONLIGHT DANCE
>
> *on the Vicarage Lawn, on Friday, August 21st.*
>
> **ADMISSION, LADY AND GENTLEMAN, 2'6.**   DANCING TO BEGIN AT 8 P.M.
>
> REFRESHMENTS.   *   *   *   WET OR DRY.
>
> *Proceeds for Improvements at the Vicarage.*

Invitation

The way it fell open said everything. It had been read a thousand times, and then a thousand times more; a fading memento of an August night; the little envelope that she probably opened every day of her life, lifting it carefully from her box of souvenirs.

A week later, the phone rang. The secretary of the Family History Society wanted to know if I would give them a talk. I had done several over the years, so whilst I started casting round for a new idea, I told him about my find. Perhaps his members would be interested in this hoard of old photos and letters? He was sure they would.

Six months later, I regretted it. I found myself sitting anxiously at my desk, devoid of inspiration. Three letters lay before me and I began shuffling them in a desultory sort of way, hoping for a miracle. There they lay: the invitation to the Moonlight Dance, the letter from Gus to his 'dear wife', and the scandalised talk of a 'vile woman'.

The invitation had been sent to a woman called Annie Johnson who had obviously lived in our house. This much was certain. Died here by the look of it, for how else had her letters and all her other possessions ended in our attic? When the invitation was sent, she was living in Gainford, a small village more than forty miles away to the west.

The name 'Bowen' kept cropping up. It was there at the top of the invitation – *Mr. and Mrs. Bowen present their compliments to Miss Johnson* - and there in the letter addressed to *Dear Mrs. Bowen.* Then there was the breathless gossip of *Mr. Bowen and that vile woman.* Finally, I was staring at Gus's signature – *I am Your husband Gus Bowen.*

Everything in pieces. Over the previous months, I had found seventeen letters from Gus. Some dated, some not. Reading them as Annie must have done, I came to know his voice, the way he cajoled her, the promises he held out of better times to come. I developed an ear for his style of lovemaking; those little declarations of love that flowed so effortlessly from his pen. Then there were the practical reasons why he couldn't see her this coming weekend. Finally, the turning points in every letter when the sinuous flow of his male charm wriggled towards money. Some letters came from London, some from Lancashire, some from exotic locations in the Mediterranean. I caught glimpses of him in Constantinople, then in Bolton, then in South Africa, and Annie, for that matter, never stopped moving either. She flitted from one set of rented rooms to another, sometimes in York, sometimes in London, sometimes in villages dotted about the Cleveland countryside, always looking for that warmer place by the fire. In the midst of this never-ending restlessness, there was talk of 'troubles' and the occasional mention of a girl called 'Beezie'. Gaps too, lots of them, so I knew from the start that I would be piecing together a broken jigsaw.

All of Gus's letters were packed into a four-year period between 1898 and 1902, so the Moonlight Dance was almost certainly in the 1890s. I went back to the invitation. The date was there - Friday, August 21st at 8pm – but lacked a year. The only clue was a smudged postmark on the envelope that seemed to have a solitary six on its edge. Friday fell on August 21st only twice in the 1890s, once in 1891 and once in 1896, so it seemed I had my year.

'They met in 1896 and parted in 1902,' I said, and then laughed. Here I was tut-tutting like a disapproving vicar, 'It's all over before it starts.'

During those endless months of emptying bags, I found more than a hundred and thirty photographs, but only two in frames. The faces that Annie lifted from her albums and placed on her mantelpiece. One of them was a picture of an old gentleman in a tweed suit sitting before the camera, a walking stick resting gently between his legs. There was no name and I gazed at the face knowing that this was someone special, a man who Annie loved. The most obvious candidate was her father. The other frame had two catches on the back and I struggled to release them. The catches were stiff but finally came free. A wooden flap fell open and I saw for the first time that Annie had written a name.

I lifted the photograph and looked at Gus's face.

'So there you are.'

Chapter 2: Talk

'Where should I start?' I said, looking at my audience.

I never counted them, but there might have been sixty people sitting in a bare church hall in Darlington; the Annual General Meeting of the Cleveland Family History Society. Behind me on a trestle-table there was a modest display of Annie's letters, photographs, newspaper cuttings and concert programmes, together with one or two of her more personal souvenirs.

'I could start,' I began, 'by telling you that she was born in Darlington. That we might describe her as middle class. I could tell you that, after a childhood spent in the town, she attended one of its private schools.'

Then I stopped and shook my head. 'But that's not the way she told it. It didn't happen like that. There was nothing neat or tidy about it.'

I recounted the tale of how I found the bird's nest. How I worked through the night to clear the rubbish and how several months later I woke one morning and remembered the bags.

'I dragged one into the sunshine. It was a lovely morning and in the bright Spring sunshine something caught my eye'

I reached down and lifted a Victorian photograph.

'Here it is.' I said, 'A studio portrait; one of those *carte de visite* photographs that filled the albums of every Victorian family. This photograph dates from the 1860s.'

Everyone gazed with a special kind of intensity, even those at the back who could hardly see it at all.

'Once my eyes were accustomed, I could see Victorian photographs everywhere."

I picked up more.

'It took months to sift through every bag, but finally we discovered a hundred and thirty.'

I turned the last one over.

'Hardly any with names.'

A collective sigh of disappointment rippled through the room.

'I'm surrounded by ghosts; faces that once meant something to someone who lived in our house. But who are they? Sometimes, I spread them out on the carpet like toy soldiers, searching for clues, and sometimes I see them, or fancy I see them. There's a fleeting glimpse of a half-recognised velvet curtain . . . a familiar chair . . . a crooked nose.'

I placed the photographs on the table and reached for a random newspaper cutting.

'I don't know how many cuttings I found. I think I just stopped counting. This one comes from *The People* in 1905. Can you see? It's the centenary celebrations of Trafalgar. Why did she keep it? I suppose it carries clues, if only I knew how to read them.'

Two bottles were waiting patiently on the table. "I know what kind of face lotion she used.' I lifted one in the air and then replaced it with the other. 'And the lingering smell of her perfume.'

Mixed in among the rest, I picked out a rough piece of cloth - "It's not the best sampler I've seen . . .' Girlish embroidery was wilting under the heavy weight of biblical commandments:

Fear God and keep his commandments
For this is the whole duty of man

Children obey your parents in the
Lord for this is right.

At the very bottom, there was a name and place: *Lydia Ann Johnson, Darlington.*

'When I discovered this, I had no idea who Lydia might be, but now I know she was Annie's sister.'

I reached for a small card with black edging:

In Affectionate Remembrance of
Lydia Ann,
the beloved Daughter of Thomas and
Annie Johnson of Darlington,
Who died January 26th 1870, in the 18th year
of her age,
And was interred this day in the Darlington Cemetery.
"In life we are in death".
January 29th

'Annie was no more than seven when Lydia died and I think she kept this as a tender souvenir of a lost sister.'

Every fragment of this woman's life had the power to conjure a story. People began jumping in, suggesting explanations, imagining scenarios. Elaborate patterns appeared, only to be broken or twisted by the discovery of new finds, and behind the mounting excitement there was a search for connections, a desire to draw things together and make a story. Some people looked for more solid ground. One lady at the back of the hall was evidently doing her sums. She had worked out that Lydia was born in 1852 and the sampler must therefore date from the late 1850s or early 1860s. She stood up and recapped this information – Annie and her family lived in Darlington and were called Johnson; her parents were Thomas and Annie. She thought this important, and sat down. And she was right. Little by little, a thread of facts began to twist and form and our fanciful stories began to pull and tug like a skittish kite at the end of a controlling line.

We worked through the rest - Christmas cards, concert programmes, household accounts, tourist brochures . . .

'This is one of my favourites,' I said as I lifted a tiny object between my finger and thumb, 'I have to be careful; it's so brittle. It's a tiny sprig of hawthorn. Or is it? Perhaps after all it might be mistletoe? Or even a rose? Over time, it's grown so old and withered it's impossible to tell. Look,' I smiled and held it higher, 'there's a homemade label attached. It reads *Souvenir from Dickey, Bolam Lane, November 21*st *1891*. She kept it all her life. How easy it would have been to lose a tiny souvenir like this, to let the memory of that November day slip, but she never did.'

And then there were the letters.

'To date, I have discovered a hundred and sixty, although I know there are more. Some are moth-eaten and unreadable but most are remarkably well preserved. It's nothing less than a miracle.'

I reached for the little envelope and read out its address, '*Miss Johnson, North Road, Gainford, Near Darlington, England.*

Opening it slowly, I slid out the card.

'It's an invitation.' And as I said it, I thought of Annie picking up the envelope and calling back to her mother.

> *Mr and Mrs BOWEN present their*
> *Compliments to*
> *Miss Johnson*
> *And request the pleasure of her*
> *Company to a*
> ***MOONLIGHT DANCE***
> *On the Vicarage Lawn, on Friday, August 21*st

'This is the night when Annie met the love of her life. I can't prove it, but no one can convince me otherwise. This is the night when she met Gus, the son of the Reverend Mr. and Mrs. Bowen and she kept this invitation all her life.'

I placed the invitation back on the table and reached for a letter. 'And yet . . .' I said with a smile and began reading: *Dear Mrs. Bowen, Your kind grateful letter received last evening too late to answer. Well dear friend I note all you said about Mr. Bowen and that vile woman . . .'* (The room sat up.) *'I am truly surprised at Mr. Bowen lowering himself in such a manner and making so little of his lawful wife, but there are some women that would tempt the best men born with their fascinating ways . . .'* (Laughter) *'. . . but you may depend, he will tire of her before long, the vile drunken <u>hag</u>.* (Gradually, the room settled) *'Now Mrs. Bowen I want you to forgive me for the part I have taken innocently enough although I am ashamed of it . . . I fenced the question with you till I would get time to tell you the real facts as far as I know them, and believe me now it grieves me more than I can tell you by letter to be the bearer of bad news . . . I suppose he will be very bitter with me for letting you know, but I will be able to stand all that, but could not have it on my conscience any longer. In fact I have been quite ill through it. So, dear friend, if I have wronged you in the least I hope you will forgive me . . . and I trust you will be happy yet . . . Wishing you to have all the happiness the world can give. I remain, Yours sincerely, Charlotte Ferguson.*

The room fell silent.

'Later that day, we found the first of Gus's letters. *My dear wife, My reason for not writing to you is that I did not think you would care to hear from me. As to my reasons for leaving you as I did I think we had better leave that to be discussed at some future time. I am very pleased to hear that you are getting well and strong & sincerely trust that you will soon be your old self again . . .*

'Perhaps,' I speculated, 'he had deserted her when she was ill? Or perhaps she sickened after his desertion? Who can say? *Well I have started work and have been on trial two weeks without pay . . . Now if you really wish the past to be of the past, and feel disposed to assist me to get what is absolutely necessary to take a position that will be worth £2 a week to me. I will endeavour to be all that you may wish in the future . . .'* (Some women began laughing.) *'Should you feel disposed to assist me in this case (in spite of what has happened) it will be for a mutual benefit, and as soon as I am settled I will look for a suitable place for you to come to - in the meantime will consider what is best to be done re. furniture etc. Should you fail me in this case I shall go out East with no intention whatever of returning. I am your husband, Gus Bowen.*

I looked up and smiled. 'In all, I've found seventeen letters from Gus and as I came across them, I read them, and as I read them I began to see how he played her. Because there were four things that Annie always got in a Gus letter. First, he gave her promises of love and better times in the future. *But if you still have a bit love left for me & I think you have . . . I will endeavour to make ammends for my past conduct.* Or this? *I must be alone when I am writing to you - then I kid myself that I am talking to you. '* Or this. *Feeling very much alone tonight . . .* (The same group of women laughed again.) *How I wish I was with you. Have quite made up my mind not to go to sea again if I can possibly help it . . . There are two bunks. How I wish you were in the other - never mind pet. The time will soon pass & we shall be in the same berth. Never mind darling - if only you care for me a little. It shall be my life's duty to make you forget the past and be happy.*

'The second hallmark of Gus's letters,' I explained, 'was his list of never-ending excuses – the practical reasons why he couldn't see her this coming weekend. *As to your coming to London - Well, in order to succeed in my present undertaking I must devote all my time and energy to business. Therefore could not be much with you - & you would find London anything but pleasant at this time of the year the fogs are something awful . . .* (More laughter.) *. . . As to my coming north - that is out of the question not to speak of the expense. What I suggest is that you remain quietly at York until I am more firmly established . . . As to my coming to Redcar . . . unless I had work to go to, would be foolish. I think I told you most emphatically*

15

that I will not leave one job till I have another to go to. For you to come to Bolton (as I shall not be here long) would be mad and cost you a good deal more than the 15/- your husband asked you to lend.

'Here is the very next letter. *I recd your letter with the enclosed 15/-, also your wire on Sat night & was all prepared for going to Redcar on Sunday but unfortunately on Saturday night or rather early on Sunday morning, whilst loading up scenery from the theatre I had the misfortune to fall from the top of a truck & hurt my back. I have not been able to sit up & write till just now. I do seem to have some jolly bad luck.*

'Thirdly, there was his constant begging. *In the meantime: as I have already told you, it is impossible for me to go without the needful. It is imperative that I should keep up a good appearance - my things are in bad condition - boots worn out & rent owing. Now I do not wish to loose what will really be a good thing, but in order to get what is absolutely necessary - Pay what I owe & succeed, I must have at least £5 by return.* There was a collective intake of breath.

'Here's my favourite,' I said, grinning: *As you will see I have been chucked out of No.1 Fairfax Street because I could not pay the rent and have not found another place yet. I have to get over this week without a single penny. If I am to come on Sunday I must ask for a P.T. not later than Wednesday - but must have the cash before asking* . . . (The laughter sputtered out as people saw the heartlessness of his bargaining.) '*I think you might have sent the clothes when I asked you.*

Finally, and less humorously, were Gus's darker moments, his moments of bullying when he thought Annie might not send the money. *Failing this* . . . Failing him getting the five pounds . . . *on Sat next I shall have to go into what we call a hard up sailors boarding house. Ship on the first opportunity and say good bye to my wife and old England for ever.*

The mood of the room chilled and an embarrassed laughter turned to silence. *Should you fail me in this case I shall go out East with no intention whatever of returning.*

'Good riddance!' someone shouted.

I picked up the last letter. 'Here's one from his mother. *My dear Annie . . . I expect Gus will have turned up at Marske by this time. He left Gainford on Saturday by the train for Skelton to go to see Beezie. Whether he would ever arrive there or not I do not know. His money was sent on to Gainford - £26/10/3. He came to Gainford a week last Saturday, took £10, went to Manchester . . . telegraphed on Tuesday for £5 more to be sent by wire . . . came to Gainford on Saturday morning, got another £5. That is the last we know of him, and if I were you I should do my worst to him. Don't think of anyone but yourself. I think his conduct disgraceful. You are quite at liberty to show him this. I have begged him to do differently and he knows it.*

Framed Photograph of Gus: His face faded

'Throughout it all,' I said, reaching down and picking up the framed photograph, 'I kept looking for a photo of Gus. It wasn't the last bag, but the second-from-the-last where I found this in a frame. Here it is.' I held up the velvet-covered frame for all to see. 'There are some brass catches on the back and when I opened them, I saw his name.' I released the catches and took out the photo.

There was a rustle in the room as everyone leaned forward.

Chapter 3: Sea

*My darling . . . Feeling very much alone tonight . . . Oh, How
I wish I was with you. Have quite made up my mind not to
go to sea again if I can possibly help it . . .*

Gus wrote several letters to Annie whilst sailing on a tramp
steamer bound for Constantinople. It was 1899 and I had no idea if
he ever served on other ships, or if this voyage on the *Aberfeldy* was
an impulsive, one-off adventure. But there was something in the
letter that hinted at a life beyond Annie; something that might help
bring him into focus. Other letters made passing references to his
seafaring life. *You seem to have had a very pleasant cruise up the
Meditean,* someone wrote in May 1899, *How delightful it must be to
be running about among such lovely scenes and in the most
enjoyable climate in the world.*

Most Victorian ships kept 'Crew Agreements'. They acted as
contracts between sailors and employers but wherever they survive,
they are often used by family historians to research mariner
descendants. It was my best chance of tracking him. Crew
agreements could tell me how much Gus was paid, where he was
living, and the name of his previous ship. If I could find the crew
agreement for the *Aberfeldy*, that would be my start. It would tell me

the name of his earlier ship and this in turn might point me back, and so I might jump from one ship to another. Yet just when I thought I had devised a plan for packing my bags and following him around the world, I learned that only ten per cent of crew agreements were kept in the National Archives. The remaining ninety per cent were in the National Maritime Museum at Greenwich, but only for the years ending in five.

Half hidden in the pages of my family history guide, I found a brief reference to a place called 'The Maritime History Group at the University of Newfoundland'. Back in the 1970s, they had managed to acquire most of the agreements that the Public Record Office seemed hell-bent on destroying and created an archive of crew agreements that could be ordered by email. Grainy photographs on the Newfoundland website showed a modest outfit boasting two tables, a row of filing cabinets and a handful of microfilm machines. There was nothing to match the pomp and grandeur of a national archive, but I liked it. Somehow or other, I could imagine the place and how it might smell, the kind of enthusiasts who might unbolt its door and begin each day. The kind of place that survives on a shoestring and keeps memory alive. Some inspired crackpot in this outfit had convinced his bosses to rescue seventy per cent of the threatened crew agreements and this meant taking possession of over two million documents.

The more I thought about it, the more I liked it. Against all odds, a plucky little David had engineered an astonishing coup. Once the family history movement took off and the internet began to stitch the world together, researchers could place orders from anywhere on the planet. All I had to do was locate a copy of *Lloyds Register*, find the official number for the *Aberfeldy*, key in the number and wait for the moment when they would tell me if anything had survived. The game was on.

Gus had shipped on the *Aberfeldy* in 1899. The Crew Agreement told me that he was hired as Boatswain at five guineas a month and this in itself was revealing. A boatswain job required skill and experience, so Gus had worked on previous boats and looked to be a seasoned mariner.

His last ship was listed as the *Fernlands* so I ordered that agreement. It transpired that he served on the *Fernlands* for two voyages and claimed that his earlier ship was the *Dunrobin*. True enough, he served on her during most of 1898. Before that, he sailed on the *Ferrum* between November 1897 and January 1898. Earlier still, he had worked as a crewman on the *Oilfield* between July and November 1896. It was a risky business jumping back from one crew agreement to another and I knew it couldn't last. Sooner or later, I would miss my footing and end in the water.

The splash came in 1896. The agreement for the *Oilfield* gave Gus's earlier ship as the *Empusa* and the researcher in Newfoundland emailed me with the bad news. They didn't have the agreement for the *Empusa*, she said, but all was not lost. As luck would have it, I had jumped back to one of the magic years ending in five, so the missing crew agreement might be in the National Maritime Museum in London. I emailed them. Well, they were not sure. Someone would have to look. According to their records, it was lodged in an external store and might take some time to locate. Not to worry, I said, lying through my teeth, I can wait. Finally, they found it and copies arrived one morning in a thick cardboard tube.

I opened it and anchored the documents down with coffee cups, key rings, a vase of flowers and a bowl of bananas.

'What's this?' Gill asked as she breezed by.

'Crew agreements,' I said, half distracted, for I was already looking for Gus and not finding him. By the time I looked up, she had gone.

I stuffed the crew agreements back. For some reason, he was not listed. It was crazy; he said he had served on the *Empusa* but he was not there. I crept down next morning and opened the tube again, half thinking that I had carelessly missed him or that he had slipped back in the night like a drunken sailor, but he was not there. And it didn't make sense. Why would he have named the *Empusa* as his previous ship if he hadn't sailed on her?

When things don't make sense, you start to wonder. A few days later I began to look for clues and turned to an online database of Victorian newspapers and typed in the name, '*Empusa*'. Over a hundred references popped up, most of them useless. They were routine scraps of 'intelligence' listing the ship's arrivals and departures from different ports. But mixed in with the rest there was an intriguing report. The ship had been sold in May 1895 to a Spanish company and renamed the *Canalejas*.

It was nearly midnight and Gill was downstairs.

'I may have found him,' I shouted. She came to the bottom of the stairs and looked up. 'The ship changed its name,' I explained, 'In 1895, it became the *Canalejas*.'

She had no idea what I was talking about.

'So he must have sailed on her before that, when it was still called the *Empusa*.'

Next day, I sent off an email to Newfoundland. 'Could you look at the earlier crew agreements for the *Empusa* and track back to 1894, perhaps even earlier?'

It would certainly cost me. I would have to pay for their research but if I was willing to do it, how far should they go? I told them 1892, but two days later they emailed. 'I'm afraid there's no mention of him.' As a final throw of the dice, I told them to go back to 1890 and two more days slipped by. 'Well,' my contact replied, 'I guess persistence pays off. I finally found C.A.A. Bowen in 1890 on two voyages.'

So there he was. Gus had spent much of his life on ships. He was a seasoned mariner. True enough, he had forsaken the sea for five years between 1890 and 1895, but for the remainder of the 1890s, he had sailed to every corner of the globe, and I started mapping his journeys. There was an almost boyish delight in doing this, sticking pins in the world – Europe, the Mediterranean, India, South America, the USA. He served on the *Empusa* in 1890, ending his voyage at St. Katherine's Dock London, and sailed before that on the *Ameer, Sindia* and *Zemindar*, all of them owned by a shipping company called the Brocklebanks. Typing their name into an archival database, I found that their company records were still held in Liverpool.

A summer squall: a ferocious burst of rain pummelling the windscreen. Every vehicle slowed to a crawl. Our sense of danger lasted only a minute or so, and during the worst of it we sat in our seats, warmed by heaters and lulled by music, but with Gus on my mind, I tried to imagine what it would be like to face this kind of fury on a sailing ship? What kind of world had knocked him into shape? The questions came and went, just like the rain, and when I reached Liverpool, the squall had gone. Suddenly, there was a blue sky. The road threaded through a landscape of rundown houses and building works until it came to The Strand, a stretch of freeway that ran beside the Mersey. Darting inside the first multi-storey car park I could find, I ditched the car and walked the last half-mile.

'My great grandfather was a sailor in Liverpool!'

I was sharing a lift with two well-dressed American ladies who were heading up to the second floor of the Maritime Museum. One of them looked over and smiled, 'He sailed out of Liverpool in the 1880s,' she said.

'You're tracing your family history?

'We are!'

I was suddenly warmed. 'So am I.'

The doors opened and we stepped out. I watched them as they walked arm-in-arm towards the main exhibition space, chatting away like lovers. Then I turned and saw a scrappy piece of paper that had been blue-tacked to a door. Someone had scrawled 'Archive' on it, so I slipped in. The room was smaller and cosier than I anticipated. There were three, oldish-looking researchers sitting at tables, swapping greetings, regulars by the look of it.

With my briefcase stashed away and my pencils sharpened, I tiptoed to a table and placed an order. I would start with the record of Gus's apprenticeship. Only two pages of information, filled with financial accounts, but just enough to give me a start. It transpired that Gus had joined the Brocklebanks in August 1885 on a four-year apprenticeship, and I found myself staring at a page of financial figures that showed how the company gave him supplies at sea and rupees in Calcutta. The aim was to train him in the skills of an officer. He was paid a nominal wage - £4 in his first year, £5 in his second, £6 in the third and £7 in his last.

It was all good stuff; solid as a rock and just about as dead. There were plenty of dates and one or two names, lots of double-entry bookkeeping, but hardly anything that gave me what I really wanted. Nothing that gave me anything about life on board a sailing ship in the 1880s. Outside the museum, I phoned Gill and gave her the news.

'So what now?'

'I'm not sure,' I said. 'I've ordered one or two new items. You never know, there might be something.'

Chapter 4: Windjammer

After lunch, an envelope was waiting for me. It was buff-brown and tempting. I peered inside and could see a battered book with a marble-effect cover, faded red binding running down its spine, much of it worn. Easing the book out gently, I laid it on the surface. After a few deep breaths, I opened the cover and all my anxiety gave way to astonishment. It was filled with drawings, vivid and bright. The first page was covered in them. A sailing ship was cutting through water, a bright red flag flying from its stern and a sky-blue flag from its mast. The ship was in full sail and each flag seemed to be stretched as tight as bliss. You could sense the exhilaration. On the opposite page, there was a frontispiece made up of more images. The author had drawn Indian palaces, palm trees, pine forests, canoes and Rocky Mountains, and at the very centre, I saw:

'A Voyage to San Francisco in the Ship Majestic, and
to Calcutta in the Ship Tenaserrim during the
apprenticeship of T. A. Parry.
Illustrated & described by a Shipmate who gives you
this short Preface.
Turn the pages over, do not be too expectant,
but if you are satisfied, my efforts will be rewarded.'

I spent the afternoon copying the journal and when I finally got home after a long drive, I woke Gill.

'You have to see this.'

I placed my laptop on the bed and clicked through the images.

'It's lovely,' she said in a sleepy voice.

'It's perfect.'

I explained that the author had served on the same ships as Gus. 'It's a fantastic view of his world.'

The next morning, I watched Gill as she clicked through the images. Her smile grew, and I knew the magic was working, just as it had worked on me. 'I think we can find him,' I said, pointing to the laptop. Alleyn had joined the Brocklebanks as a young apprentice in the early 1880s, a few years before Gus. His maiden voyage had been on the *Majestic* to Calcutta, and then a year later he had sailed to California. It was this trip that prompted his journal. He joked of coming home and spinning yarns and a journal like this was a perfect way of preparing the script. A year later, he changed ships again – 'a boon' he said, 'which all apprentices does desire' - and sailed for Calcutta a second time.

There were eighty-nine pages and most of them were devoted to his second voyage to India. Just when we needed a window on Gus's world, Alleyn slipped out of his brown envelope and gave us this gift. 'Here,' he seemed to say, 'read this. It will tell you everything.'

We soon realised that the journal was always meant as a gift. The obvious clue came from its frontispiece:

'A Voyage to San Francisco in the Ship Majestic, and
to Calcutta in the Ship Tenaserrim during the
apprenticeship of T. A. Parry.'

Alleyn had carefully crafted his journal as a gift for one of his fellow apprentices, and we saw how the two young lads had become friends. We learned that life aboard ship could sometimes throw men into this kind of intimacy. Three-month passages around the Cape were lived in tight spaces; there would be long stretches of boredom, and brief moments of excitement, and life below decks was always cramped. The claustrophobia and tensions could lead to fights, but there were friendships and sometimes love. We sent for a study of maritime apprenticeships. 'Such matters,' it said wryly, 'are as old and commonplace as the sea itself.' Young apprentices came into the 'close and intimate company of men' and learned a new kind of love. There were sexual affairs but these were fleeting and rarely viewed with alarm.

There were places in Alleyn's journal where we saw how this blossomed. The first day on board was a case in point. Probably the hardest. The young apprentices were thrown together as they faced the uncertainties of a brutal, new life. 'Surrounded by strange faces,' Alleyn wrote as he lay in his bunk, 'we manage to rub out the first day, which seems the longest, and most miserable.' Sometimes, these friendships were deepened by wonder. New places, new people, new discoveries. One apprentice might play the elder brother. 'I was aloft at the Mizen with the other apprentice,' Alleyn remembered, 'I took great pleasure in pointing out the features of the shore to the first voyager.'

Personal relationships were part of a wider *esprit de corps*. In Calcutta, the apprentices formed gangs and went about the city ransacking fruit stalls and cigar shops, 'bilking' or cheating the 'ghurries' who ferried them through its streets. The gang had to be big enough to 'strike terror amongst the Natives', and we saw with an embarrassed shake of the head how this camaraderie forged its own kind of loyalties.

The Brocklebanks had an impressive fleet of merchant ships and the *Zemindar* was one of the jewels in their crown. Built in 1885 by Harland and Wolff, it was an ultra-modern beauty, weighing 2000 tons, 300-feet in length and 40-feet wide, with a hull of hardened steel. Yet for all the technical innovations and modern sheen, the *Zemindar* was an old-style sailing ship, powered by wind and destined for the taste and smell of India. People called it a windjammer. It was Gus's home for the best part of four years and during that time, he 'doubled the Cape' each year, sailing out to Calcutta and back. This was the world that made him.

Clark Russell was a writer who specialised in sea stories; a brief biography in Wikipedia showed us a man who had a surprisingly boyish face, an ex-sailor turned author, who many reckoned the best Victorian writer on the sea. During the 1880s, he published a number of articles on seafaring life and they were syndicated in newspapers.

'Welcome aboard!' I said, as I downloaded them and sent them over to Gill. We were both settled in our chairs, each in our own study, doors ajar.

Alongside Alleyn, Clark Russell became our most trusted guide. He talked of 'the invigorating and informing experience' of a sea apprenticeship, and the glamour of a sailing ship like the *Zemindar,* cutting through tropical waters. A 'great homeward-bound Indiaman' coming into view on the open sea, her sails 'billowing on both sides, glittering uniforms on her quarterdeck, sun-burnt men in wide-brimmed hats on her castle, and parakeets in her rigging'. A workaday tramp steamer would stare in wonder as it passed her by.

'What ship is that?' the steamer would hail.

'The *Zemindar* from Calcutta to Liverpool. Hundred and ten days out.'

A ship of this dignity carried its own landscape. Clark Russell was widely admired for his gritty style of realism and always did his best to strip away the silly romance that landsmen associated with the sea, but he savoured the magic of a sailing ship like the *Zemindar,* cutting through calm waters in the burnished glow of an evening. 'The strains of the fiddle mingling with the vibratory humming of the trade winds, or the rigging glowing golden in the light of the setting sun.' As one hard-bitten sailor was heard to whisper on a star-lit night, gazing up at the sails, 'How quietly they do their work.'

Sun-burnt mariners like Gus were destined to swagger, and when they looked overboard and saw sharks flickering like indigo, they were destined to tell tales. Once home, they fell to womanizing and romancing and one of Gus's nephews remembered how he entranced them with his stories. Behind the romance and excitement, there was terror too, and this formed part of the attraction. A sailor's life was full of manliness. Gus would have to be a man who could defy the full force of nature, who could surfeit on the carnal pleasures of Calcutta, and still find the muscle to defend an empire; one of Victoria's wayward sons. He had no desire to sit on a clerk's stool because the sea was always roaring in his head. And once afloat, he learned that he must never show fear and never hold back. He must be manly above all things, and this manliness meant that he must cultivate a devil-may-care recklessness, a cool indifference to danger. 'A man may be within an ace of losing his life at sea,' Clark Russell cautioned his readers, 'but he will not suffer himself to say a word about it.'

Tests came and went and none more terrifying than climbing aloft. Some lads were bullied into it and some went by degrees. Yet even when the first climb was mastered and the initial terror faced, the danger was always there. Always waiting. There was a brief, perfunctory report of a fellow apprentice who had once sailed with Gus. A prosaic record of his death, stripped of all feeling. 'Killed – W.A. Redhouse, one and half voyages, *Zemindar* 2nd May 1887'. Alleyn's journal recorded a similar death: 'All day long this poor lad was busy in the Cabin writing for the Captain. He got through his writing business close upon 5 o'clock pm.' The apprentice was sent aloft to remove a block from the Foreyard. 'Somehow he slipped and fell upon the deck. He never spoke.'

The ultimate challenge was the crew. The men gathered in the forecastle and tested each other, sometimes with knives. An apprentice like Gus would have to survive, or go under. Growling was endemic because sea voyages were long, the money poor, the food unspeakable, but whenever a sailor reached home, all this was forgotten, because for a few brief days he would play the 'lion', prowling the streets. At the end of each voyage, Gus was tougher, leaner and browner. He stood out against pasty-faced 'stay-at-homes'. Friends sought him out and bought him drinks. People loved his stories. Girls sat on his lap. The world was his oyster.

Chapter 5: Calcutta

Alleyn remembered the scene. Friends and relations huddled on the quay, waving and cheering; sailors and apprentices standing on deck, cheering back. Everyone putting on a brave show. And he remembered how the bravado turned to melancholy. The harbour fell from view as the ship moved sluggishly into 'lumpy water'. Down below, the metal cups and pans hanging beneath the men's bunks began to rattle and chatter. The ship rolled. Crew members looked at each other with a familiar kind of hollowness and tried to lighten the mood with whisky. Soon they would be on deck and things would start; their first taste of a regime that would last for months. The daily routine of washing and painting. Day by day, the *Zemindar* would journey south until one day Gus looked up and saw albatrosses and molly-hawks in the sky and found himself breathing warm air.

The old customs were dying out but Gus caught the last of them. As the ship crossed the equator, one of the sailors would turn himself into Father Neptune, the rest of the crew would be his mermen, and Gus would be brought before them. A ducking in salt water followed and then a shave with soot and grease. Like everything on the ship, he must take it like a man and laugh it off, just as he must laugh at storms. 'We shipped large quantities of salt water,' Alleyn recorded and talked light-heartedly of a man being washed overboard. 'He was picked up with his mouth badly cut and beauty spoiled by the loss of three teeth.' That was the way. Always joke about it, make light of it. The devil-may-care attitude that would carry you through.

Gradually the ship moved south and the world lightened. Oilskins were shed and Gus walked about the deck with a new kind of freedom, feeling the sun on his back. 'Old Jamaica' they called it. Damp clothing and sleeping togs were dried and cleaned. Drinking water became scarcer and you made do with daily allowances skimmed from barrels.

Then the doldrums. 'Humbugging weather', Alleyn reckoned. The days and weeks when they toiled under the sun and hardly moved at all. On Gus's second voyage, the *Zemindar* left Liverpool on May 5, telegraphed an 'all well' message a month later, and aimed to be in Calcutta by late July. A typical three-month affair. 'Eyes wearied with the waste of waters,' one veteran recalled, 'watched eagerly for the first glimpse of the palms of Saugor Island'. And Gus learned to read the signs like everyone else; the cry of macaws floating down from the rigging; a faint whiff of bamboo in the air; the brown stain of Calcutta spilling into the sea.

A satellite map of India came into view. Gill ran her finger over the screen and traced the river. 'The Hooghly,' she intoned, savouring its name. Calcutta was a hundred miles inland and approached by this shape-changing river. The Hooghly never stopped mutating. Sometimes it was narrow and deep, sometimes as wide as a lake. Several of the narrower channels were notorious. Only a single ship could pass at any one time, and places like this might change during the rainy season. One of the worst was the fabled 'James and Mary Bank', about forty miles from the city. A ship took the ground here and was swallowed up. 'When a ship sinks in mud or quicksand', Kipling warned, 'she regularly digs her own grave.'

The land on either side was flat. A copper sky overhead. The jungle seemed to squeeze the river and it stretched out on either side as far as the eye could see. 'There is no <u>scenery</u>,' one European complained. Others were entranced by the greenness of it all, for this was greenness on the grand scale. As Gus leaned over the rails, he would see tiny villages peeping out from the lushness. 'The natives were nothing new to me,' Alleyn boasted, 'Their manners and scant clothings, their queer jargon.' Gus probably laughed too, for here were 'comical and interesting jokers' who he could talk about when he got home.

And all the while, they were sailing into the most fertile trap in the world. The bones of past imperialisms were rotting away on all sides. Dissolving wherever you looked. 'There! Can you see? The old Dutch fort of Budge-Budge', one of the last relics of an earlier age. It was already eaten by the jungle. The steamy sultriness of the place was overpowering. Here was a climate that was wonderful for vegetation but terrible for men. 'Men do not die in Calcutta', one resident warned, 'they wither.'

Within forty miles of the city, the jungle gave way to industry. Jute mills and brickfields for the most part, and beyond them, a place called 'Garden Reach', once the favourite suburb of rich Calcutta merchants, and now the makeshift palace of the King of Oude. He had been settled here by the British when they annexed his kingdom in the 1850s. Tall towers housed his exotic court and menagerie. At the top of each tower, Gus could see Bengal tigers circling in cages, their vivid stripes glistening in the sun. High in the burning sky, immense flocks of pigeons swirled and swooped making ever-changing patterns, orchestrated by bands of coolies who controlled them with long poles. Beyond the imprisoned opulence of Garden Reach, the Hooghly became a melting pot. There were ships here from every part of the globe: clippers from America, 'buggalows' from the Laccadives, old East India liners, Chinese junks.

Once berthed, the gangplank was thrown down and the *Zemindar* opened for business. An army of Indian traders scurried aboard. The most welcome was the 'Captain's Sircar' who brought letters from home. Alleyn remembered the moment. 'The men reading their letters and joking to one another. We all felt happy as we read the loving words penned by our dear friends, so far away in Merry England.' A time for relaxing, for smoking pipes, for dozing and lounging. Some of the older hands tried a spot of bargaining. 'Changee for changee' they called it, bartering old clothes for bread and eggs and, best of all, for bananas.

Come the night, the sultry and mosquito-ridden river did its best to break them; a night to be endured until it finally ended at five-thirty with a watchman's cry - 'Three Bells!' The men lounging in their beds, soaked in sweat. A second formal call and a lazy breakfast of coffee and smokes. Abdoul elbowing his way through the crowd. 'A young fellow,' Alleyn tells us, 'who knows every ship in the employ and every officer and apprentice.' We learn that Abdoul brings news. He has the details of ships in the river and recites the names of shipmates. Half an hour later and it's, 'Turn to!' The men loosening the sails, overhauling the gear, spreading canvasses against the sun. Soon, the Customs Officer strides aboard and breaks the seals. The hatches open. 'Eight bells' and it's a full breakfast. A thin Calcutta tailor with a measuring tape round his neck, darts about the ship doing his own kind of brisk trade. He knows exactly what the men want. 'We apprentices do cut a dash,' Alleyn laughs, 'our jaunty cheese cutters look quite killing with a snow white cover and black braiding. In the evenings we can wear our uniforms.'

I turn to Kipling, for he knows the place. 'This is a city,' he tells me, 'there is life here, and there should be all manner of pleasant things.' The City of Palaces, the Second City of Empire, the fabled *City of Dreadful Night*. He came to Calcutta at the same time as Gus, towards the end of 1885, when Gus was seventeen and Kipling only twenty. Two men in search of life. The first year of Gus's apprenticeship when his wages were spent on pleasant things.

Kipling hires a guide because he wants to go deeper and explore the darkest recesses of the city.

'Where are we now?' he asks.

'Somewhere off the Chitpore Road,' the guide says.

Kipling nods and takes stock. 'Calcutta is a fearsome place for a man not educated up to it.' The city has its grandeur and there's no denying it. There are streets of luxurious shops and sumptuous hotels. The central area is stunning.

'If you get into the centre of the *Maidan*', Kipling smiles, 'you will understand why Calcutta is called 'The City of Palaces'.

But behind the grandeur, the place reeks of corruption. It is blighted he says with 'the Big Calcutta Stink'.

'It is faint, it is sickly, and it is indescribable,' and Kipling reckons it is best savoured at night.

The imperial centre and western quarter fall silent. We meet our guide by a tower. Sailors are gathering in coffee shops and we hear them singing: "Shall we gather at the river? The beautiful, the beautiful river?" He reckons there are about two thousand of them from perhaps fifty nationalities adrift in the city - 'This great growling beast of a city'- and two hundred of them are sodden with drink.

The pavements filthy, the air heavy.

'Aha! You want to see?' the keeper of an opium den smiles as we stumble into one of the poorest quarters, 'Very good, I show.'

'How long does it take to know it?' Kipling asks, for the place oppresses him.

'About a lifetime,' the guide nods, 'and even then some of the streets puzzle you.'

We come to a squalid hut where a group of women are cooking. 'There are no men here!' they shout as we enter. 'Na–na! Na sailor men ee–yah! Arl gone!' But we see a door and behind the door, the room is black. A 'white hand with black nails' reaches out from the surrounding gloom.

'A sailor from the ships,' the guide reckons, 'He'll be robbed before morning.'

It could be Gus.

'The man is sleeping like a child,' Kipling sighs, and bends down to examine him, 'both arms thrown over his head, and he is not unhandsome.' He looks closer. 'He is shoeless and there are huge holes in his stockings. He is a pure-blooded white, and carries the flush of innocent sleep on his cheeks.'

Towards the end of the night, we come to 'the lowest sink of all'. A winding road of 'cramped stalls' where women stand by their doors. Behind them we see mock displays of domesticity - glowing lamps, toilet tables adorned with plaster dogs, glass balls from Christmas trees, statuettes of the Virgin Mary, cheap chintz.

'Isn't that a European woman at that door?' Kipling asks.

'Yes. Mrs D-------' someone says, 'widow of a soldier, mother of seven children.'

Her head goes back in a laugh, 'Nine if you please, and good evening to you.'

'Then the secret of the insolence of Calcutta is made plain,' Kipling thunders. 'Small wonder the natives fail to respect the Sahib, seeing what they see and knowing what they know.'

We go back. Kipling is all for climbing a tower and shouting to the world, 'O true believers! Decency is a fraud and a sham. There is nothing clean or pure or wholesome under the Stars, and we are all going to perdition together!' but he decides against it and trails home.

Next morning, we meet him by the river, appetite restored. 'There must be some sort of entertainment where sailors congregate', he reckons, rubbing his hands, but this is the hard-bitten world of 'Bombay Jack'. The world where sailors buy cheap cheroots and raw whisky. The place where they drift and sleep. Some of them are sitting outside a building, their backs to the wall, smoking impassively. The Shipping Office. A captain strides in looking for men. There's plenty available: Italians with gold earrings; tough-looking Yankees; red-faced Danes, Cornish lads; Germans and Cockneys, one or two Welshmen 'spitting and swearing like cats'.

Kipling points to a man in the shadows. We try to make out his face and see only ugly gashes. 'What comes to them in the end?' Kipling wonders, 'They die at sea in strange and horrible ways; they die, a few of them, in the Kintals, being lost and suffocated in the great stink of Calcutta; they die in strange places by the water-side, and the Hooghly takes them away under the mooring-chains and the buoys, and casts them up on the sands below . . . They sail the sea because they must live; and there is no end to their toil.'

Prophecies. Little by little, Kipling has revealed a secret. The way we must see Gus.

'He's a loafer,' I told Gill. For two days, I had immersed myself in Kipling's Indian tales. They came at the end of three months of searching. We had been tracking Gus, as best we could, pillaging the sources, digging out the clues. Hundreds of extracts from newspapers and novels, maps and histories. But Kipling was the one who guessed Gus's secret; the sweetest secret of all: 'There is no life so good as the life of the loafer who travels by rail and road; for all things and all people are kind to him.' I stared at Gill and then carried on. 'As every soul on the ship is a loafer like myself, no one is discontented. Imagine a shipload of people to whom time is no object, who have no desires beyond three meals a day and no emotions save those caused by a casual cockroach.' Then another: 'You know the unadulterated pleasure of that first clear morning in the Hills when a month's solid idleness lies before the loafer, and the scent of the deodars mixes with the scent of the meditative cigar.'

Gus charmed and seduced Annie, he betrayed and lied to her and milked her of money. There was no denying it. Anyone who read his letters could see it. Yet here he was, barefoot and brown, in all his simplicity, stretched out on the deck of a sailing ship or exploring the streets of Calcutta; the free spirit of Empire who lived for the moment. A loafer who followed his instincts and gloried in the feel of the sun; a man who made no bones about drinking and sex, who knew Calcutta and pleasure. Kipling and others fell in love with loafing, and so did Gus.

In 1908, W. H. Davies published his *Autobiography of a*

Supertramp and George Bernard Shaw was happy to write a preface. He loved the sound of Davies's life. If Davies was right and loafing the best way to live, 'then British morality is a mockery, British respectability an imposture, and British industry a vice.' The sheer outrageousness of the idea appealed to Shaw. 'Another effect of this book on me is to make me realise what a slave to convention I have been all my life,' he laughed, 'When I think of the way I worked tamely for my living during all those years when Mr. Davies, a free knight of the highway, lived like a pet bird on titbits, I feel that I have been duped out of my natural liberty.'

Shaw's enthusiasm was shared by others. A zeitgeist, an overturning of Victorian ideals, a wilful delight in louche living. We found no poetry from Gus. He never sang about the pleasures of loafing, or if he ever did, the tune is lost. Why should he? Loafing was a tune in itself. The simplest kind of poetry. We could see him stretched on the deck of the *Zemindar*, his eyes shut, his bare back on the warm wood.

Before this, our only view of him had come from Annie's letters. The dangerous man who seduced and betrayed her. Yet there was more to Gus than that. We could see it now. For much of his life, he had lived beyond Annie, and in truth beyond us, but like her, we were drawn to his mystery.

Chapter 6: Family

Sometimes it might be a bundle of papers tied in red ribbon rising gently and solemnly from the depths of a provincial archive. Sometimes the musky-smelling contents of a chest that sit like a mystery at the heart of an English house. Or perhaps it's the rusty padlock that needs to be forced before a forgotten room can be entered and explored? Our chance discovery of Annie's papers in that cold December attic was the kind of discovery that every historian dreams of making, but it came at a time when the world was changing. Over the next few years, we learned that the internet was the attic of all attics: the place where anyone might rummage and find gold.

Gill and I were looking for Gus – the hidden Gus – and came across a name; an unusual name that kept cropping up: *Ed. & Liebe have left the Spen,* someone wrote in 1898, *They are now at Holly Cottage, Haxby, York. I thought Liebe and Ted were going to Cornwall,* Gus asked, *you say London? . . . Remind Liebe she promised to let me have the ring . . . Liebe says she thinks of me every time she sees the sweet peas?* At one point, Gus wanted Annie to live with Liebe. *It is my fault if you cannot. You <u>must</u> speak darling & get whatever you want. Surely Liebe must understand . . . You must not show this to Liebe poor darling. I know it is not her* *fault - God help her she is too much like me - I know that she would give one anything. I take very little interest in either Liebe or Edward,* another snapped. *I just forget about them.*

It was an exotic name and easy to find. I typed it into Google and the alchemy fizzed. There she sat on a website in Oklahoma, the creation of George H. Graham, a family historian who had built an elaborate family tree based on shipbuilding dynasties in the North of England, and instantly and effortlessly, we stepped into his world. Here amongst the hundreds of people who had been so lovingly researched was the name of 'Liebe Mary Bowen'. She turned out to be Gus's sister, as well as the wife of Joseph Edward Davies, and this explained the *Ed and Liebe* or *Ted and Liebe* of the letters. Better still there were scores of other Bowens sitting beside her, gathered on that summer night in Tulsa as if for a reunion. There were elaborate family trees tracking the Bowens over several generations, one or two photographs, snippets from obituaries – everything we could possibly want. 'Special thanks,' the website said, 'to Cindy Hatchett, née Wheelan, of South Africa for many of the details provided.' I emailed George and told him of our discoveries. Could he put us in touch with Cindy? Yes, he said, he could do that. Off went his email and within a day, Cindy was laughing across five thousand miles. 'Jeepers!' she cried, 'I am so excited, I don't quite know where to start!'

She was descended from one of Gus's brothers. He was called Greg and spent several years with the Brocklebanks, just like Gus. But Greg had done grander things and risen to become a ship's captain. Cindy told us how he went to India in the early 1890s and settled in Calcutta where he met and married the daughter of a surgeon. He did well, became a commander in the Royal Indian Marine, had four children and one of them was a spirited young woman who married the secretary of the Viceroy of India. By all accounts, she was headstrong. Not content with her high-ranking husband, she abandoned him and ran off with a guardsman, and like many of the Bowens, had a talent for music and rebellion and often played in concerts, music halls and pubs. Later in life, she wandered into France and earned money by picking flowers for the perfume industry and finally, so the story went, she lived with a poet. One of her brothers was a poet in his own right, and another became an officer in the merchant navy. This last brother was a prolific author on maritime history, retained a life-long interest in Eastern philosophy and served in both wars; he married twice and one of his daughters lived on a farm near Johannesburg. She was Cindy's mother.

Cindy had researched her family's history, so if anyone could tell us about Gus, it was her. That weekend, she and her mother ransacked their family archive. Everything was pulled out - letters, photographs, certificates - and at the end of a feverish day, she sent the news. There was nothing. Not a thing. Cindy was sorry, but they couldn't find a thing. Gus simply didn't exist in the family record. She had badgered her aunt in New Zealand, but she too found nothing. The silence was heart breaking, and in a sense it was hollowing, but it said something. This charming loafer who we had stumbled across by chance was the black sheep of the family and banished from memory.

And perhaps it was inevitable. Cindy had researched the facts and passed them on to George Graham, and George had posted them on his website. We skipped from one solid fact to another and saw how Gus's father and grandfather were both clergymen, and that many of his relations were clergymen, solicitors and academics. Solid middle-class types, respectable and comfortable. It was easy to see how they had distanced themselves from Gus.

Then we discovered a bundle of letters by Gus's father in Durham Record Office. By this point, we knew that he was a clergyman and gloried in the name of Craufurd Townsend Bowen, but the letters opened a new window. The family had lived in a tiny rural community called Bolam, and at the end of a long day in the archives, we drove over to see for ourselves. The village stood peacefully in the rural landscape and occupied a ridge overlooking green fields.

They had moved into Bolam vicarage in 1885. Over the next twenty years, Craufurd and his wife worked tirelessly to convert a seventeenth-century hall into a family home. There was never much money in the kitty but they kept at it. Craufurd was a keen gardener and the lawn he laid out at the back of the house was a step in the right direction, for it offered stunning views of the countryside beyond. Here was a lush space where the life of a Victorian vicarage could be lived in style. The world that Gus rejected: croquet on warm afternoons, fund-raising bazaars, open-air sermons on hot summer Sundays. Improvements kept coming and they were still beavering away at the fabric of the building when Craufurd had his moment of inspiration. A composer of music and passionate student of astronomy, he conjured up the possibility of a moonlight dance on the vicarage lawn. Invitation cards were printed, personal names added by hand, slipped into envelopes and sent to anyone who mattered in the community. Bolam was a work-a-day village made up of farmers and labourers, so there were few guests to be garnered there, but only a few miles away was Gainford, with its genteel mix of professional and landed families, and Gainford of course was where Annie lived. A local newspaper caught the moment: 'On Friday, the vicarage garden at Bolam was the scene of a function quite new in these parts . . . All around the lawn, banners and flags of various devices floated from tall masts and the entire space was encircled with a cordon of Chinese lanterns. After the dancers had assembled, the movements of the throng of merry-hearted young people, flitting to and fro in the moonlight which flooded the whole scene, produced a *tout ensemble* quite enchanting. The dancers continued to trip to and fro till the small hours of the morning.'

'So this is the night,' I said, 'when she falls for Gus. She keeps the invitation all her life.'

Over the next few months, we came to know Gus's father. Like many clergymen in the Victorian landscape, he was a gifted man living quietly and modestly in his parish; a talented musician and composer, an enthusiastic painter and a knowledgeable astronomer. One of his descendants described him as 'an all-round genius', but this would have embarrassed him. He never liked parading his gifts. Far from being the stern autocrat of our imagination, he was a likeable man who moulded himself over the years into a self-effacing servant of the church; the kind of loveable hero that you find populating Victorian fiction. Brought up in a long tradition of Christian humility and English reserve, he made much of his limitations, and talked from an early age of devoting himself to a quiet ministry, preferably in a country parish, and people rather liked him for this. 'A living requiring much ability and energy', he explained, 'I should never dream of applying for, but I trust, should Bolam be offered me, that with divine assistance I should be enabled quietly, humbly and diligently to perform the duties of a pastor in that retired village'.

Part of Craufurd's humility was learned from his father, the Rev. Jeremiah Bowen. We often wondered whether Gus knew his grandfather, for the old man lived in the Fenlands, and died there in 1875 when Gus was only eight, but even if they never met, the boy would have seen his sermons and poetry on the shelves of the family library. I found them in the British Library.

In a poem written towards the end of his life, Jeremiah remembered his own childhood in a rambling old house, filled with ancestral portraits. It was an image that gave us the first clue to the family's aristocratic connections. Cindy confirmed this. 'My mother always told me that we are connected to the Duke of Norfolk somehow, but I have not been able to prove it.' Nor could we. But in a sense, it hardly mattered, for this was how the Bowens saw themselves; the way they raised their heads and faced the world.

The pages of Jeremiah's poetry were uncut, so I was forced to wait patiently until someone in the British Library could make a decision. Two hours dragged by as they debated the pros and cons of making a book readable, until finally someone thought it could be done. Once opened, the book's sadness was released. 'I love to gaze upon the full-orbed moon', Jeremiah sighed, as if that melancholy sigh had been held in for more than a hundred years. I found him sitting in a comfortable rectory in rural Cambridgeshire, recalling his life by moonlight. The long-lost scenes all returning: the lonely bedroom of his childhood approached across a moonlit gallery filled with family portraits; boyhood pranks in moonlit woods, and the enduring memory of Oxford by moonlight. Cindy confirmed that Jeremiah went to Oxford in 1821, and graduated in 1825, having enjoyed 'a gentleman's education'. After Oxford, he took a curate's position in Staffordshire where five years were spent in rural isolation. For most of the time he was deprived of congenial company and often felt that he was preaching to lumpen congregations, 'too dull to understand'. The story would have been told many times and Gus would certainly have heard it. His grandfather had been rescued by a wealthy benefactor, a benevolent ghost, who flew in one day and transformed his life.

Chapter 7: Relations

There was always something phantasmagorical about Chauncy Hare Townshend. His family background was a rich mix of aristocratic blood and high City wealth, with extensive estates in Norfolk, London and Switzerland. Chauncy inherited a fortune. When young, he was thought good-looking: 'Those who knew Byron,' Bulwer Lytton recalled, 'said it was Byron with bloom and health.' After Eton, he went to Cambridge where his undergraduate poetry dazzled tutors and won him the Chancellor's Gold Medal. A sample was sent to Robert Southey and the poet invited him to stay in the Lake District where he rubbed shoulders with Wordsworth and Coleridge. Later, he forged a close friendship with Dickens and the great man dedicated a novel to him. A gilded man stepping confidently into a gilded world.

Yet, for all that, he was never happy. 'Chauncy Hare Townshend's life has been my *beau-ideal* of happiness,' Bulwer Lytton said, 'elegant rest, travel, lots of money but he is always ill and melancholy.' In 1856, Dickens found Chauncy on a cross-channel steamer, tucked up in his private carriage, and surrounded by a bizarre collection of invalid paraphernalia. 'I found Townshend on board, fastened up in his carriage, in a feeble wide-awake hat . . . He looked like an ancient Briton of weak constitution – say

Boadicea's father – in his war chariot on the field of battle.' When Dickens clambered aboard, he found the carriage 'perforated in every direction with cupboards, containing every description of physick, old brandy, East India sherry, sandwiches, oranges, cordial waters, newspapers, pocket handkerchiefs, shawls, flannels, telescopes, compasses, repeaters (for ascertaining the hour in the dark) and finger rings of great value. He asked me the extraordinary question 'how Mrs Williams, the American Actress, kept her wig on?' I then perceived that mankind was to be in a conspiracy to believe that he wears his own hair.'

Strange to relate, Chauncy was a close friend and patron of Gus's grandfather. They probably knew each other as boys; Jeremiah was born in Cambridge and spent much of his childhood there, and Chauncy's family had estates nearby. Then there was Eton; several of Jeremiah's friends attended the school, including Chauncy himself, although there is no mention of Jeremiah in the records. As for university, Jeremiah went to Oxford and Chauncy to Cambridge. In truth, it was hard to see how they met. Perhaps after all there were hidden family ties? Jeremiah's wife came from a noble family that claimed ancestral blood, so this was a distinct possibility. Finally, lacking any evidence to the contrary, we saw Chauncy as a benevolent ghost who entered Jeremiah's life at exactly the right moment.

Chauncy was ordained a clergyman but never needed to work, yet in 1828 he officiated at Jeremiah's wedding, and a year later, became a sponsor to his child. The closeness between the two men was obvious, and more amply demonstrated when we tracked Chauncy's papers to a museum in Wisbech where one of his personal albums had two silhouettes of Jeremiah.

Chauncy's silhouette of Jeremiah

Several well-paid clerical posts were in Chauncy's gift, including a wealthy living in Norfolk, so in December 1829, he offered it to Jeremiah and the relatively poor living in Staffordshire was exchanged for something that brought in a handsome four hundred pounds a year. Thirty years later, Chauncy raised the stakes still higher and presented him with a living worth eight hundred pounds.

One way that Jeremiah could express his heartfelt gratitude was to name some of his children after Chauncy, so Gus's father was christened Craufurd *Townsend* Bowen.

'What about Craufurd?' Gill wondered.

Sir George Craufurd turned out to be another patron, influential and powerful, and it soon emerged that Gus's grandfather lived for much of his life in privileged circles. He sat at tables where people talked routinely of royal drawing rooms, of the latest literary and artistic levées, of county politics and estate management. A well-educated clergyman like Jeremiah might not have much money, or indeed any titles, but at least he could be a lively conversationalist. The rich livings and comfortable rectories that Chauncy bestowed upon him were all well and good, but they were never his. And this was the problem: his children would never inherit. The hope was that Chauncy would support them, but who could tell?

Jeremiah fretted. Somehow or other, he had let them down; his children would have to make their own way in the world. 'This is the last will and testament of me, Jeremiah Bowen, made this day of September 1871.' He had not drafted a will before, he said, because his property hardly merited the effort. 'It is little enough now.' Nothing of any substance was left. Craufurd received a few personal items – his telescope, watch and books - and that was it. What little there was went to his unmarried daughters.

Gus's 'Aunt Em' had married a lawyer and might have prospered famously, but her husband took to drink and started bringing prostitutes home, so they divorced. The scandal was embarrassing but the family survived. Later, she opened a boarding school for girls and was joined by 'Aunt Charlie', who never married. Both sisters needed help.

Much of that help came from Jeremiah's two other daughters who both married well. Gus's 'Aunt Grace' married a wealthy clergyman who lived in a very grand house in King's Lynn; it still has the power to impress. 'We live in a pleasant house,' their daughter wrote in her journal: 'It is a large old-fashioned house with a good entrance hall. Many of the rooms are wainscoted . . . There is a room with four windows in it, here we often have tea and watch ships coming into the harbour . . . Miss Pycroft is the morning governess and Miss Street gives music lessons in the afternoon.' Later, they moved to Snettisham Hall, an even grander house, and Aunt Grace surveyed the scene with pride: 'How I wish I could sketch! If I live till my children are grown up, what a treasure the scene now before me will be.' 'Aunt Mary' did well too. She married a well-off university man and had a charming villa near Cambridge, complete with pleasure gardens, lawns and croquet grounds, vinery, orchards, stables, cow-houses, barns, coach-houses and pastures.

As a boy, Gus would visit these relations and sample their world. They would take him on tours of university colleges, encourage him to rub shoulders with well-off cousins who were studying at Eton, and introduce him to high society. There were moonlit walks through pleasure gardens, visits to ancestral tombs, glittering garden parties, champagne and claret.

He would taste it all.

Chapter 8: Vicarage

Rich relations; poor relations. Most families have them. Some people inherit; some don't. Some people marry well and some badly. Craufurd followed Jeremiah and made a career for himself in the church. His first post was well away from the rest of his family and took him north. In 1859, he came to the small village of Skelton-in-Cleveland and accepted the position of curate. The job was hardly well paid. People often referred to these appointments as 'starvation livings', and Craufurd earned only £150 a year. It was a start, and not dissimilar to the start that Jeremiah made himself. There would be a time of hardship and a time of preferment.

Hannah Tate was nineteen when he arrived. Young and pretty and poor. She lived with her family in a cottage overlooking the Town Green where Craufurd came to lodge. A simple watercolour survives in Hannah's family that shows the cottage. A venerable pear tree winds lazily between windows and doors. The building is divided in two and the door to one side stands open. The solitary figure standing in the picture, leaning nonchalantly against a gate post, is probably Craufurd himself. An empty carrier's cart stands beside him in the street, and may have belonged to Hannah's father who scratched a living as a common carrier and labourer.

Watercolour of Pear Tree Cottage, Skelton

Beyond the cottage, the road slips away. Half way down the hill was the parsonage house where Craufurd's senior clergyman lived. Then at the bottom, there was the church itself, a simple eighteenth-century structure untouched by Victorian ideas of restoration and nestling quietly in a leafy hollow. When Craufurd opened the door, he would have heard the sharp click of the latch as it echoed in the bare, whitewashed interior. We knew this because we went there one Sunday afternoon in Autumn and absorbed the gathering twilight. When Craufurd climbed the three-decker pulpit (as we did) he looked out over a maze of box pews with family names emblazoned on the sides.

'Nothing's changed,' I whispered and held my breath. There were rooks outside.

'What's this?' Gill said, walking over to a raised pew complete with fireplace.

A dog-eared pile of damp pamphlets gave the story. It was the squire's pew. By all accounts, he would poke the fire vigorously whenever sermons dragged on too long. Craufurd was spared this indignity when his senior clergyman took pity on him and sent him to the tiny village of Upleatham across the valley, half hidden in the blue mistiness that forms a backdrop to the painting. It was here that he stumbled through his first sermon.

The Tates were not well off. Hannah's father struggled to make a living. Always at the beck and call of farmers, and sometimes in the depths of winter never called at all, John Tate earned something like three and sixpence a day. 'Hard addlings,' the locals called it. Never enough to keep a family. So there was no other option for it: wives and children would work too. Children went out to the fields, some to scaring birds, some to weeding, some to running errands, some to haymaking and harvesting. Single and married women would clear stones, scale manure, set potatoes, make hay, shear corn. The sight of them sweating away at haystacks, or 'beclarted' with muck, offended modern notions of decency. 'It is the most primitive society,' one newspaper in the 1860s complained, 'as rough as the old Norse colony from which it sprang years ago.'

Yet others were fascinated. Here was a customary world sharpened by want. A population that was wedded to the soil, with its own voice and its own folk ways, and if you doubted it, all you had to do was listen to the talk. A *Glossary of the Cleveland Dialect* appeared in 1868 and for many years it sat on my desk like a family bible. Each day I would turn its pages and savour its sounds. I was trying to find a few dialect words that might describe Hannah.

'Do you think she might have been a 'bamsey'?' I said, pointing to an early page. 'A fat red-faced female!'

Gill grimaced.

'What about this then - a 'brole'? An impudent hussy who is bold and unblushing?'

In truth, Hannah's mother came from farming stock and brought some pride to the table. As far as we could tell, Hannah and her brother were never sent to the fields but were educated and encouraged to speak properly. Her brother managed to secure a post in a local solicitor's office whilst Hannah herself, according to stories preserved in the family, was sufficiently well educated to work as a governess.

Hannah in later life

Flirtations and affairs between gentlemen and lower-class women were not uncommon in the Victorian years but almost always short-lived. Their liaisons came and went; allowances were made; eyes averted. So when Craufurd seemed to be drawn to Hannah and all her country-girl prettiness, there was nothing to suggest a scandal. There would be shy glances, whispered conversations, keepsakes and country walks. He lodged with the Tates and brushed against her every day, so this closeness was only a matter of time.

But then a letter was sent back to Norfolk that changed everything. Craufurd talked of marrying Hannah, and Chauncy Hare Townsend was so flabbergasted that he withdrew his patronage on the spot. Three years later, he presented Jeremiah to a new living and could easily have given Craufurd a plumb post worth £400 a year, but this hot-headed romance with a pretty country girl destroyed everything. From this point on, he was entirely cut off.

Craufurd married Hannah in August 1860, barely six months after coming to Skelton, and their first child was born nine months later. There may have been some illicit lovemaking. Chauncy disapproved of the marriage but the Bowens accepted it. Eyebrows were raised and heads shaken, but his marriage to Hannah was weathered. It happened in another part of the country, well away from Norfolk and Cambridgeshire, so there was no immediate threat to the family. From this point on, Craufurd and Hannah made their own way in life, unaided by patronage and high connection, but still in touch with the wider family.

News reached him in July 1866 of a desirable living in the rural community of Bolam. Here was a chance to better himself. He had been tipped off by one of his sisters and personal connections counted for everything in this oily game of preferment. The Rev. Edleston was the resident clergyman for Bolam, so Craufurd's sister reminded him that they had known Edleston's wife in Cambridge. It was exactly the opening card he needed to play. 'Dear sir, I have just received a letter from my sister . . . about the Bolam Curacy. I should like to come over at once to see the place . . . I will bring testimonials with me. Please remember me very kindly to Mrs. Edleston whom I had the pleasure of knowing very well some years ago. I remain, Yours very faithfully, Craufurd Townsend Bowen.'

A written testimonial was provided by his rector, sealed in an envelope, and popped in Craufurd's pocket. He took a train to Gainford and found a pretty village on the banks of the Tees where the river ran through green and peaceful country. The Edlestons lived in a handsome house overlooking the village green, with a splendid garden running down to the riverbank. The tiny village of Bolam was about five miles off and formed part of Gainford parish. The place was perfect; a rural parish in lush countryside where Craufurd could live out his quiet life. Gainford village had an air of southern softness about it, and the changes that rolled over its lichen-covered roofs were the kind of changes that Craufurd liked best, slow and seasonal. During the afternoon, the two men talked, and Craufurd renewed his acquaintance with Mrs Edleston. Everything seemed to go well and he journeyed home that evening confident that he had made a good impression but, before leaving, he gave Edleston the testimonial.

'I am sorry my incumbent had so little to say in praise after the good service I have done him.' Craufurd wrote to Edleston a short time after, nonplussed by the news that the reference had been less than flattering. 'Not a word about preaching; not a word about love for, or devotion to the work . . . But I need not commend myself; I would fair leave that for others to do for me, but I think without any undue self-commendation on my own part, I may say of the people both in Guisborough and Skelton, my former curacy, "they are my epistle" . . . I wish it had been unnecessary for me to say all this as it seems to savour of self-praise, but I must do myself justice.'

All was not lost. Craufurd sent his regards to Mrs Edleston and hoped she might rally to his cause. She did. With an imperious sweep of her hand, she dismissed the poor testimonial and put her trust in family ties. Craufurd would need rooms in the village and she began making enquiries. Meanwhile, her husband dithered.

'Dear Doctor Edleston', Craufurd whispered a year later as he roused the old rector from what appeared to be a long and fitful nap: 'I am afraid if I do not take care that I shall soon be left in the lurch. My Rector, as soon as I told him that I was likely to be leaving . . . gave me to understand that he could not work with a man that was on the move, and gave me notice to go . . . If the appointment to the district of Bolam is to be made in the course of a month or two, I will not seek another curacy but should be negligent beyond this time . . . With very kind regards to yourself and Mrs Edleston.'

A week later, Edleston offered him a temporary curacy. It was hardly the ideal solution but it would tide him over till Bolam could be sorted, and Edleston was sure that Bolam would be sorted, sooner or later. One of the problems, he said, was finding a suitable vicarage. He hinted at the possibility that Craufurd's father might step forward and help? Perhaps Jeremiah would contribute to the building of a new house? When Craufurd broached the subject, there was a predictable wringing of hands and the matter dropped. In the meantime, lodgings were found and Craufurd settled into the village, leaving Hannah in Skelton with her father and mother. She was expecting their third child. Craufurd rolled his sleeves up and got down to business. Yes, he said to the organisers of an evening concert, he would be delighted to give a reading, and hit upon the idea of a Longfellow poem. Whenever he could, he travelled back to see the new baby, who they christened Charles Arthur Augustine Bowen. Soon, however, he would be known as Gus.

We could see how Craufurd fell in love with the place. Gainford stood near the river and one summer afternoon we sat on the riverbank throwing stones in the water. A soft breeze rustled through the trees and the air hummed with insects. During the morning, we had walked the fields between Gainford and Bolam. In one lush meadow we stood for ten minutes listening to a tracery of lark song rising high above us. Here was a place where Craufurd could minister to a genteel congregation, paint his watercolours, keep one or two hens, and spend his peaceful nights gazing up at the stars.

If only Bolam could be sorted. Trinity College had the final say for it was in their gift. His precarious position dragged on for two years until news reached him in 1869 that Bolam would go to an ex-fellow of Trinity.

'I have but little hope of obtaining the appointment', he urged Edleston, 'unless my application be well backed by yourself,' and for once, he cast aside his reserve and spoke plainly. 'Permit me to remind you', he said, 'that I left a good Curacy . . . and a diocese in which I had made many valuable friends, both amongst the Clergy and Laity of high standing and position, solely and entirely because all-but-certain preferment was offered me . . . In the circumstances,

I hope I may rely upon you for giving me what help you can to render my application for Bolam successful.'

For his part, the Bursar of Trinity College was not optimistic. 'It is a question between yourself and another gentleman, and the Seniority will have to decide the matter. But as your competitor was formerly a member of the foundation of this college and is strongly recommended by his Tutor, I think he will be preferred.'

When Edleston went to Cambridge, there was little hope of success. It seemed to be a *fait accompli*. Yet against all odds, he pulled it off. Craufurd was appointed. There was still no vicarage, so he would remain in Gainford and walk the five miles to Bolam every day. Five miles there and five miles back. And soon it became a kind of personal pilgrimage; the way he entered the landscape. During the 1870s and 1880s, the sight of him walking the narrow lanes between Gainford and Bolam became as familiar as the cows in the fields.

Then, in 1884, the Old Hall at Bolam was put on the market and several wealthy patrons were persuaded to organise a fund-raising campaign to turn it into a vicarage. The house was in poor condition but at least it would give Craufurd a home in the village. An estimated five hundred pounds was needed to make it habitable, but for all its problems, the old place had some attractions; there was a venerable seventeenth-century fireplace, acres of eighteenth-century wainscoting and a general patina of old age. Donations trickled in and a fund-raising bazaar was organised. At the end of the bazaar, Craufurd made a little speech. 'It is very gratifying to me,' he began, 'to find this kindly feeling expressed in this very pleasant way towards myself. You all know that I have walked backwards and forwards to Bolam, a journey occupying an hour and half each way, during the fourteen years I have been vicar here, and it has begun to tell on my health.' People smiled and clapped. The money was raised.

Craufurd and Hannah: Bolam Vicarage

By the following year, renovations were complete and the Bowens moved in. In truth, the house was still unfinished and a good deal of work was needed to make it comfortable, but this would come. The Moonlight Dance was one of many fund-raising events that finally turned it into a delightful home. But for now, they had arrived.

'Gus's world,' I said with a smile.

We were standing outside the house on a frosty morning, and the place looked idyllic. There was an old-fashioned holly wreath hanging on its door.

Chapter 9: Spooning

One day, Cindy emailed in a state of great excitement. She had found a website dedicated to Chauncy Hare Townshend and decided to post a message on it. Did anyone know anything about his friendship with Jeremiah? Incredibly, someone did. Her name was Patti Bergh, and she and her husband lived in Canada. A day later, Cindy emailed a second time. Patti had rooted through her family papers and come across some journals written by Gus's brother. It was almost too good to be true. A flurry of emails followed, twenty-one in all, each with a batch of attachments, and by Christmas, we had a full set.

The journals began in July 1880, five years before the Bowens moved to Bolam and were still in Gainford. Gus's brother was eighteen, almost seven years older than Gus, and known as 'Bro'. The first entry set the tone: 'Sunday, the 25th of July, 1880: Very hot. Church in morning. Went down by riverside with Nap & Anna Grieveson. Spooned Nap.'

Flirting with girls never seemed to stop. I pointed to a drawing that Bro made of two faces kissing; it was one of many drawings that we came across in the margins of his journal. After evening service, he was doing it again. Bro and his friend took the same girls for a walk. One Spring evening, we did the same, heading into the countryside. The lanes were narrow and always bordered by wide-open fields. One or two farmhouses were dotted about in the emptiness of it all, but that was it. Open countryside on all sides and plenty of space for spooning.

We already knew something of Gainford from Annie's papers. When she came to the village she was in her twenties - twenty-seven to be exact - and her happiness can be measured by the number of souvenirs she kept; the programmes and posters that were her mementoes of a special place and time. We cleaned and sorted them and gradually pieced them together. There were church bazaars and amateur theatricals, harvest festivals and cricket matches, the cosiness of winter recitals and the worthiness of fund-raising concerts. One Sunday, we sat cross-legged before a roaring fire with a patchwork of programmes before us.

'Carriages at 10.30!' I laughed, handing a newly discovered programme to Gill. It was a fund-raising concert for Gainford Cricket Club.

'It's rather good,' she said, blowing off the dust. 'Fine-quality, cream-coloured paper. Fashionable illustrations – very *fin-de siècle*.'

We saw that a Miss Donkin opened the concert with a song by Elizabeth Barrett Browning, set to music by Theo Marzials, one of Oscar Wilde's set. We found no trace of Kate Donkin in Gainford but soon discovered that she was the daughter of a wealthy ship-owner from Northumberland, and now based in London. Kate was engaged to a young officer who lived on the outskirts of the village, described as an 'all-round good fellow'.

Local talent performed too. The Rev. Ryan got up and gave a rousing rendition of 'The Gallants of England':

> Ho! Fill me a flagon as deep as you please,
> Ho! Pledge me the health we all quaff on our knees,
> And the knave who refuses to drink till he fall,
> Why the hangman shall crop him

The hangman shall crop him,
The hangman shall crop him
Ears, love-locks and all . . .

Not, by the look of it, a teetotal fanatic. Nor for that matter was Gus's fun-loving brother. 'Friday, 4th March 1881: Beastly day. Turned teetotal. Saturday, 5th March 1881: Ditto. Broke teetotal.'

Bro was apprenticed to a civil engineer and his diary made passing references to work, but mostly it was a celebration of youthful delights – the joys of spooning, smoking, drinking and larking. The kind of pleasures Gus loved. There was ample opportunity to enjoy them; a glorious two-week holiday in August, free Saturdays and Sundays, early finishes at work, and endless larks in the evenings. They were part of a prosperous, easy-going world. Charles Penney, one of Bro's friends, worked for his father in their printing business. The Grieveson girls were daughters of a 'commercial traveller'. Bro spent many evenings with the Simpsons, a wealthy banking family. Then, there were the Adamsons, who were builders; Henry Tennant, a National Schoolmaster, Frank Homfray, the son of a physician. All having fun.

Craufurd and Hannah gave Bro and Gus the freedom to be gentlemen; the chance to make the right connections, to handle themselves well, to live a little wild and act the part. They were learning the rules. Sometimes Bro went to Cambridge and tasted the real thing, spending days with 'Aunt Mary' and her wealthy family. It was all within reach. On his final day with them in 1880, he left Cambridge by the 10.05 train, landed home in Gainford by five, joined the Grievesons for a picnic by the river, spooned a bit, stayed for supper, and got home after midnight.

What we assumed to be the dull isolation of a village like Gainford turned out to be a myth. Cambridge or London were less than a day away. The village had its railway station and the Bowens could travel where they pleased. One August Bank Holiday, Bro wheeled his penny-farthing up to the station and loaded it on the

7.20 train for Penrith. From here, he bicycled to Pooley Bridge, hired a boat, rowed across Ullswater, had lunch in a nearby hotel, rode back to the station, and was home in time for tea. Later that evening, he called on friends and took a girl out walking. 'Went to bed early.'

A few days after, he took another girl out but was stopped by rain. Undeterred, he whisked her into the back room of a pub and did a little spooning. Afterwards, he went to another pub, and then to the village dance, where a gorgeous girl gave him 'the blue devils'. Then there was Maggie Barker. Maggie came from Seaton Carew, a seaside town on the North East coast. In the first week of the summer holiday, Bro and a friend cycled over and had a glass of sherry with Maggie. She and her sister met them in the upstairs room of a hotel. That evening, they attended the theatre in Hartlepool and watched a performance of *Lady Audley's Secret*, Mary Braddon's sensational romance of family secrets and murder. The next day was a sizzler. A Sunday. 'Not at church at all', he wrote. He wore knickerbockers and a Tam o' Shanter, and frisked about with two girls on the beach. That evening, there was another stroll, this time with new girls. The day after that, they went to the beach again and larked about with a group of very 'jolly girls', one of them 'an unsophisticated damsel.' They swapped hats and played games until midnight.

Spooning was fun. So too was drinking. A riverside picnic near Barnard Castle was a marvellous chance to get tight; 'the quantity of liquor imbibed,' he boasted, 'was something terrific. I fell in the river.' In September, he made the acquaintance of an artist who turned out to be a 'splendid fellow'. Bro posed in the nude, smoked a pipe, and drew a picture of himself in the margin of his diary, just to prove it. Later that week, they crossed the river and sat all night on the roof of an old pigeon-cote drinking whisky. They were both keen swimmers and shared dips with Gus. Craufurd joined in too. He loved swimming.

Then there were Saturday games of football and hair-brained

expeditions that nearly ended in catastrophe. In 1880, Bro and friend paddled two canoes down the Tees and into the North Sea: 'It was very rough & we thought we ought to have made our wills before leaving, but got to Redcar safe but utterly exhausted after a very rough passage. The sea much calmer at Redcar. We had a bottle of champagne & then a big dinner at the Coatham Hotel. Jolly band playing outside. Caught 9.13 train to Stockton. Went into Bays & liquored'.

We lost count of the times he crept home in the early hours of the morning. Or never came home at all. 'My people never knew', he admitted. One time, he scrambled through a window while the family slept. There were no reproofs, or none that we could find. One of his friends was censured for taking too many liberties with a girl, and Bro was given a pamphlet about the dangers of smoking, but these were the only times when adults thought they should lecture or disapprove. Apart from one notable Sunday.

A stick figure appears in the margin of Bro's journal, standing in a pulpit and glaring down at a sinner below. A black line runs from the eye of the clergyman to the eye of the sinner. The Rev Blackburn Clarke was the new curate of the parish and had heard of Bro's exploits. 'Clarke stared at me awfully in church. Great excitement.' By the following evening, Craufurd weighed in, not against Bro, but the poor curate. He had overstepped the mark and Craufurd 'sat on him'. Social connections meant everything and Miss Nesham, an influential spinster in Gainford Hall, was persuaded to sit on him too. This was not a straight-laced community.

Come Christmas, Bro was on the shoulders of the bank manager, putting up mistletoe in the church porch. On Christmas Eve he went to the Simpson's and stayed till three. Then on Christmas Day, he did the decent thing and attended church. Straight after, he ran up to Headlam Hall where the new love of his life was living. Her name was Laura Pape. On Boxing Day, he went to Headlam again and skated with Laura. Then, on New Year's Eve, he attended a 'Servant's Party' and stayed the night.

I hope you will have a very happy Christmas, one of Annie's friends wrote, *don't forget your old pal in the midst of all your festivities . . . Gainford is always so wildly gay at Christmas time.*

Gus was part of this scene and so too was his sister, Emily. She was courting a young man called Richard Elgey from a wealthy family on the outskirts of Gainford. The Elgeys had a farm of six-hundred-acres and were well off. Like Bro and Gus, Richard lived wild. He was two years older than Bro and three years older than Emily.

'You needn't run, Mr. Elgey,' a local policeman shouted when he caught him daubing paint over Gainford Railway Station in 1885. 'I know you.'

He was hauled before the magistrates and found guilty.

'It is always a source of regret,' the Chair of the Bench sighed, 'to deal with persons of the defendant's position.' But this was par for the course. Gainford was full of young people from perfectly respectable families who were living on the wild side. It was a revelation.

Patti sent more journals. Some had been lost and there was a gap of eight years between 1880 and 1888. Once we picked up the story, Bro's wild years were over. He had settled down. By 1888, he and Laura had married and had three children. He was working as an engineer for the North Eastern Railway and doing well. Gus had grown up too and was sailing with the Brocklebanks: 'Saturday 27th October 1888: Guss turned up about 10 o'clock having driven from D'ton (Darlington) in a cab. 130 days voyage from Calcutta to Liverpool. He landed on Friday night. Of course it was late when we got to bed, about 2 next morning.'

Gus stayed three weeks, sometimes in Bolam, sometimes in Gainford. Every now and then, he went to Darlington where he was spooning a girl. She may even have been Annie. The days passed: 'Sunday 18th November 1888: Packing Guss' things & mooching about generally all day. Bed rather late. Had a dip in the morning.

Monday 19^{th:} Guss went off to join his ship, the 'Sindia' at Liverpool. This will be his last voyage before he is out of his time.'

The last tangible whiff came in Bro's journal as he waved good bye. It was 1888. Newspapers of the time said the ship reached Calcutta in April 1889, and Gus stayed a few months before returning on the *Ameer*. Where once it would have taken a sailing ship three months to sail from England to India, a steamer like the *Ameer* could do it in less than a month. The ship reached Liverpool in November 1889, and then went back to Calcutta in the early part of 1890.

After that, we lost him.

Bro in later life

Chapter 10: Tom

Down he went. Down to an almost impenetrable depth, loafing in a world of subterranean pleasure. Occasionally, we caught sight of him as he rose to the surface and saw for a moment the life he was leading, but only a moment.

We tried to follow the leads. The *Ameer* steamed into London from Calcutta on May 14, 1890 and Gus packed his bags. He headed home to spend time with Bro and his parents, but a month later, he was off again. Loafing in Bolam was no longer enough. He might play the lion here, telling tales and spinning yarns, but Gainford and Bolam were tame places for a man who knew Calcutta.

'This might be the first time that Annie sees him,' Gill said, 'Doesn't she come to Gainford in 1890?'

If so, it can't have been for long because Gus was on the move. He made another voyage around this time. The *Empusa* sailed to Middlesbrough where it collected a cargo of steel. Most of the crew had signed up for the voyage in London, so Gus was the last to join. There were twenty-four men in all, including a Second Mate called Tom Sadler. They sailed to the port of Aguilas on the coast of Spain where a group of British capitalists were building new railways and mines. The boat arrived towards the end of June, unloaded its cargo, took a fresh consignment, and remained a week. It left again on July

7 and returned to Newport. A few days later, Gus and Tom signed for another voyage, this time to Patras in Greece. They were becoming shipmates and by early September 1890, they were back in England.

Both came from similar backgrounds and it was easy to see why they became friends. Tom's father had been a clerk in a well-to-do legal practice in Lincoln's Inn, and might have done well for himself had he not contracted tuberculosis; it killed him when he was only twenty-seven. Tom was three at the time. His mother did the best she could to keep things afloat, taking in work as a needlewoman and renting rooms in the East End. Their fragile middle-class world had been destroyed at a stroke, and the precariousness of this existence was not lost on Tom. What was the point? Better to live life as a loafer. Better to grab what you could before it was too late. Tom's mother never stopped hoping they might recover the ground they had lost and she taught him to read and write, first drilling him with words of one syllable, then two, then three and four. It was simple and crude but it was her way of keeping hope alive. When he was nine, she scraped a little money together to pay for his schooling. Tom studied for six years and then found a job as a clerk. The chance was there; he might have accomplished what his mother wanted and reclaimed the ground, but it was not to be. He grew discontented. Clerking was a dull business and worse still, it was unmanly. 'Born a man, died a clerk.' was a favourite jest of the period. Slumped in his office, gazing at ships and mariners who had touched the four corners of the world, he resolved to break free.

'I bitterly regret that day,' his mother said.

Something happened after that Greek voyage. Gus gave up the sea and never went back for five years. We didn't know what caused this, but something happened. At least it meant that he was somewhere in the country and we could find him, so I began looking. I searched and searched the 1891 census and found nothing. There was no sign of 'Charles Arthur Augustine Bowen'. Plenty of Charles Bowens, all of them checked, and none like him.

'So perhaps he is back at sea?'

I shook my head. 'In 1896 he says the *Empusa* was his last ship. If he served on other ships he would have given their names. There's no reason to lie.'

Our best guess was that he was somewhere in London, but the prospect of checking millions of Londoners on the off chance of finding him was crazy. I turned to newspapers but they were equally daunting. Typing in the name, 'Bowen' produced 21,323 hits between 1890 and 1900.

'What about the *Empusa*?' Gill said.

It was worth a try. I typed the name and there were 119 hits. A little less daunting but daunting enough. It seemed impossible, but just as I was about to give up, I saw something. The record of a conversation:

'I opened the gate and said, "What ship?"'

He said, "The *Empusa*."

That ship belongs to the same firm as the *Fez*, and the two vessels were lying in St. Katherine's Docks.

I said, "What are you?"

He said, "A donkeyman."'

A chance discovery. Something wholly unexpected. A serendipity moment that took us deeper. During the next few weeks, we seemed to sink into a grotesque form of darkness; the buried subterranean holes where Gus and Tom were taking their pleasure.

A gatekeeper at St. Katherine's Docks had remembered a testy confrontation with Tom when he was trying to return to his ship after a wild night in Whitechapel. It was reported in the newspaper. Confronted by the gatekeeper, Tom called himself a 'Donkeyman'. This was a piece of sailor slang for a 'Fireman', one of the hard-bitten men who sweated below decks on tramp steamers, shovelling coal into boilers.

Tom was older than Gus and married. Back in 1877, he had come across Sally Chapman, a young woman of only twenty-six to his weather-beaten thirty-eight. A 'pleasant-faced, comely, and hard-working' lass someone said. She married him and instantly regretted it.

'I was married on Thursday,' Sally said, 'but I knew by Sunday I'd made a mistake, and I've known it ever since.'

Tom's mother thought the marriage changed him, and not for the better. He was becoming harder, drinking heavily, acquiring an unpredictable edge, and sometimes turning violent. His mother and wife knew his moods and took a pride in handling him.

'He didn't go for me,' Sally boasted, 'I always looked after that. I always kept him at a distance.'

Living with Tom was an up-and-down affair. One Sunday morning, he woke in a loving mood and made Sally breakfast, but soon he went off to his Radical club and came back drunk.

'There's papa!' his daughter shouted, 'he's tight.'

Sally trained her as best she could: better to coax and flatter him, she said. Better to say, 'Shall I get your slippers?', but the little girl was frightened and ran away. Most of the afternoon Sally was cooking Tom's dinner, but now she thought to herself, 'It's all for nothing. I've got a drunkard's home.'

They were about to start the meal when there was a knock at the door. Sally went to answer it, and half way down the stairs she saw a woman's head through the skylight, and thought it might be her niece.

'How can I ask her up?' she asked, and ran back. 'This is a nice place to ask my friends. It is nothing but a drunkard's home!'

Tom exploded, hurling his dinner across the room and overturning the table. Sally ran downstairs, opened the door, and discovered that it was a Sunday-school teacher wondering why their daughter had not attended chapel. As the two women tried to sustain a polite conversation, they could hear Tom destroying the room upstairs. He took a hammer to a mirror, a pair of lustres and eight pictures. Sally reckoned he would have started on the furniture, but the drawers and washstand were too heavy.

Most days, he was sober and tender-hearted. 'Why,' Sally said with a brave smile, 'if a strange cat came into the house, he would not turn it out again till he had sent for a 'penn'rth' of cat's meat.' It was a pity that he drank, but a man wanted a glass of beer. She was proud of him. Proud of his learning. He could read newspapers and knew something of the theatre. He knew about politics too. Did you know he could write a beautiful hand? Well, he could, and she knew it. Most of the time, he hid this from everyone. Kept it secret. And only she knew about the little diary he kept; the curious record of his voyages and the things he had seen. There was no doubt about it, Tom had a secret side, an air of mystery, a submerged intelligence that only Sally knew about. Half proud and half frightened, she boasted of his strength – he was as 'strong as an elephant with wrists like iron'. Never a big man, he was thick set and just like Gus, walked the streets with a sailor's jaunt and swagger. His dark complexion made him stand out. Sally loved him.

She wanted him to quit the sea. Why couldn't he settle down and make a life with her? Tom tried to please her but it was no use; he always went back. So, when he signed up for another voyage in August 1888, Sally told her friends that he had left her, and she went back to her mother where she made a living of sorts as a washerwoman. Nothing was heard from Tom for over a year, and then out of the blue, he wrote to her. Would Sally meet him in London? She agreed to see him but soon they fell to bickering. That night, they tried to get a room in a coffee house but Sally was crying and the manager wouldn't let them in.

'I will tell you what we will do', Sally said, 'You go your way, and I will go mine. I will never live with you anymore.'

And off she ran.

'Now, Sally, what do you mean?' he said, catching up with her. 'You're not afraid of me?'

Gradually, he calmed her down. What they should do, he said, was get a bite to eat. She would feel better after that, so he took her to a stewed-eel shop.

'Halloa, Tom!' a brassy woman shouted as the two of them

walked in, 'How are you?'

'I am all right,' he said, looking away.

'That party you were with the other night,' the woman said, 'She's gone to Manchester.'

It was no use. Sally left him and they lived apart. She saw nothing of him for two years, then out of the blue, he turned up again. It was just before Christmas and he stayed for two days. He left on Christmas Eve, telling her that he was joining another ship. It was called the *Fez* and they were sailing to the Canaries. She never said it, but he looked older. His hair and beard were grizzled, his face worn and tired. He was changing, and she could see it. Some things were still the same though. He was still wearing his favourite double-breasted jacket, and his black and white scarf stained with tobacco spit.

Chapter 11: Whitechapel

The *Fez* and the *Empusa* belonged to the same company. When Tom's ship docked in London on February 11th 1891, the two ships lay together. Off he went for a night in Whitechapel, and led us in the fullness of time to Gus.

His first port of call was a public house in Goulston Street where he downed a glass of gin. Next, he moved onto *The Princess Alice* where he bumped into Frances Coles. The previous year, they had spent a night together in a common lodging house, so he bought her a glass of gin and they chatted. Off they went to the next pub. Around eleven, Frances led him to White's Row Chambers, a lodging house with 'doubles' – special rooms where prostitutes and clients could spend the night. Frances knew her business. They got there before the pubs closed so they could beat the rush. She often used this lodging house and the people liked her. She never caused any trouble; she was quiet and good natured, sometimes a little drunk, but never violent.

Tom and Frances surfaced next day around lunchtime. He was the first to admit that they'd been drinking heavily; mainly gin and cloves, but sometimes gin and peppermint, rum and milk, whisky and beer. Frances waited till the moment was right. When he was well-oiled, she asked if he would buy her a hat. A nice black one.

She'd been fancying a black hat for long time.

'You had better have some underclothing,' he said, 'for what you have is old and dirty.'

No, she said, she fancied the hat. So off they went. Tom stood outside the shop until she brought it out. He inspected it and agreed to pay. They parted company but met up again in another pub and decided to spend the night in Thrawl Street where Frances was lodging. The only trouble was, she owed rent. At the last minute, she decided it was too dangerous and thought they should go back to White's Row Chambers.

'We will go to Thrawl Street,' Tom bawled, beating his chest and challenging the world, 'I'm afraid of nothing.'

Just then a woman walked by and felled him. She'd been carrying a bottle and hit him over the head. He slumped to the ground and a well-organised gang surrounded him. They kicked and punched him and stole his valuables. When he came to, he accused Frances of helping them and they began arguing. Finally, they parted.

Back in White's Row Chambers, Frances flopped in front of the fire. Several lodgers admired her new hat. Yes, she said, it was a nice one and threw her old hat on the flames. One of the lodgers jumped up and rescued it. There, he said, you'd better keep it, just in case. Lulled by the warmth, Frances fell asleep, her head on the table. An hour later, Tom turned up.

'Well, there she is,' the doorkeeper said, pointing to Frances, 'asleep with her head on the table.'

He tried to wake her but she was gone. There was blood on Tom's face so the doorkeeper took him out and cleaned him up. When they returned, Tom did his best to wake Frances but it was hopeless. She had spent all his money and there was nothing left. Anxious to find shelter, but with nothing in his pocket, he pulled out his discharge papers and asked if anyone would lend him two shillings. He would pay them four shillings the next day.

'Come along old chap, 'the doorkeeper said, taking him by the arm, 'you had better get out; you are only getting into trouble.'

There was only one thing to do. He would sleep on his ship. At half past one in the morning, he arrived at the dock gates where Henry Sutton was on duty.

'What ship?' Sutton asked.

Tom was fuddled. He should have said the *Fez* but thought he was on the *Empusa*, the ship that he and Gus had sailed on.

'What are you?' Sutton asked.

'A donkeyman.'

Sutton was about to let him through when he looked at Tom's face. 'How do you account for that?' he said, pointing to the blood.

'I got it in a scuffle in Brick Lane.'

'I can't admit you. You're not in a fit state to be admitted.'

Tom stood his ground so Sutton pushed him. He staggered and fell, and lay there half dazed. A policeman came up and tried to rouse him.

'I want to get to my ship.' Tom groaned.

Then a group of dockers appeared. 'What's up, old man?'

'I want to get to my ship and he won't allow me.'

'I'll give you a lodging,' one docker said, and tried to lift Tom, but he lashed out and caught the man's face. It was almost as if he wanted a beating.

The policeman winked and walked off. For the next few minutes, the dockers kicked Tom and gave him a thrashing.

'Don't touch him anymore,' the policeman said when he finally came back, 'he's had enough.'

Tom staggered away. A waiter in a coffee shop saw him coming up the street and talking to other policemen. One of them examined Tom's ribs and thought they were bruised rather than broken.

'No, I don't think I'm so much hurt,' Tom admitted. It was just past two and he made his way to White's Row Chambers again.

The doorkeeper noticed the fresh blood. 'Have you been at it again?'

Tom asked if Frances was there.

'I've not seen her,' the manageress said, 'She went out a little after twelve.'

'Can I go in the kitchen? I feel so faint.'

'No, we don't allow any strangers here, and no one is allowed to stop in the kitchen. There would be a £5 penalty against us.'

'Look at me,' Tom pleaded, 'I am all over blood. Look at my head!'

'Well, I can't help you; you must get out.'

'You're a very hard-hearted woman.'

Tom headed towards the East End where he knew there was a hospital. About the middle of the Whitechapel Road, a young policeman stopped him. Where was he going? He told the policeman he had been assaulted and thought he had been cut with a knife. The policeman stared at him, 'Have you a knife about you?'

'I told him,' Tom said, 'that I didn't carry a knife. My shipmates, one Matt Curley, and another named Bowen, know that I have not carried a knife for years.'

Gus was being sucked in. The young policeman found no knife and let Tom go, and just before five, he reached the hospital where a night porter examined his wounds.

'I've been with a woman and she's done me,' Tom mumbled. He was shivering. The porter looked at all the blood. There was too much. Tom told him he had cut his finger but the porter shook his head, 'That would not cause all that blood.' A nurse was called and she dressed the wounds, and then they allowed him to sleep.

At six-thirty, they kicked him out. A waiter in a nearby-by coffee shop agreed that he could sit in a corner and keep warm. Around half-past eight, Tom pulled himself together and wandered off, heading in the direction of the shipping office where he planned to collect his wages.

'I got into a row in George Street, Spitalfields,' he told the clerk who asked about the blood on Tom's face, 'I was knocked about by some old hags.'

He picked up the money and went to a Sailor's Home. On the

way, he heard the newsboys shouting the latest headline.

'There has been another murder in Whitechapel,' the *Daily News* reported, 'The victim was of the "unfortunate" class. She was butchered with one terrible stroke.' It was enough. The mere mention of a murder like this in Whitechapel was a sure sign that the Ripper was back. 'In its general features, this bears a close resemblance to all the other Whitechapel crimes.'

The horror that had haunted Whitechapel three years before was still fresh in the mind. Unfinished business. 'Jack the Ripper' had mutilated his victims and walked away coolly into the London night. He was now the new bogeyman of the streets. Sooner or later, people said, he would be back. He was just taking his time.

And here he was, just as they predicted, back to his old tricks. Stepping out of the shadows. The police were quick to link this death to the five other murders that had taken place in 1888. Less than an hour after the body was found, a telegram was sent to every police station in the city – 'Another Murder in Whitechapel' – and everyone knew what it meant. Twelve hours later, the police issued a statement claiming the crime was probably the work of the previous killer and ordered the docks, wharves and steamers to be searched. London newspapers carried the story in their afternoon editions, and by evening it was global.

Reporters gathered at the scene and were jostled by sightseers. A gang of youths offered makeshift performances. Matches were lit so they could see the spot. It was under a railway arch and the police had chalked an 'X'. The youths conducted mock searches and seized girls to show how 'Jack' operated. Then a piano-organ came and they started dancing.

A bizarre clue had been found. As the police turned the body, a woman's hat emerged. It was nestling under the victim's skirt and everyone read the portents. One detective talked of their suspicions that the Ripper must be a woman. But then he stopped. 'What strange inducement,' he wondered, 'must have been offered to get one woman to accompany another to such a spot?' The room fell silent.

The two hats were curious. When a lodger from White's Row Chambers heard about them, he knew what had happened. He ran to the house and asked if Frances had been seen.

'Let us go and see if it is her,' they said, and walked in procession, first to the police station and then to the mortuary.

Chapter 12: Ripper

Tom lay low. Bruised and battered and nursing a hangover. Outside his window, he could hear people shouting the news and beyond the door, sailors were talking and laughing. Everyone wondering if the Ripper was back. Suddenly and unbelievably, Tom was the most wanted man in the world. Scores of witnesses had seen him with Frances. They had been drinking together for almost two days, so he knew it was only a matter of time. Somebody would collar him. One of the lodgers at Whites' Chambers was already giving evidence and touring Whitechapel with the police, looking for him. All they had to do was track him down.

Next morning, Tom went for a drink. Hair of the dog. He would face the inevitable. He leaned against the bar and waited. The witness finally came in, saw him and ran out to tell the police, and they ordered him into the street.

'I expected this,' Tom said, as he sauntered out. On his way to the police station, he turned and smiled. 'I am a married man, and this will part me from my wife. But you know what we sailors are.'

'This is the man,' the police said as they marched him into Leeman Street Police Station.

'Am I arrested for it?'

'No, certainly not,' the officer said, 'but it is necessary to take a statement from you to help us throw light on the matter.'

Tom struggled to remember anything. The drink was fogging his mind. 'The prevalent belief amongst all who have had occasion to investigate the circumstances,' the *Daily News* reckoned, 'is that the person who has earned for himself the name of Jack-the-Ripper has once more commenced his terrible operations.' Back in the Autumn of 1888, there was talk of a sailor being the man in question, and now it looked to be true. Admittedly, there were a few uncomfortable disparities between the current crime and the previous murders. Frances had not been mutilated like the earlier victims, but a young policeman had disturbed 'the fiend', so perhaps he had not been given time?

Amidst this fevered speculation, an old sailor stepped forward. The previous evening, he had been staying in a seaman's home close to the docks when another man joined him.

'I'm nearly dead', the sailor sighed as he sat down. 'I've been out all night and I've got robbed. I'm dying for a drink.' He produced a knife. 'Will you buy it?'

The old sailor offered a shilling, throwing in a bit of tobacco for good measure. He examined the knife and opened it. 'This is not an English knife?'

'No, I bought it abroad.'

'Where?'

'In America.'

An hour later, he took the knife out and examined it, for he had heard the news. 'I felt the big blade and a clammy feeling came over me. I then got a basin of water and dropped the knife into it. I left it about a minute, at the same time rubbing the knife with my fingers. I then took out the knife and wiped it on a dirty towel. I then looked at the water and saw that it was slightly salmon-coloured.' He put the knife back and went to bed. Next day, he had second thoughts and decided to sell it.

'Oh,' the buyer joked, 'it looks like Jack the Ripper's knife.'

Armed with this evidence, the police confronted Tom. 'Sadler, have you sold a knife lately or at any time to a sailor at the Home?'

'No, certainly not. I never had a knife to sell. The only one I had was an old one worth two-pence that I used to cut tin with.'

'Are you sure you haven't sold one this week?'

'Yes, certainly I am.'

'You answer to the description of a man who has sold a clasp knife to a sailor on Friday morning. You will have to stand for identification.'

He was taken to the basement and lined up with a group of other men. Gas jets flared against the walls. After a moment of hesitation, the old sailor came in and walked straight up to him. Could Tom take his cap off?

'Yes,' the sailor said as the cap was removed, 'you are the man I bought the knife off.'

A knife was part and parcel of a sailor's life; a handy tool and sometimes a weapon. Sailors who carried knives could draw them, and two shipmates who fell to fighting could easily end up stabbing. Sometimes there would be confrontations with First Mates or Captains, although most knife fights happened after heavy drinking. Newspapers were full of them. Rival gangs would clash. Friends would fall out. There would be arguments over women. Many sailors couldn't even remember why they stabbed someone because they were too raddled with drink. In a world where violence could flare in a second, sailors made it their business to know who carried a knife, and who had a reputation for using one. Tom knew this, and most of his shipmates knew it too. They could tell the police that he never carried a knife. Just ask Matt Curley or someone called Bowen.

'Why Gus?' I wondered, 'There must have been other shipmates? Why pick him?' I stopped for a moment and thought. 'Are we sure it's him? Sadler just talks about somebody called Bowen. It could be somebody else.'

I opened the online catalogue of the National Archive and looked for any surviving records of the Ripper murders, and came across MEPO 3/140, the mystical shrine where countless generations of Ripperologists have come to worship. This was the file that contained all the official records of those gruesome deaths. There were sixty pages devoted to Frances's murder, including interviews with Tom's wife and statements from a lodger. A week later, I was in London looking for myself.

There were reports from the inquest and a depressingly bleak picture of Frances's body. Several police reports had been entered, including interviews with Tom's shipmates, the two men who Tom reckoned could testify that he never carried a knife. 'Matt Curley and one called Bowen.' That's how he told it. Tom had struggled to remember the second man's name, but here he was in the flesh.

I got up from my seat and wandered off. The police had tracked Bowen to a house in Whitechapel. It was not Gus. This was another sailor called Frederick Bowen. I walked downstairs and stood in the rain. 'It's not him,' I said as I phoned Gill. 'It's unbelievable – there's another sailor called Bowen.'

'It could be Gus?' she said, 'Maybe he was giving a false name?'

'It's possible. We need to check. I don't think we have the crew agreement for the *Fez*. We need to check if Frederick Bowen was serving on the ship with Tom.'

When I got home, we contacted Newfoundland and they sent us the crew agreement. He was there. Frederick Bowen.

'So it's not Gus,' I sighed and pressed my hands to my temples.

'How did Gus know that? He must have read the papers like everyone else. None of the papers said it was Frederick Bowen?'

I nodded.

'I bet he thought it was him,' Gill said, 'I bet he thought Tom was pointing to him.'

It made sense. Gus and Tom had shared voyages and were both in London. Tom's two nights in Whitechapel had given us a glimpse into the life that Gus was leading. When the story broke and Tom was the centre of attention, Gus would have sensed the danger. Like everyone, he read the papers, and saw that his old shipmate was calling on someone called Bowen. He was being sucked in. So he went to ground, fearing the worst. We had never been able to find him in the 1891 census, and this was why.

Once Tom was identified as the seller of a knife, the police charged him, and everyone marvelled at his coolness. Except us. This is what sailors did; their 'studied indifference to danger'. For a brief moment he broke down, but only for a moment. As the police walked him to the cells, he recovered his courage and smiled. 'The old man has made a mistake about the knife,' he said, 'I never saw him before.' As the door closed, he affected a brave smile, 'Make it as light as you can, gentlemen.'

Later that day he went to court. An immense crowd gathered and members of the press jostled for places. When Tom appeared there was an audible gasp, for this was not the man they expected. A rough-looking sailor with a grizzled face? What had happened to the Ripper of popular fantasy? The suave gentleman with a sharp knife? Still, they said, he was remarkably cool. Look at how he sauntered into the dock, cool as a cucumber, his hands in his pockets. And his performance in court was remarkable. He cross-examined witnesses and claimed the police were denying him food. Next day, the papers were full of it. He might look rough, they said, but behind that grizzled face and those tattered clothes, there was a cunning intelligence at work. Here was a man who was the master of disguise.

Several papers carried a portrait of Tom. 'Seldom has a man's face been more eagerly scanned,' the *Pall Mall Gazette* admitted: 'There were many who saw, or fancied they saw, all the devilish cunning and malignity which one would imagine the Whitechapel murderer to possess . . . Sadler showed considerable acuteness . . . He listened to the evidence with great care, saw instantly when a point was made against him, and in a rough, but not ineffective, fashion, endeavoured to meet it . . . For himself, he affected to regard the proceedings with an air of unconcern.'

The discovery that a rough sailor could handle himself like this was hardly new. Tom and Gus were a matching pair, each of them well educated; each living as loafers. They were 'gentlemen loafers' in a world of heavy drinking, casual sex and murderous knife fights. Both were capable, if the mood suited, of disarming the world.

The police did their job. They painted Tom as 'exceedingly artful.' A master of disguise. What people saw in the courtroom, they said, was what victims saw in the street. A likeable, slightly shambolic man. And that of course was why his victims dropped their guard and went like lambs to the slaughter. A fascination with disguise ran through everything, not least among journalists. 'I cannot tell you exactly when this idea came into my mind,' one reporter confessed, 'A secret voice seemed to whisper to me, "Go to Whitechapel. Who knows but that you really may succeed in catching Jack!" . . . So I left home at nine in the evening, dressed as a ship's engineer.'

The Sherlock Holmes stories were full of disguises. *The Man with the Twisted Lip*' appeared that year and told of a middle-class man in suburbia. One day he disappeared and the celebrated detective was asked to find him. Doctor Watson was sent in search of the man and the doctor's trail took him to an opium den. There, he found a decrepit figure. When Watson left the den, the figure followed. 'For two streets he shuffled along with a bent back and an uncertain foot. Then, glancing quickly round, he straightened himself out and burst into a hearty fit of laughter.' It was Holmes, delighted as ever with his own performance. And finally it emerged that the missing gentleman had been a master of disguise too. For years his fortune had been made from begging and not from legitimate business. He had learned to disguise himself as the man with the twisted lip, and established a pitch in the City where he cadged money from passers-by.

The intriguing idea of disguise ran deeper still, deeper than moustaches, old clothes and twisted lips. The great theory now was that Jack the Ripper had a fractured psyche, a man with a split personality; a gentleman by day; a demon by night; a 'Jekyll-and-Hyde' figure. Stevenson's story appeared in 1886, and was an immediate sensation. People were entering a new age of psychological complexity. There were no out-and out villains anymore, no heroes to cheer, just characters who seemed to be lost in their own labyrinthine mysteries.

The more we found out about Gus, the more fascinating and complex he became. We stumbled from one dark tunnel to another. He was hiding in London. He may have donned a false moustache, or assumed a fake limp, but the most obvious ploy was to change his name. He was keeping low, avoiding the storm. Tom's time in Whitechapel had turned into the biggest news story of the day, and Gus was in danger. If the police tracked him, and he was called upon to act as a witness, his name would be known across the world. Up there in the headlines, beside Tom. We thought of his parents reading the paper, and their scandalized neighbours in Bolam and Gainford. He had to find a place of safety, somewhere discreet, well away from Whitechapel, a cheap room in some part of the city where he could go to ground. A place to ride out the storm.

Then, out of the blue, Tom was saved. With surgical precision, the coroner dissected the facts and concluded that Tom was innocent. He could not have killed Frances, for he had been seen elsewhere in Whitechapel when she was killed. The case crumbled and Tom was freed. He was whisked away in a four-wheeled cab, his head out of the window, his hat in the air. His sailor bravado never deserted him.

Two months later, a reporter tracked him down. He was lodging in a coffee shop in Shadwell, recovering from a bout of bronchitis, and feeling low. He denied carrying a knife, but made no mention of any shipmates, and reckoned they had all deserted him. He was probably right. We saw from the police reports that the press had stumped up a sizeable sum for Tom's story, and the police were still convinced of his guilt, so it was not over.

Gus went to ground. The census was taken on the 5th of April, a month after the case ended, when Gus was still worried. He had probably changed his name, and this meant he would be hard to find, but perhaps he had not changed his age and birthplace? If he kept these, we might still find him. After all, how many men, who were living in London in 1891, could have been born in a small, Yorkshire village called Skelton?

The answer was twenty-two. None had first or second names remotely like Gus, and half could be discounted immediately; four were servants; there was a soldier, and six men were living with their parents. So that left eleven. We began double-checking. There was Lancelot Broadley, a restaurant waiter, married with three children. Frank Brown, a civil servant. George Chester from another part of Yorkshire. John Lynas, a clerk and book-keeper. Frederick Mart, a cab-yard foreman. William Martin, a 66-year old trimmer, who worked in an iron foundry. George Morgan, a carpenter. Edward Penty, a married man, and Isaac Scarth, a physician and surgeon. Then there was John Wood, who ran a small tobacco and stationer's business.

Which left one. Someone called 'Charles Smith'.

We clicked the entry. A street in Marylebone, up in the north of the city, well away from Whitechapel. A place called Carburton Street. A man called Charles Smith appeared on the page, living in a building that had been sub-divided. The main part of the house was occupied by a general dealer called William Palmer. Above him, was Mary Woolmore, whose husband was temporarily away; she was sharing two rooms with her daughter, a female visitor, and a male lodger. Two more rooms were occupied by a man called John Clark. At the top of the house, there was a commercial traveller, and then Charles Smith. He was calling himself a sailor, a Second Mate in the Merchant Service, and was twenty-five. It had to be Gus.

The name was hardly imaginative, but enough to throw people off. Then, as we turned the page, we saw he was sharing the room with a woman.

Chapter 13: Venice

This much we knew, or thought we knew.

Gus was living with a woman who came from Ireland. Her name was Mary, and this is why we called her, 'Irish Mary'. She was the same age as Gus, but that was it; there was little else to go on, apart from the fact that Gus seemed to be breaking the rules. The poverty-stricken Irish carried the mark of Cain. The people that almost everyone scorned. The crude stereotype of 'Paddy' living in a pigsty, always drunk, congenitally stupid, and forever in trouble, was a firm favourite with many English writers. If anyone wanted to capture the horrors of a Victorian slum, an Irish woman rolling in the gutter was a perfect start. That would do it. Let her wallow in her rags, and scream her curses, and the scene would be complete.

In truth, Irish Mary was nothing like this. She was as silent as the grave. We could find nothing about her, and the fact that she was born in Ireland, and called Mary, didn't help at all; Irish records were hard to access, and only gave up their guarded secrets reluctantly. The one thing we knew was that her surname was almost certainly not Smith. Nor could we find her in any English records, apart from this bogus entry with Gus in 1891. At some point in her life, she must have found her way to England, perhaps alone, perhaps with family, and was living in London in 1890, but there was no evidence to link her with Gus, or with anyone else in the story. It was ironic: Gus did his best to hide, but failed to pull it off; Irish Mary, was invisible.

London offered plenty of options; cheap rooms where they could hide. Alongside most of the poorer people in the city, the two of them probably kept moving. Best to keep ahead of the game. We guessed that Gus had met her when he sailed into St. Katherine's Dock on the *Empusa*. When Tom Sadler came in February 1891, they were still in Whitechapel, or so it seemed. A boozy, fractious binge may have started well enough, if you were partial to that kind of thing, but soon it spiralled out of control. Finally and apocalyptically, it crashed. Frances was murdered, and Tom arrested, and the world looked on, picking over the grim details with fascinated horror. We could see how Gus was doing his best to hide, shunning the publicity, desperate to shield his parents from the worst. He did his best to dissolve into the city, melting into its mass.

This much we knew. Or thought we knew.

April 1892, more than a year later. A bleak Easter with freezing temperatures. An influenza epidemic sweeping the city, and soon decimating the population. The improbable end of Gus's year of hibernation; his year of lying low. Out of the blue, he surfaced again. Thousands might be falling prey to the new virus, but suddenly the world was looking safer, at least to him. Gus stepped out of the shadows and into our sights.

Liebe, his favourite sister, had arrived in London and was planning to marry. She had chosen a man called Ted Davies, who the Bowens did not like, so Liebe ran off with Ted and turned to Gus. She wanted him at the wedding, so he came. His signature was on the certificate.

'Joseph Edward Davies,' I said, looking at the certificate and trying to squeeze as much juice out of it as I could, 'Better known as Ted.' I hunted down a couple of references in the letters. *Ed. & Liebe have left the Spen. They are now at Holly Cottage, Haxby, York.* And again: *I thought Liebe and Ted were going to Cornwall, you say London?* According to the certificate, the young couple were renting rooms at 15 Howell Street, Paddington. Charles Booth spent much of the 1880s and 1890s, colour-coding London streets, and the notes accompanying his maps described Howell Street as a place where many of the houses had broken windows, and where respectable people mixed with rougher types. According to the 1891 census, the houses were big, with a family living on each floor. Not quite a slum, but certainly down-at-heel.

Ted and Liebe

We wondered why the Bowens disapproved of Ted. The marriage certificate described him as an 'Usher at "Venice"', which only served to deepen the mystery. We had no idea what it meant. Turning to our database of Victorian newspapers, we typed in 'Venice AND London', and a tidal wave of information swept us away - shipping news, commercial intelligence, diplomatic telegrams, everything. Yet in the midst of this surge, we saw it. The 'marvel of marvels' – 'VENICE IN LONDON'.

Imre Kiralfy was the man of the moment; Hungarian man of mystery, and undisputed marvel of the modern age. The man who was the presiding genius of London's latest extravaganza. Two years earlier, he had staged a colossal recreation of Nero's Rome, and we learned that he was a member of the new cosmopolitan set that gave the Victorian public its regular jolts of sensation. Described by one paper as a 'citizen of the world', Kiralfy was always on the move, flitting between Europe and America. 'Today he may be here,' the *Pall Mall Gazette* said in wonder, 'next week in Venice . . . the week after at Madrid . . . and the week after that in America.'

The first hint of Kiralfy's grand design came in March 1891. He would recreate his own, 'Venice in London', complete with the Piazza San Marco and Grand Canal. Visitors could take lazy trips in real Venetian gondolas, and shop in Venetian bazaars. By August 1891, the idea was taking shape and the great man granting interviews.

'Mr Kiralfy,' one reporter enquired, 'let me ask who put the idea of this your latest and most wonderful spectacle, in your head?'

'The thing was suggested to me by a few London friends . . . I propose to take the whole of this immense hall,' he said, pointing to the cavernous spaces of Olympia, 'The entire centre portion of the hall will consist of an elevated stage, with a lake in the front. Upon the stage will be produced a magnificent spectacle . . . Over twelve hundred people will be employed.' Kiralfy was nothing if not confident. 'I have made arrangements for a climate. The water representing the seas will be warm. Consequently, the atmosphere of the hall will possess a geniality entirely foreign to your English climate; and visitors will pass at once from the cold dank fog of a London winter into the presence of the warm air and brilliant transparent skies of Venice.'

'Do you think public taste is tending in the direction of these colossal spectacles?'

'I have been twenty years in the business,' he smiled, 'and my experience is that the demand for amusements of this character is increasing. You have however to set yourself a bigger task each time, as the public appetite grows by what it feeds upon.'

It was true. Late-Victorian society was growing fat on spectacle. *Nero* had been a gorgeous triumph, but Kiralfy now considered it paltry, hardly more than 'a Punch and Judy show'. His new entertainment would be grander. This Venetian extravaganza would eclipse everything that had gone before. It would be stupendous.

In part, this love of spectacle came from the theatre. Victorian melodramas relied heavily on scenic effects. Sir Augustus Harris, the best-known exponent of this style of theatrical bombast, was christened 'Druriolanus for the overblown productions he made synonymous with Drury Lane; everything on the epic scale. He came to the first night of Kiralfy's show, and sat in the front row stamping his foot; he simply loved it. There was something in Kiralfy's style too that drew on the international exhibitions that were appearing in Europe and America, and something from the American razzamatazz of Barnum and Bailey, and something from Buffalo Bill and his Wild-West showmanship.

Asked what profits he made, Kiralfy demurred, 'I don't think the matter is of any general interest.'

'There I must join issue,' the reporter insisted, 'The public clearly loves to be taken behind the scenes. It is rumoured that fortunes have been amassed?'

'Venice in London' was a vast moneymaking machine. For 'a democratic sixpence' the inhabitants of Cockneydom could take an omnibus across London, pick their way down a muddy street in Kensington, pay their money at the door, and become Venetians for the day. Newspapers couldn't help but savour the delights of 'Arry and 'Arriet, eating macaroni and spaghetti, reclining gracefully in a gondola, and singing 'Ta-ra-ra-boom-de-ay'. Yet this plebeian end of the market was just a start. Kirafly wanted the middling and upper ranks too, and hit the jackpot in December 1891, when he persuaded the Prince and Princess of Wales, the Duke of Clarence and lesser members of the royal family to take a box.

'The hiring of a great hall and the engagement of a chorus girl', he explained with characteristic conceit, 'are equally worthy of attention'. He liked to present himself as the master of all things. So perhaps he hired Gus, as well as Ted? We could imagine them both in their gondolier's gear. In truth, the ushers and extras were paid a shilling a performance, which translated into twelve shillings a week - a hopeless wage in the context of the 1890s. But forget all that; they were part of an exotic extravaganza, rubbing shoulders with Italian artists, Venetian gondoliers, French scenic painters, Viennese costumiers, English dancers and actresses.

The opening night was on Boxing Day 1891. Kiralfy staged the event in two halves. The evening kicked off with a performance of Venetian history, made up of mimed sections from *The Merchant of Venice*, intercut with battle scenes, processions and pageants. The action stalled in places, and the audience grew restive. One reviewer complained that the whole thing ran on and on like Tennyson's brook, but most people were delighted.

Everyone agreed that the second half was a brilliant success. A veritable sensation. It offered Londoners a new form of entertainment, a chance to *experience* Venice. Visitors could saunter beside canals, and sample Italian restaurants, browse in Venetian shops, and buy Venetian crafts. For an extra sixpence, they could take a gondola ride and dip their fingers in warm Venetian waters. This gigantic recreation of Venice worked like a charm and continued to delight. For a fantasy two hours, Londoners could lounge and gaze, flirt and socialise. One lady remembered how she spent her days sipping chocolate, and nibbling sugary cakes served by dark-eyed waitresses. Her favourite place was a lofty gallery where she could watch the crowds. Beneath her, there was a life-size bridge where a smart gondola moored each day, and the gondoliers serenaded her with guitars and violins.

'I for one,' she sighed, 'will never taste chocolate again without being reminded of that pretty scene.'

Male visitors were less impressed. They found themselves

competing with the charms of Italian gondoliers, not to mention English loafers: 'Solemn youth: "An awful bore! Are you not tired of it?" Brilliant brunette: "Indeed, no! It is such a relief to escape from this cold, grey London, with all its serious faces, and to forget them among the warmth and colour and movement of Venice. I've been five times already, and hope to come as many more." Solemn Youth: "Aw, sorry I spoke."'

The 'superfine' were sceptical too. The whole thing, they said, was bogus, which was clearly true. They admitted that the gondoliers were authentic, and so too were the *carabinieri*, but the male attendants! Dear me! The male attendants. Men like Ted and Gus . . . They were horribly counterfeit.

Most visitors ignored this. *Nero* had given them a glimpse of the semi-barbaric pomp of Rome, but this was different. The experience now deepened and intensified. In Kiralfy's fantasy, the Victorian audience lived and breathed a 'fairy Venice of their own.' Over a million came during the first year, and most of them loved it. So when Kiralfy closed the show in December 1892, it came as a terrible shock, not least to the people employed. 'Venice in London' had run its course. A year in one place was more than enough, and Kiralfy was moving on. In truth, he was preparing a bigger and better show for the World Fair in Chicago.

'This modern representative army', one London journalist noted as the cast disbanded, 'is of necessity composed of mercenaries – men who march and fight for so much a day.' Gus and Ted would have known this. They were loafers and mercenaries of a modern kind, and life in London was a mercenary business. Looking after yourself and moving on were the best ways to stay afloat. A city with few loyalties. Public-house pals might laugh and joke, but you could never trust them. Capitalist entrepreneurs like Kiralfy hired and fired at will. You watched your back when you walked in Whitechapel. In a fix, Gus moved on, secure in the knowledge that there was always a corner to turn.

Chapter 14: Corners

Finchley Road Baths; a magnificent building designed in the English Renaissance style. Another proud monument from late Victorian civic life. Gus landed a job here as a swimming instructor and soon turned himself into a professor. Men in the Victorian era who made a living as swimming instructors were often called professors, and the absurdity of this appealed to us. We liked the sound of it. 'Professor Bowen'

'My dear madam, let me introduce you to my esteemed colleague, Professor Bowen.'

There were two excellent articles on the fascinating details of this arcane world, and I contacted their author, Dave Day. I told him the story of Gus's adventures, including his stint as a swimming instructor.

'There was never any real requirement for instructors to be excellent swimmers,' Dave said. 'Many of them came out of the services, or like Gus from the navy. The key qualification was the ability to instruct which is why some of these men had been drill instructors or fencing instructors in a previous life.'

'Could he claim to be a Professor?'

'Generally men who claimed the title of Professor had well established credentials as public performers before they turned to teaching.'

Professor Pearce was a case in point. He ran Hampstead Baths and according to one newspaper, earned £500 a year. A colossal sum for the time. We dug out several articles and saw that he was an accomplished entertainer and publicist. Under Pearce's guidance, the baths boasted a yearly programme of aquatic fetes, life-saving competitions, polo matches, escapology stunts, novelty races and comic routines. His own specialism was acrobatic diving, and his *piece de resistance* was a twin dive performed with the resident lady professional, Ida Lewin, better known as the 'Real Mermaid'. A newspaper illustration caught them in mid-air, diving into the water, arm in arm. Another paper summed up Pearce by calling him a 'Professor of swimming and illusions' and this is how he made a living; the sporting professional was part competitor, part entertainer, part promoter, part 'professor'.

In the 1890s this flamboyant style of management came to an end. The new middle-class administrators of the sport had a different agenda, and swimming henceforth would be promoted as an activity that guaranteed both health and fitness. As one newspaper put it, swimming was to be encouraged as a sport that would build 'a sound body' and a 'perfectly sound mind'. Anyone making money from the business was now viewed with increasing suspicion, and flamboyant characters like Pearce and Gus were told to pack their bags. Time to turn another corner.

Before we followed Gus, Dave emailed with fresh news. He had passed our original message onto his partner, and she had found something: some Attestation Papers that Gus had signed when he tried, without success, to join the army in 1890. Something that we had completely missed. He wanted to join the 16th Lancers, a prestigious unit, and was committing himself to seven years of service, with an extra five in the army reserve.

The document was dated 10th June 1890, and harked back to a time when Gus had returned from India, two years before the Tom Sadler affair. It was a revelation, not least in Gus's physical description. He was only five feet-eight tall, really quite slim, weighing a feathery nine and half stones, with a 'fresh' complexion, blue eyes, and dark-brown hair. He already had three tattoos: one on his left shoulder, one on his right arm, and one on his left arm.

And then we saw it. The doctor rejected him, claiming he was suffering from heart disease. There were no details. It was anyone's guess how Gus reacted to this news, but it was hardly something that a young twenty-two- year old would want to hear. A body blow. An early intimation of mortality that was bound to change his whole view of life. What was the point of planning? Why bother? Better to live your life for the moment. Better to be a loafer. And the doctor was not finished. He rejected Gus a second time, because now he suspected this young man was not as young as he claimed. 'Probably not under 30 years of age' he reckoned, and Gus's wild nights in Calcutta seemed to be catching up. They had taken their toll. In point of fact, he was only twenty-two, but looking older.

Turn the corner. Keep ahead of whatever is coming. After his time as a swimming instructor, Gus took a new job as a London cab driver.

'I never take a cab if I can avoid it,' one lady admitted. She was writing to a newspaper, 'You never know what you will have to pay, and I always feel I shall be insulted and abused if I don't pay whatever is asked.' Her letter was mocked by the male readers. They thought she was demonstrating the 'inexperienced nervousness of an infrequent cab-rider'. Learning to handle cabdrivers was a masculine art. It was one of the skills that a man-about-town acquired in his personal mastery of the city.

Henry Irving knew this only too well. Towards the end of his life, he reminisced affectionately about the relationships between actors and cabbies. 'There was a time, 'he said, 'when a hansom, by a slight stretch of the picturesque, might have been described as my address. That was in the days of youth and high spirits.' He fondly remembered sitting under 'the charioteer of the sun, and snatching a fearful joy from sharp corners and a sudden congestion of traffic.' Irving reckoned that no one with any claim to urbanity and style could move across London without the aid of a cabby. For all his faults, the cabby would be your guide, and he would steer you through the 'reefs and rocks of the city'.

Avoiding the rocks was Gus's way of knowing them; finding the secret of the streets, taking shortcuts, keeping ahead of the pack, being endlessly streetwise. Every street had to be known and memorized, and this labyrinthine knowledge had to be mixed with daring. The best drivers were the men who could travel at speed and take risks. London traffic was the worst in the world. Tons of horse droppings were scattered each day, and were then left to dissolve in rain, spreading a slurry across the surface. So skids were all too common. Fallen horses were a familiar sight, and spills like this could shoot passengers out like cannon balls. Pedestrians were in constant danger too, and the ageing Gladstone was nearly run over twice. As Henry Irving moved into middle age, he relinquished the helter-skelter of the cab, and resigned himself to making do with a sedate 'growler', or four-wheeled coach that lumbered along at a leisurely six miles an hour, but he never forgot the excitement of those early days. Whenever a hansom flew by, he felt a pang of regret. There was a reckless glamour associated with it. This was 'the brotherhood of the whip'.

For the most part, cabs catered to the rich and famous; aristocrats, wealthy bankers, rakish libertines, celebrated actors, politicians, music-hall stars. These were their bread-and-butter customers, the money-making side of the business. But not everyone was a celebrity. Hailing cabs and speeding through the city became the fantasy adventure of every impoverished clerk. What better way to impress your sweetheart? And then there were the anxious hordes of visitors. You could see them, staggering out of the railway stations with their luggage, blinking and bewildered. Perfect victims.

The roguery of cabbies was legendary.

'What is the fare?'

'I leave it to you, sir.'

'Will you please tell me the exact fare? Then I can give you whatever extra I may feel disposed.'

'Three shillings, sir.'

'Now, that is not so; why do you not tell me?'

'Well, sir, half-a-crown is the fare, but we generally get three shillings.'

'Well, I'll give you half-a-crown, but that is more than the exact fare.'

Sometimes they were stung back. Notorious 'bilkers' like Leicester Serrell could turn the tables. Gus had played the game in Calcutta and knew how it worked. You hired a cab, drove around for hours on end, and then ran off without paying. Simple. In September 1896, Serrell hailed a cab in the Caledonian Road.

'Do you know you're driving the champion bilker?' one cabby warned as he drove by and saw who was inside.

Later that week, Serrell did it again. He hired a cab at 11.15 pm., drove for five hours, and then claimed he was short of cash. He told the cabby to wait. There was a public house nearby and he knew the people who ran it. Once inside, he would get the money. He strolled into the bar, bought a round of drinks for everyone, turned to the cabby and said, 'I don't know about you, old man, I've no money with me at present. I shall have to write a cheque.'

A typical working day for a cabby started at dawn and stretched till midnight, although much of it was spent lounging in cab ranks, or crawling through the streets looking for fares. They worked all weathers; sweltering under sun, soaking in rain, freezing in snow. Gus would have hired a cab like the rest of them, and the cost had to be covered before he could earn anything for himself. One of the leaders of the drivers reckoned that in the old days they could make thirty shillings a week, but by the mid-1890s, it had dropped to a pound. Barely a living wage.

Yet for all that, cab driving was perfect. Free and easy. It never tied you down. There were no regular hours. Gus could skip work for days at a stretch, and then loaf as much as he wanted. The working days, when they came, were long and tiring - sixteen or seventeen hours at a stretch – but this is how he liked it. Feast and famine.

One reporter wondered how cabbies ever found time for a settled home life, but he was missing the point. What did Gus want with a settled home life?

Chapter 15: Lovers

Gus's love life. Best treated as a minor work of art. Expertly forged and beautifully crafted. Much of it counterfeit, yet even when you knew you were looking at an outrageous fake, you had to admire the style, the expert craftsmanship in every line.

We went back and subjected every letter to a closer reading. Every line had to be examined for new clues, because we now realized they were everywhere.

I dug out Annie's invitation, and as I lifted it from the battered shoebox, the little envelope fell open. It always did.

Mr and Mrs BOWEN present their
Compliments to
Miss Johnson
And request the pleasure of her
Company to a
MOONLIGHT DANCE
On the Vicarage Lawn, on Friday, August 21st

The night when Gus and Annie met. We knew that Friday fell on August 21st only twice in the 1890s, first in 1891, and then in 1896. A blurred six was still visible on the envelope's postmark, so we had our year. The year when Gus left London. Five lazy seasons of loafing were coming to an end, and he caught a fresh whiff of the sea. The crew agreements told us he signed up for another voyage in 1896, the year of the 'Moonlight Dance', the year when his life in London ran out of corners. He came north, and Irish Mary came with him.

Gus sailed from North Shields in June 1896. He was bound for Philadelphia, and then Rouen, and only returned towards the end of July. Three weeks later, we imagined him packing his bags and making his way to Bolam. This would be the night. The moonlit night when he and Annie met.

'So at some point in 1896,' Gill said, 'just to get this straight, he leaves Irish Mary and meets Annie'?'

I shrugged my shoulders. The romance was looking a little tarnished, there was no denying it. As we approached the scene, I looked at the crew agreements again, and saw that Gus had signed up for another voyage in 1896, this time to France, where his ship collided with a pier at Le Havre. Perhaps the accident delayed things? Perhaps that was the reason? But whatever the cause, he didn't get back until September 15th, two weeks after the dance.

Everything went slack. The invitation lay on the desk, and I remembered the line that I always trotted out at the start of every talk: 'Well,' I would say, lifting the invitation as high as I could, 'I can't prove it, but no one will persuade me otherwise. This is the night when Annie meets the love of her life! This is the night when she meets Gus.' No one questioned it, for everyone wanted it to be true. It seemed so right. Yet here we were, seeing it for the first time with steady eyes, and realising it never happened.

We knew that the Moonlight Dance could only happen in 1896 or 1891, so we began to think that it must be 1891. Why else had Annie kept the invitation? Gus was embroiled in the Tom Sadler affair that year, and hiding away in London, but there was nothing to stop him jumping on a train and coming north. So it was possible.

'He can make it,' I said, 'He needs to get out of London, away from the press and the police. He's just back from his Indian voyages. He might even tell Annie about the Tom Sadler affair? His sensational brush with the Ripper. An exciting secret between the two of them?'

'He's playing a dangerous game if he does.'

All of which was perfectly feasible, until Patti Bergh emailed from Canada, and sent us an image. She had just come across one of Bro's scrapbooks, and there was a page where he pasted his own invitation to the moonlight dance. Better still, he had dated it. It was 1896 after all.

So Annie had gone to the dance, and kept the invitation all her life, but not because of Gus. The story was all wrong. And if this part of the story was wrong, what else might be wrong? Did we really know anything about Annie and Gus? And what of the other women in his life? Irish Mary and the mysterious *vile woman*?

'When did Mrs. Ferguson send her letter about the *vile woman*?' Gill asked, trying to collect her thoughts.

'Sometime in 1900.'

'So if Irish Mary is the *vile woman* mentioned in that letter, it means that Gus lived with her for ten years. We know they were living together in 1891, so it's ten years. Where does Annie come in?'

'Much later.'

'Which means we're missing something.'

Mrs. Ferguson's letter had been sent in March 1900. *Well dear friend,* she wrote sympathetically, *I note all you said about Mr. Bowen and that vile woman.* So it was clear that Gus was seeing another woman in 1900 who Annie loathed, and who she had called *the vile woman.* Probably Irish Mary. Next, we found a memorandum dated May 15th 1901, sent by a Station Master on the outskirts of Manchester: *Your marriage certificate is herewith returned. I am keeping all your correspondence as I intend if possible to prosecute the woman who has been receiving your money since February last. You will receive your payment early in*

June for that month in advance. Please be careful not to talk about this or this woman may escape.

Irish Mary? It was difficult to tell. We could see that Annie was sending a certificate to prove that she was Gus's wife. Our best guess was that Irish Mary had been masquerading as his wife, and that Annie was now exposing her. But her determination came as a surprise; she was urging the authorities to take action, and we saw for the first time that Annie was not a woman to be crossed. Her vendetta continued for another year, for there was a second memorandum, this time from the Chief Constable's Offices in Manchester, dated November 8th 1902: *Madam, I have to acknowledge the receipt of your letter of the 7th instant and to acquaint you in reply that you had better consult a solicitor on the subject.*

The author of the memo had given a name, and it was not 'Irish Mary': on the very top, he had written, *re Agnes McWilliam.* It reminded me of a letter that Gus sent to Annie in December 1900, when he was trying his best to placate her. *As to Miss McWilliam,* he wrote, *she had some money left when her uncle died - went to her relatives here & has since taken a situation. I have not heard anything of her since.*

Irish Mary? Agnes McWilliam? Annie? It was impossible to tell. What on earth was happening? At least we had a new name to chase. And not only that. Manchester took on a heightened significance, and we began scanning the letters looking for clues. Passing references. There were two; one where someone was telling Annie that Gus had gone to Manchester with ten pounds in his pocket, and a second that simply said, *Auntie knows this street in Manchester very well.*

We started trawling the 1901 census, looking for a woman in Manchester called Agnes McWilliam. As it turned out, there was only one, but she was fifty years old, and a bit too long in the tooth for Gus. So we cast the net wider. There were several McWilliams who were closer in age, but none called Agnes. It was possible that she had changed her name, but if she had, we were never going to find her.

Spreading the net wider, we looked for sightings in Lancashire, and several emerged. There were two Agnes McWilliams working as domestic servants in Liverpool; an 'Agnes S.B. McWilliam living with the family of a lithographic designer in Bolton; an Agnes McWilliam who was described as the daughter of a commercial traveller in Cheshire, and another who was the daughter of a boiler-maker and storekeeper in Liverpool. Any one of them might be her. Or none.

It was dark. I stood by the window and put my head on the glass. Nothing was certain anymore.

Chapter 16: Deceit

Doubt, they say, defines our modern life, and we must learn to live with it. Perhaps it's true. Yet sometimes it feels as if we are hurtling through the night, our hearts pounding, our eyes shut, hell-bent on experiencing the next sensation. One day we are thrilled; the next day broken. Historical research was my trusty companion, a way of facing the chaos, a time-travelling GPS system that would get me through. I would plan projects, collect evidence, test theories, find destinations. Chaos would be conquered, order would be restored.

But this? The endless uncertainties of the story were frightening. Sometimes I would kid myself that this was good, that it would make me more receptive to events. Going with the flow. But here I was with my head on the window, my eyes aching, and my brain spinning. The more we found, the less we knew; the less we knew, the more we were obliged to find. All in all, it was a bottomless pit.

Time for tea. Whilst I went downstairs to make a pot, Gill sat at the computer and carried on searching. She was looking for Gus and Annie's marriage. Annie had sent her marriage certificate to a Station Master in Manchester, so there had to be a record. This at least seemed certain.

'It looks like they got married in Middlesbrough,' she shouted, 'It was 1899.'

The date was wrong. So was the place. Why had they not married in Bolam or Gainford, where dear old Craufurd would have done the honours?

'Let me see,' I said, as I got back upstairs and peered over her shoulder. 'It can't be. It's too late. This is 1899. I'm sure we have a letter from Gus before this, where he calls her *my dear wife*.'

'How many Charles Augustine A. Bowens can there be,' she said, and pointed to the screen. 'It's got to be him.'

After a while, I found the letter. Gus was sending it to Annie in December 1898, six months before this marriage in Middlesbrough. He was calling her *my dear wife*. A second letter had been sent from the same address, and this started with *my dear wife* too. Then I realised something: the other letters started differently. Usually with *my darling*. It was a small detail, but crucial. For some reason, these letters were different; he was calling her *my dear wife*.

Here was Gus calling Annie *my dear wife*, six months before he married her, and *my darling* after. Everything was wrong. I stopped for a moment and smiled. There was only one explanation: these two letters had been sent to someone else. Either to Irish Mary or to Agnes McWilliam.

The first letter was sent on December 14, 1898, six months before he married Annie. Gus was in London, and the letter had been sent from the Kings Cross Road. *My dear wife, I recd your welcome letter this morning, and felt with you that it is not going to be a particularly happy Xmas for either of us.*

For reasons best known to himself, he seemed to be keeping her at arm's length. *As to your coming to London - Well, in order to succeed in my present undertaking I must devote all my time and energy to business. Therefore could not be much with you - & you would find London anything but pleasant at this time of the year, the fogs are something awful. As to my coming north - that is out of the question not to speak of the expense. What I suggest is that you remain quietly at York until I am more firmly established & am able to contribute to the home we will make here in the future*

And then there was his usual begging: *In the meantime: as I have already told you, it is impossible for me to go without the needful . . . 'It is imperative that I should keep up a good appearance - my things are in bad condition - boots worn out & rent owing. Now I do not wish to loose what will really be a good thing, but in order to get what is absolutely necessary - pay what I owe & succeed, I must have at least £5 by return.*

Whoever it was – Irish Mary or Agnes McWilliam – she was getting the same treatment as Annie, but there was something darker too, for he sometimes threatened her. *Failing this, on Sat next I shall have to go into what we call a hard up sailors boarding house. Ship on the first opportunity and say good bye to my wife and old England for ever.*

Then, very quickly, his charm returned. *But if you still have a bit love left for me & I think you have (I see you still think of Beezie) - this can be averted and I will endeavour to make amends for my past conduct. Your erring Husband. PS I should be grateful if you would also send parcel per return.*

We stopped for a moment. Gus's reference to his *dear wife*, and the way he signed the letter, calling himself rather honestly her *erring husband*, suggested they were married, but when we worked through the records, there was no mention of any marriage to either Irish Mary or Agnes McWilliam. So something was amiss. And the second letter suggested that he had abandoned her. *My dear wife, my reason for not writing to you is that I did not think you would care to hear from me. As to my reasons for leaving you as I did I think we had better leave that to be discussed at some future time. I am very pleased to hear that you are getting well and strong & sincerely trust that you will soon be your old self again.*

More threats followed: *Should you fail me in this case I shall go out East with no intention whatever of returning, I am Your husband, Gus Bowen.*

I picked up the letter. According to our thinking, it had been sent in December 1898, either to Irish Mary or to Agnes McWilliam. If Gus had married either of these two women, and then gone on to marry Annie in July 1899, his first wife must have died, or the second marriage was bigamous. And if she died, it must have been between December 1898, when Gus was writing to her, and his marriage to Annie in July 1899, the following year. By the late nineteenth century, almost all deaths were registered, and the system had come as close as possible to being fool-proof. It was hard to die without the authorities knowing. A doctor had to write the original death certificate, and then copies were given to the local registrar and undertaker. Only then could a burial take place. Suffice it to say, there was no record of either of these two women dying.

And there was something else. I was convinced that Gus was at sea when the letters were written. For reasons that we couldn't yet divine, he was trying to fool this woman, and make her believe he was in London. I spent a few minutes arranging the crew agreements. He was on a three-month voyage in late 1896 to Philadelphia and France. Then there were two weeks ashore before he signed up for a trip to the USA. Then he quitted the sea for a year, but in November 1897, he went back again. He joined a ship at Middlesbrough, and sailed for Scandinavia, finishing the voyage in January 1898. Twelve days later, he joined a new ship at Stockton and sailed for South America; a much longer voyage which lasted five months. He called at Rio de Janeiro, Buenos Aires, Rosario, and finally returned to Liverpool on July 12th 1898. By the look of it, he took a month off, and then signed up for another voyage that left Liverpool for South America, and this meant that he was away for four months, from August to December 1898. He had visited lots of places, but never London.

How on earth had he written these two letters from Kings Cross? For reasons best known to himself, he was trying to persuade someone that he was living in London. I went back to the crew agreements, and saw that Gus's last voyage finished in Cardiff.

Before reaching there, his ship had called at London.

'What's the date of the letter?'

'December 13th.'

'The ship docks in London. There's a stamp on the agreement from London. It's dated December 13th.'

We could suddenly see it. He docked in London on December 13, 1898, and sprinted through the city to his handy address in the Kings Cross Road, where he picked up his letters. To all intents and purposes, it was his clearing house, the place where he collected mail and sent off new letters. As soon as we saw it, we realised how simple it was. He could write to this woman from South America, and send it to this man who lived in Kings Cross Road, who would then open the letter and find another inside. All he had to do was post the enclosed letter. By the look of it, the man was called Burnett. Probably an old friend from a previous voyage. The letter would have a London postmark, and that would be enough to convince whoever received it that Gus was living there. The master forger at work.

But if these letters had been sent to another woman, and not to Annie, how on earth had they ended in our attic? In truth, neither of us had an answer.

'I give up,' Gill sighed.

'No, we're right,' I said. 'These letters are to another woman. Somehow or other, they've ended in our attic.'

We fell back on the available facts. Gus and Annie had married in Middlesbrough in 1899. The obvious next step was to get a copy of the certificate.

'Tomorrow,' I promised.

Chapter 17: Mary

'I'm sorry,' I said, 'Can you say that again?'

'Bowen and Johnson,' the archivist confirmed.

'That'll do.'

It had been remarkably simple. After giving my final lecture, I buttoned my coat, avoided all contact with staff and students, slipped into town, and made for the archives. It was a frosty day, and the building no more than ten minutes away. I dodged through the crowds, my breath vapouring in the air. The archivist found the volume, the page was scanned, the photocopy sealed in an envelope, passed over to me and popped in my bag. A few minutes later, I was heading for a coffee.

'You were right,' I said, as I quickly phoned Gill, 'Annie and Gus got married in Middlesbrough in 1899. The two letters in 1898 must have been to somebody else.'

'Does it give us anything new?'

'I don't know!' I laughed. Why on earth had I not read it thoroughly? 'I'm off for a coffee. I'll ring later.'

The coffee shop was crowded. One empty stool stood by the door, so I bagged it, unbuttoned my coat, sat down, rubbed my cold fingers, and pulled out the envelope. With laboured precision, I placed it on the worktop, squared it up and looked down.

I rang Gill ten minutes later. Ten revelatory minutes. Ten minutes of watching bodies come to the surface.

Gus and Annie's Marriage Certificate, July 8, 1899

According to the certificate, Gus and Annie were living at the same address when they married, and this looked suspiciously like 'living in sin'. In truth, the net curtains of history were twitching. If people wanted to marry in a different parish from their own, they sometimes applied for a license. One of them would then establish residency by living in the parish for a time. It was possible that Annie had done this, and that Gus had simply used her address as a lazy way of completing the form.

Gus described himself as a widower, so we were right, he had previously married another woman - Irish Mary or Agnes McWilliam – and this woman had died. Except, of course, we could find no record of a death. Or, for that matter, the original marriage.

'And guess who turns up to the wedding?' I asked, pausing for effect. I was looking at a signature that was bursting with its own body language. 'Agnes McWilliam! And wait until you see her signature.'

Agnes had scribbled her name in what seemed to be a terrible temper, and I could see it exploding across the page, knocking the poor vicar's to the edge. If ever a signature was telling us something, this was it.

Things to ponder when you drive home. Blurred lights on the cars, everything abstracted by rain and suddenly made beautiful.

Was it possible that Annie and Gus were living 'in sin'? Victorians had their fair share of immoralities. Novels and melodramas were full of eloping couples, or cautionary tales of torrid affairs. Newspapers regularly reported on rougher types who lived in sin and seemed to end up throttling one another. As a social historian, I'd seen plenty of this. Then there were the intellectual bohemians who had the social confidence to flout marriage and live with their lovers, some of them openly, some discreetly. I began counting - George Elliott, Wilkie Collins, Charles Dickens, Mary Braddon . . . By the end of the century, the sanctity of marriage was openly debated, and Mona Caird's articles in the *Daily Telegraph* were legendary. They asked the shocking question, 'Is Marriage a Failure?', and the paper claimed that over 27,000 readers answered. Many of them thought it was. So yes, it was possible. And then there was the newly-discovered enigma of Agnes McWilliam. What part did she play in Gus' life, and what could have prompted her to come to Annie's wedding? Her signature kept exploding in my head. In the midst of this new melodrama, it was easy to forget Irish Mary. What had happened to her? And finally, there was the tantalising figure of 'Gus the Widower'.

When I got home, Gill had her own explanation. 'Gus did one of them in.'

'Well, it can't have been Agnes McWilliam because she was at the wedding.'

'Irish Mary then.'

Out of the blue, Cindy emailed and told us that she had stumbled across a Bowen descendant who seemed to be living in Long Beach, California. Someone who might be Gus's granddaughter. She gave me a telephone number, but I hardly knew what to do with it. Three weeks elapsed, and I kept delaying the call, for I was nervous about initiating a conversation with a woman half way across the world. A woman who knew nothing about me. Then one night, just before Christmas, I summoned up all the courage I could muster, checked the time in California, and dialled the number. An answering machine kicked in and I began leaving a message.

'Hello, Mrs Tibbs, my name is Tony Nicholson. I'm an historian working in England . . . '

The phone clicked and someone answered.

'Hello?'

I began again and told her the broad outlines of the story. She listened patiently. Some of Annie's letters, I told her, were written by a man called Gus, and we believed he might be her grandfather?

'That's right, he was my grandfather.'

'I thought you might like to see them,' I said, trying to keep calm, 'There are several, and at least one photograph. I was hoping you might be able to give us more information.'

'I think they told me that my great-grandfather was a clergyman?'

'Yes, he was! His name was Craufurd Townsend Bowen. He lived for many years in a pretty village called Gainford in South Durham, and was vicar of Bolam nearby.'

'Incredible.'

'In fact, we have material on *his* father – Jeremiah Bowen – who was a rector in Norfolk and Cambridgeshire. I could send you a silhouette of Jeremiah, if you want?'

'Well, if I can help . . . '

A few weeks later, Pat found a family history that had been typed by a member of the Bowens in the 1960s, and she sent it. Mixed in with the rest, there was an entry on Gus. Not much, but it gave us this: 'Married Mary Frances Loughan in Lady's Chapel, Grove Rd. St. John's Wood, Marylebone, 16th April 1892'.

'I don't know about you,' Gill smiled, 'but Loughan sounds Irish to me.'

We checked the internet and saw that the church was still there in Grove Road, and indeed it was Catholic, so I emailed the priest and asked if he could copy the entry from their register. No problem, he said helpfully, but next day, he was less sure. Did we have the right date? He could find no reference to them. There was no entry for that date, and no whiff of Gus or Mary at all. He had gone the extra mile and checked six months before, and then six months after, but there was nothing. We scanned the online indexes of marriages, but there was nothing there either. And slowly we began to realise that this was the master forger at work again. Gus had lived with Irish Mary, but he had spun a yarn about marrying her. Our best guess was that he was trying to reassure his parents. Making things respectable. And by all accounts, they believed him.

The Bowen family history carried a brief mention of a child. It turned out that Gus had a daughter called Liebe Mary, who was known in the family as 'Beezie', and this immediately rang bells. The name, 'Beezie', had cropped up in several of Annie's letters. *My dear Annie,* Gus's mother had written, *Beezie will do when quite convenient to yourself.* It seemed that Annie was taking her for walks, and we could see that Gus's father adored her: *She's a sweet dear good child,* he said, *and everyone loves her.* On one moth-eaten page, Gus had shared a fantasy: *I guess they will miss Beezie when we take her away,* he told Annie, and then, *Can you not get Beezie to write to you?* A correspondent from the Edwardian era was a nurse and worked with Beezie: *Did you know I had Beezie as my probationer. It is so nice for us both, and she has grown such a nice useful girl . . . We have just been in the wood getting honeysuckle.* Another friend asked, *Have you heard from Beezie, have you?*

We found Beezie in the 1901 census, and saw that she was living with Craufurd and Hannah in Bolam Vicarage. She was nine years old, and this meant that she had been born in 1892, the same year as Gus's mythical marriage, and suddenly it began making perfect sense: he had tried to make Beezie's birth look legitimate by concocting a bogus marriage to Irish Mary, and everyone in Gainford and Bolam believed him.

The pieces were falling into place. Beezie had been mentioned in one of the two mystery letters to *my dear wife*. After threatening to leave this woman, Gus softened his approach: *But if you still have a bit love left for me,* he said, *& I think you have (I see you still think* *of Beezie) - this can be averted and I will endeavour to make ammends for my past conduct.* That settled it; the letters were to Irish Mary.

We searched for Beezie's birth, but never found it. It was possible that a harassed registrar had somehow bungled the name, for there was nothing in the records. We combed the indexes and scanned the entries. The hours spent looking for her seemed wasted, until one day we discovered that Gus had never registered her birth at all. It was his way of doing things, and we really should have guessed. If in doubt, he concocted a lie, or kept silent, or went to ground. In Gus's world, disclosure was dangerous.

'He's dumping Irish Mary,' I said.

As to my reasons for leaving you as I did I think we had better leave that to be discussed at some future time.

He was moving on.

I am very pleased to hear that you are getting well and strong & sincerely trust that you will soon be your old self again.

Chapter 18: Agnes

'I have a sister,' Pat told me. 'Her name is Grace.'

It was two weeks after our first conversation, and we were talking on the phone.

'I was telling her about this strange man in England,' she laughed, 'and wondered if she was willing to talk. You might like to visit her. She lives in Morpeth.'

I laughed too, for here was the power of the internet. How would I have found Grace, who lived only seventy miles away, if I had not gone via Oklahoma, South Africa and California?

'I think she has a few photos you might like to see.'

It was the day before New Year's Eve. We were preparing for company and Gill was busy. I would go alone. A grey morning with heavy clouds in the sky. I set off and rattled up the A1. Once in Morpeth, I found a coffee shop and made a few notes, filling two sides of paper with eager questions. During the short walk to Grace's house, I think I forgot most of them, and so with an almost empty head and a nervous smile, I knocked on the door and glanced at my watch. It was exactly two o'clock,

'Grace?' I said, as she peered out.

'Tony!'

She seemed to be lame and walked with a stick. We shuffled

into a cosy room, decorated in the cottage style, with windows looking over the river. I could see several photos on the table.

'Would you like a cup o' tea?' she said, mimicking the English phrase in her strong American accent. She might be lame and frail, but I could see that she was sharp. She would take over. Once tea was made, and we were sitting on the sofa, she asked if I could pass her a photograph.

'This is my grandmother,' she said and stared at the image.

Agnes McWilliam

I was looking at a woman from the 1890s, or perhaps the Edwardian era. A studio portrait. My best guess was that she was in her twenties or thirties. She was gazing with an artistic kind of intensity into the middle distance, looking away from the camera. Fashionably dressed, she sported a stylish hat that was topped by an elaborate feather, a tight velvet jacket, leather gloves and a light-coloured skirt. In one hand, she carried an umbrella, and in the other, a glossy cylinder. Neither of us had any idea what the cylinder was.

'What was her name?' I asked.

'Agnes.'

My throat constricted. I had formed an image of the *vile woman* as a classic *femme fatale'*, a woman who was beautiful and full of dark intent, but this was not her. Not a flesh-and-blood woman who carried an umbrella. Not a woman who grew old, and then became a grandmother.

'Can you remember her maiden name?' I asked.

'It was Scottish.'

'McWilliam?'

She gazed at me, 'You've come across her?'

'Yes,' I laughed, 'you could say that.'

'Agnes lived with us,' she said, 'Not permanently, you know, but for long periods. My father liked her. He loved to have a laugh, and Agnes was full of fun. My Mom, bless her, never had a great sense of humour, but Agnes was different. She was a lovely singer and a marvellous cook. We loved the days when she baked bread or made pancakes – she made the best pancakes in the world - and sometimes she would sing. Scottish airs. The smell of that baking and the sound of her singing . . .' Her voice trailed off. 'I can remember taking one or two trips to Scotland, when I was a girl. I think we called on her relatives who were farmers, somewhere near Stranraer.'

When I got back, I told Gill all about this and we began searching for Agnes. There were two potential births that might be her: the daughter of a schoolmaster near Ayr, and the daughter of a joiner in Greenock. Neither was near Stranraer, so I tossed a coin and we went for the joiner. He was called William McWilliam, and his wife's first name was Jane. With a bit of luck, there would be a record of their marriage. I keyed in the details and braced myself for a tidal wave of hits, but only two trickled in, and one of them announced, with perfect timing, that William McWilliam was married to a spinster called Jane Moffat in the Original Secession Church, Sun Street, Stranraer, on June 23, 1862,

Six months later, we went to see for ourselves. The short sea crossing to Larne and Belfast transformed Stranraer during the Victorian years. A tiny market town on the edge of Scotland was turned into a bustling seaport, and the port was still operating when we got there. We wound our way down to the harbour, where our B&B was part of a curving row of houses, some of them brightly painted, all facing the sea. We wheeled our bags across the road and rang the bell.

From the doorway we could see Ailsa Craig, better known as 'the floating mountain'. It was an apt description, for it seemed to hover in the distance, floating on the surface of the sea. I thought about Agnes and that phantom mountain. A young woman dreaming of other worlds. It was late afternoon and we made for the library.

'What name?' the librarian asked.

'McWilliam. William McWilliam.'

I thought her father would be easier to find, but after ten minutes, the librarian came back with a glum face and admitted there was nothing, only a brief notice of his death in 1892. So we browsed the library shelves, looking for anything that might give us a feel for Agnes's world, and found *Galloway Gossip*, a collection of local tales that had originally been serialised in newspapers, most from the 1870s when Agnes was growing up. The book's main theme was the loss of traditional customs, killed off, as the author joked, by that 'terrible complaint called gentility'.

The next day, we drove through the narrow lanes that criss-crossed Galloway, and hardly saw another car for miles at a stretch. Sometimes grass was growing in the middle of the road. Our little flirtation with wildness. It was a patch of country that still felt unspoiled, detached from the modern world. We parked the car in a quiet lane, and looked over green fields to the sea. There in the distance was Aisla Craig, as luminous and mysterious as ever, yet all the farmhouses looked the other way, their windows facing inland. On a hot day like this, it was hard to fathom. We were basking in sunshine. Then we noticed the hedges, all bent and buckled, and thought of winter with its ferocious storms blowing in from the sea, laying the hedges flat.

Agnes's father worked as a joiner in Galloway, but came from farming stock. He was drawn to Stranraer in the 1860s because it offered work; a wooden pier was being constructed as part of the town's transformation into a ferry port. There was even talk of transatlantic ships sailing in from America. New ferry links with Belfast and Larne tempted Agnes's parents to move, and they settled for a brief period in Ireland. They lived there for most of 1863. A year later, they were back, and stayed for a short time in Greenock where Agnes was born. By the early 1870s, they had returned to Stranraer, where William established a cattle-dealing business and seemed to do well. Things were bright. Then, in 1873, Agnes's mother died and her father remarried, and there was little else to tell. The broken bones of a childhood.

Brought up in the strict covenanting traditions of the Presbyterian Church, Agnes became an 'honest worthy lassie', and we found her in the 1881 census, working as a domestic servant in one of the local Presbyterian manses where the resident minister was called Smellie (pronounced Smiley). During our Stranraer trip, we found the manse and tried to imagine what it was like in Agnes's time. We knew all the classic stories of Presbyterian ministers and hell-fire sermons, so it was easy to imagine the place as gloomy. Yet Smellie was a master storyteller, a man of vivid imagination, and anything but gloomy. When we got home, I downloaded his *Men of the Covenant*.

At the start of each chapter, I seemed to edge closer to the fire, anxious to catch every word. He returned me to a world that I had lost. There was a voice in that book, a poetic voice, that reminded me of my father. He was a Methodist preacher, and every Saturday night he retreated to his study and rehearsed his sermons. Sometimes I would open the door of my bedroom and stand quietly on the landing, just listening to his voice. Smellie's stories were like that. They were a revelation, for I knew nothing of the Scottish Covenanters' history, but the real pleasure lay in the way he talked, the words he used, the images he evoked. I found myself listening again, as Agnes must have listened. The sound of poetry coming through a closed door. And when Smellie talked of the field and hill preachers, who formed the heroes of his book, he talked of them in summer finding a place for preaching in the sheepfold, and gathered in winter around a peat fire, blazing on a stone-flagged floor. 'Their images,' he said, 'scarce ranged beyond the red horizon of the moor, and the rainy hill-top, the shepherd and his sheep, a fowling piece, a spade, a pipe, a dunghill, a crowing cock; bleak, austere, but genuine, and redolent of the soil.'

Agnes must have heard that voice. Those stories. That simple poetry. Yet she drifted away, just as I did. Congregations thinned, personal faiths crumbled and churches closed. Yet the poetry remains, always bubbling up, always there, coming from deep down – deeper than geological time – from a place that Smellie called, 'the darkness where God is'.

Chapter 19: Barmaids

A Victorian gentleman enters a city bar:

'A glass of sherry, please, miss', he asks, trying to catch the attention of an elegantly dressed and magnificently coiffured barmaid. She admires herself in the mirror and chooses to ignore him.

'A glass of sherry, miss, please,' he repeats.

'Do you want two glasses?' her ladyship asks, still not looking round at him.

'No, one glass if you please.'

'Oh!' says the beauty in mock astonishment, 'I thought perhaps you wanted two, *as you asked twice*.'

The Victorian barmaid. The licensed flirt of the gin-palace playing her part with all the venom she could muster. The barmaid as feisty performer. A woman holding her own in a man's world, and emboldened for a few brief years with an air of mystery and power. Barmaids fascinated and infuriated the Victorians.

'We suppose nobody knows how many barmaids there are in England', one man mused, 'How they became barmaids; what they do and where they go when they cease to be barmaids; how they acquire that supercilious air and that tone of indifference.'

We knew this one. She came from a Presbyterian family in

Stranraer. Agnes turned herself into one of the fine and handsome women of Victorian gin-palaces, who bedecked themselves out in cheap jewellery and gaudy clothes, and were hired by astute publicans to make a show. They were part of what the Victorians saw as the modern world – their own world – and were first spotted in the 1830s. 'Her hair is dressed in a profusion of curls,' one journalist noted, as he looked too longingly at this voluptuous specimen, and his eye moved down, 'It hangs luxuriantly over her bare neck and but half-hidden bosom.' As his eyes lingered, he realised she was always on display, always coiled in an act of mock seduction. Something had changed. The old-fashioned barmaids, who came and went whenever customers called for them, were now relics of the past. These new women were meant to put on a show, and placed under the hot insistent glare of male desire, their every move hyper-sexualised. 'Who can but admire,' one male customer smiled, 'the manner in which she gently tries a new cork into the neck of a bottle?'

Transformations. We had found Agnes working as a servant in the Rev. Smellie's manse in 1881 - the 'honest young lassie' of her parents' hopes, the girl they wanted her to be – and ten years later, we found her again, this time working as a barmaid in Glasgow. Rebellion was the most obvious explanation. Here was a young woman who was breaking free, shaking off the confines of her religious upbringing, escaping her background, rejecting her Presbyterian world.

We dug out Agnes's photo. Her feathered hat had caught my attention when I first saw it, but now it looked more saucy, like her hairstyle and jewels, her bustles and padding. I could see how she played the part, deploying the props. Victorian barmaids were chosen for their natural charms, but they dressed to kill, and used every trick in the book; fancy hats, low-cut dresses, rouge and ivory-powder, hairpieces and padding. 'It would be interesting to know who invented the barmaid', one contemporary asked, 'Drinkers did without them forty or fifty years ago, and they do without them now in France and America.' Nobody quite knew how to explain the mystery. Truly, it was a riddle. 'Young men, ay, and old . . . lean over the white marble or zinc, and seem to hear Circe's song in the rather trite or meaningless syllables that fall from the overdressed girls who serve them.' The scheming barmaid, flirting with customers and making endless conquests, was becoming a stock figure in Victorian mythology.

'Hot or cold, sir?' inquires the fair damsel of a stout gentleman who has just made his appearance, and requested a glass of gin-and-water.

'Hot,' he replies, catching some portion of the lady's soft manner, and looking as amiable as he can.

'With sugar?' says she.

'A little,' replies he; and while the lady is brewing the liquor . . . the gentleman is eying the fair belle with a glance of fond love.

'Beautiful gin-and-water, this,' says the old gentleman, the figure of the barmaid in his eyes, and the fumes of the turpentine, hot water, and lump sugar mounting in his head.

'Another glass, my dear,' says he, having by the aid of the last grown extra loving.

'As the first?' inquires the fair one, in the same tender tone as before.

'Yes, my love,' is the reply; and the old gentleman feels as though he could make love all night.'

The way a barmaid flirted with some men and snubbed others meant that she was loved and loathed in equal measure. In a world ruled by men, attractive women like this were designed to catch the eye, especially when William Holland's 'Barmaid Shows' hit the headlines in the 1870s. Holland was one of the great impresarios of the age, and ran a pleasure garden in North Woolwich where you could always have a good day out. He promised a jolly time; trashy and bizarre, saucy and crazy - a day to be remembered. There were fish dinners in his riverside saloon, after-dinner smokes in his geranium garden, fun and games in his 'wondrous maze', a visit to a well-known fortune-teller, shocks from an electric machine ('Kiss me! Kiss me!' the girls cried, as the electric current ran through them, and they delighted in flooring any young man who was mad enough to respond); pop-guns, rifle ranges, archery grounds, holidays swings, shrimp teas, fruit stalls and Holland's Grand Scenic Depiction of the Paris Commune. In the midst of this lunacy, he furnished a room with four handsome bars that were backed by gilt mirrors. Potted plants were brought in to give the place a classy look. 'English barmaids, Irish barmaids, Scotch barmaids, Welsh barmaids, giant barmaids,' he trumpeted, 'All serving in a Fairy Palace.'

Some thought it indecent, so Holland slapped on a thin veneer of respectability; the potted plants helped, but his rules forbade any forwardness or frivolity, and he established strict codes of dress. Customers were urged to judge the girls by their 'neatness' and 'dexterity', as much as their beauty, although no one was fooled. The women were there to titillate. And it worked. Thousands flocked to the shows, including 'swell gentlemen' from the West End, sailing down this workaday stretch of the Thames in their private yachts.

Everyone who entered William Holland's 'Fairy Palace', paid their sixpence and then received a ticket that acted as a voting card. Each barmaid was placed in a stall behind the bar, with a number over her head. Male customers would circulate and pass judgement. A journalist who had been sent to the scene, overheard the typical male banter: 'There is the second one in the left row, a girl with ribbons of chocolate hue, stuck amid the frizzles of her golden hair. She will surely be the winner. No – stay, I will not bet upon her; the other one, a little further on, with the blue velvet tied across her forehead.'

Holland was unapologetic. 'The public want a sensation,' he said, 'and I give it them. I engage a score or two of respectable young girls to serve at a bar in the concert room. It constitutes a Barmaid Show, and yesterday ten thousand people came into the gardens. Conclusive! The public delight in what they condemn; they like to 'snatch a fearful joy' in witnessing what they would like to persuade themselves ought not to be witnessed.'

And what was wrong with that? Barmaids were forever on show. Some metropolitan papers nodded. Several provincial papers were less sure. One Irish paper was appalled: 'The wit and ingenuity of the world would seem to be on the side of frivolity and wickedness.' Holland's barmaid shows were symptomatic of the age. Victorian society was going to the dogs, and wherever a man looked, there were saucy plays being performed, or risqué novels being written, and any self-respecting gentleman would never let his family and servants see them. A man who invents a 'monstrosity' like a Barmaid Show, is 'instantly elevated to the rank of benefactor.' Thankfully, it was an English disease, brought on by idleness and indulgence, and could never spread to Ireland. 'What is often called our provincial narrowness saves us from many of the degrading eccentricities of our rich neighbours.' Scottish papers were much the same. Barmaids were less common in Scotland, and often nicknamed 'London barmaids', which was never meant as a compliment. For the most part, they were confined to city hotels.

Yet even here, the wickedness of the modern age crept in. In 1897, *The National Police Gazette* ran a series of barmaid competitions across the country, and chose Glasgow as one of its venues. A coupon could be cut from the paper and sent as a voting slip. Readers would name their favourite barmaids. Never fear, they could send as many coupons as they wished (the more the merrier). The poll would last a month, and once the votes were counted, the most popular barmaid would receive a handsome bracelet. We never did find out if Agnes won.

But she was there. We found her in the 1891 census, working as a barmaid in St. Enoch's Hotel, Glasgow, a colossal building thrown up in the grand chateaux style and catering to a high-class clientele. The hotel was opened in 1879 by the Glasgow and South-Western Railway Company, and most of the men who Agnes met here were wealthy merchants and businessmen, theatrical agents, politicians, railway directors, visiting celebrities, together with one or two aristocrats. They made the hotel their centre of operations. Some stayed a night, some took suites on a semi-permanent basis, and some used it as a handy base for political and business campaigning.

It flourished under the guidance of Ernest William Thiem. According to the Glasgow press, Thiem 'excelled in the management of great functions', combining grandiose vision with close attention to detail, and when Agnes joined his staff, she became part of a cosmopolitan world. Thiem had experience of running hotels in London, Paris and Edinburgh, and knew the business well. Even down to advertising for a barmaid:

> 'Barmaid required for the Refreshment Rooms, a Young Lady about 25 years of age as Head Barmaid: must be experienced in this class of business; salary to commence at £30 per annum, with board, lodging and laundry – Apply, stating age, full particulars of previous engagements, enclosing photo.'

The job brought its fair share of perks. A barmaid like Agnes could meet a wide range of men. National and international celebrities came and went, but the great and the good of Glasgow society were always there, propping up the bar. They swanned in for public dinners, confident that Thiem would always provide a sumptuous spread.

We scanned the census to see who was staying here in 1891, and found Zelie de Lussan, a well-known American opera singer. She was holding court in the hotel and touring with the Carl Rosa Opera Company.

'Anything about her in the papers?'

Plenty, as it turned out. Carmen was her great role, and one critic reckoned that her special gift was to balance Carmen's sexuality with modern ideas of female modesty. Quite a feat, but one that Agnes and other barmaids were doing every night of the week.

We tried to work out how Gus and Agnes met. Either Gus came north and met Agnes in Glasgow, or she went south and met him in England. It was possible that Gus had sailed into Glasgow and spent time there, although the bar of St. Enoch's Hotel would have been too expensive. We went back to the Crew Agreements and found no clues. No mention of Glasgow. Gus's letter to Irish Mary had been sent from Liverpool in December 1898, when he was planning to abandon her, so the most likely scenario was that Agnes went south and met him there.

This was the only way to make sense of it. And it explained why Gus had been fooling Irish Mary with fake letters. He had met Agnes in Liverpool, and had fallen for her. They were spending time together, and he was taking care to cover his tracks, using his clearing house in London to make Irish Mary think he was there. We never did find anything to link Gus and Agnes to Liverpool. Nothing that looked conclusive. No census enumerator who surprised them in a seedy upstairs room. No newspaper report. No letters. No employment records. By the look of it, Gus had done an impressive job. He had covered his tracks.

So the broad sweep of the story took shape. Gus had lived with Irish Mary for almost a decade. Then, in 1898, he sailed into Liverpool and met Agnes. By the look of it, he fell for her. He left Mary and moved in with Agnes, and shortly after, his daughter, Beezie, was taken from Mary and brought up by Gus's parents in Bolam vicarage. Irish Mary simply disappeared from view.

But what about Annie? Where did she come in? We knew that Gus married her in July 1899, shortly after falling in love with Agnes, and that looked odd. We were still missing a key piece of the jigsaw.

Chapter 20: Emily

Buried among the rest of Annie's possessions, there was an enigma.

My dear Annie, I am very sorry that you have not confided in me. I wanted to hold you to that day at Dton (Darlington) *but you would not give me a chance. You little know how sorry I am, it has been quite a trouble to me for ever so long and I have been looking for a letter from you but it has not come. I wish you had left Gainford before this. I am feeling very angry with you but the same time you know I would do anything to help you* (if) *I could. For Goodness sake get out of Gainford at any price. I often think of the dream I had about you in January. It was strange. Now dear write to me, unless you have a better friend. I wish I could have seen you. It would have been more satisfactory than writing. I shall be here until a week on Wednesday. Then I go to another case. With love, Your sorrowing friend, ???*

Mysterious and coded. Written in crisis.

We understood hardly anything of what was going on, but saw that a sense of panic was running through every line. An address was printed on the top, embossed in red letters – *4 Trafalgar Terrace, Coatham, Redcar* – so it seemed the writer was staying there, although this was not certain. The rest was murky. No date, no obvious meaning and everything signed off with an unreadable signature.

The sound of an incoming email. Five thousand miles away, Cindy was sitting at her computer. She laughed and told me that her teenage children were whooping it up in the background, somewhere in that sprawling house of hers in the suburbs of Johannesburg. Over the previous months, we had emailed each other, swapping information, ticking off names, filling gaps, and during that time, we had mapped out most of the territory. All of Gus's family had been ticked off: his grandfather; his father and mother; the larkish Bro who finally settled down and lived in Gainford; Greg, who sailed to Calcutta; Liebe, who went with Ted to London. All of them accounted for.

Except for Emily. She was Gus's older sister, and somehow harder to find. All we knew for certain was that in 1885 she married Richard Elgey, the tear-away son of a rich family who lived on the outskirts of Gainford. Their daughter had been born only a few months later. They fled to Middlesbrough where no one would recognise their faces, largely because Emily was the daughter of the vicar and her condition embarrassing. After the birth of their daughter, the two of them disappeared. A week or so earlier, I wondered if Cindy could find them, although I wasn't sure how she could do it, but then reminded myself that she was better at this kind of thing than me.

'You asked previously about Emily Elgey,' she began, and I could sense an unmistakable whiff of triumph in the air. She was probably sitting at her desk with a smile on her face, and a glass of wine in her hand. 'I have found her on the 1901 census, and she is listed as a widow, though I couldn't find a record of her husband's death. She's lodging with an older widow, but it's difficult to see her occupation. There's something there, but I can't read it.'

With a little help from Cindy, we found the page. She was right, it was Emily; no doubt about it. Back from the grave, or at least from her husband's grave, for she claimed to be a widow. The page had been badly mangled by a civil servant running amok with a brutal pencil, and somehow or other he had contrived to obscure everything. We tried to decipher Emily's job, approaching the page from every angle, experimenting with different techniques, trying to shine a light on what was there. And none of it worked.

But slowly, we began to see it. In a nearby house, a domestic gardener had been allocated a 'G', and then a 'farm labourer' had been labelled 'Ag', and it was clear that people were being classified by occupation.

'So what does he say about Emily?' Gill asked, and squinted closer, 'Looks like "Sick", then "Draper's" something or other.'

The label, 'Sick', had been scrawled across Emily's line and was obscuring everything beneath it, but then we saw for the first time what was really there: 'District Nurse (Trained)'.

I grabbed the mysterious letter from the table, *I shall be here until a week on Wednesday. Then I go to another case.* I turned the letter over and stared at the signature.

'Look, can you see? It's *Em*! It's Emily.'

The letter was written in Redcar and, according to the census, Emily was living in a village called Marske, only a mile or so away. She was a nurse and nurses definitely have *cases*. There was another letter from 'Em' to Annie that talked proudly of her work, and was dated *Redcar, Jan 4th 1897*: *I have been pretty busy since I came, this being an operation case. I have been in my element, quite a field day last Wednesday. We had Dr. Murphy to operate. Quite a special man. Dr. MacKinlay to give chloroform . . . I had prepared an operating room after my own heart and things went off first class. It was an abdominal section, so of course a critical operation. She is doing splendidly . . . I expect this case will only last until next Monday and I shall be glad as I want to see more of Gus before he goes . . . Well goodbye my dear and mind and be a good girl. With much love, Yours ever, Em*

Annie was close to the Bowens and particularly close to Emily. Gus was back in Gainford after quitting his merchant sailor's life.

Then, at some point in the summer of 1898, he went back to the sea and sailed into Liverpool where he met Agnes, and everything changed. He abandoned Irish Mary. Beezie was brought to Bolam to live with her grandparents. Occasionally, Gus left Agnes and came to see his daughter at the vicarage, and it was during these visits that he probably met Annie, a close friend of his sister. So Emily turned out to be a key player, and her story unfolded.

After the birth of her daughter, Emily and Richard separated. It had been a hasty marriage, and only a year later, Richard abandoned Emily and headed off to make his fortune in the Australian gold fields. It was 1887 and we found him on a ship heading for Townsville in Northern Queensland. The Queensland gold fields had been making news since 1872, but in the mid-1880s there was a fresh burst of activity. British newspapers were full of advertisements for new mining companies, and these were egged on by Queensland officials who kept dangling the prospect of 'thousands of square miles of mineral wealth yet untouched.' One or two letters appeared in the press from disillusioned emigrants who openly complained about the few jobs that were to be found in this remote territory, the high price of provisions, and the intense heat. None of it mattered. The flow of migrants never stopped. As soon as the Queensland officials exhibited a gold 'cake', worth £5,923, in the Colonial and Indian Exhibition of 1886, the fever was as high as ever. As far as we could tell, Richard never made a fortune, nor for that matter did most of the migrants, but he settled in the area, married a second time, and raised a family. Some of his descendants are still living there.

He left Emily with a young child, but his disappearance in 1887 happened to coincide with Queen Victoria's Golden Jubilee, and this in its own way was fortuitous. Part of the Jubilee celebrations encouraged women to make donations to a special Jubilee Fund. Whatever money was collected would be devoted to a specific project for women, selected by the Queen. She chose a district nursing scheme that would establish professionally-trained nurses throughout the towns of Britain. Whilst this project gathered momentum, a new system of nurses and midwives was formed in villages. Its chief instigator and secretary, a formidable woman called Elizabeth Malleson, publicised the organisation in the press, and almost every metropolitan and provincial newspaper carried her story. Nursing was now in the news.

'No vocation is more eagerly sought after by women of the educated classes'. A new culture of professionalism emerged, and this made nursing increasingly attractive. Under the scheme, district nurses would be trained in an approved hospital or infirmary for at least a year, and then receive more training 'in the field'. Here was something that a respectable middle-class woman could tackle with pride. 'Of all employments open to gentlewomen there is none more suitable than that of a district nurse, as so much tact, discretion, and good breeding are required to introduce sanitary reforms without hurting the feelings of those who are to benefit by the change.'

There was no denying the hardships. The job had its fair share of 'repulsive' work, but this only heightened its appeal. By a strange logic, menial work was said to be best suited to women of the 'higher stamp'. They would become the 'servants of the poor'. It was a new and secular version of a much longer Christian tradition, based on self-sacrifice and service. A tradition that Emily knew only too well. The hard realities were revealed when we came across a *Guide to District Nursing* that had been published in 1889.

According to the guide, Emily would forsake any feminine adornments; her hair would be made smooth, and there would be no fringes or frizettes. She would remove her rings and jewellery, and learn to wear the simplest of uniforms. Fancy footwear was out, and she would adopt flat shoes that made no noise in the sick room. Above all, she must be clean. Once this personal form of renunciation was adopted, and a period of training completed, she would enter the homes of the poor. Here, she would 'sweep and dust and empty and wash out all the dirt and foulness she finds'. And the conditions could be foul. 'Sometimes there is a plague of flies in the room,' the guide warned, 'which can be traced to some foul or decaying animal or vegetable refuse.' She would clear it out. There might be damp walls, blackened ceilings, filthy wallpapers, and houses infested from top to bottom with vermin. Every conceivable horror.

She must carry a notebook where the details of each patient would be entered, and this was kept alongside a box of matches and a rolled-up piece of wax taper. Why? Because she would find herself in dismal, dark houses in winter and need to light her way. She would carry a second bag containing a spare notebook for special cases, two clean temperature charts, an ink bottle, a pen and three pencils (red, blue and black for colour-coding), a penknife, a sheet of writing paper, an envelope and two blank postcards; if a place was found that was particularly bad, the postcards would be sent to the local sanitary authority, alerting them to the problem. More bags were needed for medical equipment - probes, forceps, spatulas, thermometers, catheters, razors, tins of caustic, crystals of carbolic, spirits of turpentine, insect powder, zinc ointments, flannels and bandages, glass syringes, vaginal tubes and enemas.

If this wasn't enough, she would have to 'nurse' the sick rooms too. Beds would be moved from against walls to avoid draughts and vermin infestation. Light would be controlled by improvised blinds. She would look under the bed for soiled linen, dirty utensils, boots and coal, and then clear them out. Floors and carpets were mopped and scrubbed, furniture and mantelpieces wiped. Fires lit: 'I was helping one of the district nurses to light a fire,' the author of the guide recounted, 'when the poor patient exclaimed, "Please, nurse, don't use more than three pieces of wood. I never do!' Every cinder would have to be replaced because the poor could never afford to throw them away. Then the ashes themselves would be carried to the dustbin. The state of the dustbin inspected. She would ensure that bedpans, chamber utensils and urinals were washed, and leave water inside to absorb the smell. Where she found them very neglected and stained, she would scour them. Slop-pails made of zinc and lacking a lid, would be covered with towels or old newspapers.

Ventilation and temperature were crucial. In cholera cases, it was important to keep rooms warm, but dysentery required a cooler environment. And then the nurse would have to improvise a wide range of devices: bed-pulleys and bed-rests that were cobbled together from a mixture of old towelling, inverted chairs and pillows. In cases of bronchitis, diphtheria and croup, a moist atmosphere was essential, so peashooters could be slotted into the spout of a kettle and placed on the fire; as the kettle boiled, a thin plume of steam would emerge.

Bed linen had to be changed regularly, but in a particular way that never exposed the patient. Many patients needed washing or sponging. Hair had to be combed and brushed and cleaned with spirits of turpentine and ointment. Lice and bed vermin were eradicated. A regular brushing of the bed linen was necessary, and any cracks in the bedstead filled with a special paste made of carbolic powder. Where bugs infested the flooring, the nurse would show the family how to fill the crevices with another cleansing paste. Blankets and bedding would be sprinkled with insect powder.

Then there was the body and all its fluids. Bedpans might be improvised from dustpans, soup plates, jam jars and sauceboats. If there were no proper 'mackintosh sheets', a double fold of newspaper might be placed beneath any incontinent patient. Many of these daily procedures required an intimate knowledge of bodies, and there was a lingering anxiety about middle-class nurses having to handle working-class, male bodies. 'And here I must again repeat what I have always maintained,' the guide stressed, 'that where a woman has to bath a man, no exposure is either necessary or justified. A blanket should always be thrown round him as his clothes or night shirt are removed.'

So whilst Emily learned to look away, she also learned to observe. It was her job to note the kind of cough a patient had, the kind of phlegm he brought up, the pain he complained of, the colour and texture of his lips, the state of his teeth, discharges from his eyes, ears and nose, bowel evacuations, urine samples, breathing and sleeping patterns, temperature and pulse.

If this wasn't enough, she might have to do some basic cooking, cobbling together iced drinks, beef teas, stews and broths, puddings and gruel. If there was no proper oven available, a large saucepan might be pressed into service with a well-fitting lid, the pan placed on the fire and the lid inverted. Red-hot coals would be placed on the lid and then sticks added, so the top was always hot.

Finally, she would face death. Helping patients to be comfortable during their final illnesses. Washing the body in a prescribed way, cleaning wounds and clearing away discharges, closing orifices, brushing hair, tying chins, composing features. She might even place a small bouquet of flowers in the folded hands.

We found Emily working as a housekeeper in a large convalescent hospital in Rhyl in 1891, only four years after Richard left. This was her start. The way she set about making a new life for herself. Then she trained as a District Nurse in Stockton, and by the late 1890s, she was a fully-qualified practitioner. By the sound of it, she sometimes worked as a private nurse and moved from one case to another, but by 1901, she was a District Nurse in Marske, ministering to the needs of a mining population.

Meanwhile, her daughter lodged with people in Bolam, only two doors from Craufurd and Hannah, and the crisis was weathered. Several members of the Elgey family were nearby and it was hard to see how Richard's flight to Australia could ever have been kept secret. People would have talked. Yet for all the embarrassment and scandal, something happened. Emily became a new woman. A District Nurse who could cope with almost anything. Someone who Annie could turn to.

My dear Annie, . . . I am feeling very angry with you but the same time you know I would do anything to help you . . . For Goodness sake get out of Gainford at any price . . . Now dear write to me, unless you have a better friend . . . I shall be here until a week on Wednesday. Then I go to another case. With love, Your sorrowing friend, Em.

Chapter 21: Trouble

Annie and Gus were married in Middlesbrough in July 1899, just like Emily and Richard ten years before. After the wedding, they spent two weeks together before Gus signed up for another voyage, this time as a boatswain on the *Aberfeldy* bound for Constantinople. He wrote to Annie and some of his letters ended in our attic. They were sent at different times in the voyage and several of them were moth-eaten. The first was from Antwerp, and two chunks had been chewed out so its sentences kept fading away:

S.S. Aberfeldy, Antwerp, July 30th, 99, My darling, I am wondering if you . . . (I have got such a bad pen and cannot use it). Feeling very much alone tonight (Sunday) . . . Oh, How I wish I was with you. Have quite made up my mind not to go to sea again if I can possibly help it. Well, there is no letter from you yet, but . . . to get one tomorrow . . . my third to you. Hope . . . them all right . . . not expect to get away . . . before the end of the . . . so you can safely . . . this - I do not know how long letters take . . . I feel very . . . not having heard from . . .

Gus gave some inconsequential news of the ship's crew and then began snuggling closer: *I have my berth to myself. There are two bunks. How I wish you were in the other - never mind pet. The time will soon pass & we shall be in the same berth . . . keep a good heart . . . remember I think of you . . . I wonder what letters . . . had since I left . . . write you.*

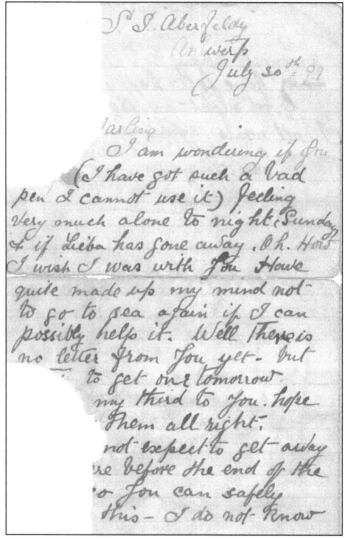

Gus's damaged letter to Annie: S.S. Aberfeldy, Antwerp, July 30, 1899

The sentences kept coming and going. *Weather here is simply roasting. Expect you are having it fine too. There is really no news to tell you but writing to you is the only bit of pleasure I have. I am*

*just going to turn in & shall think of & pray for my darling until
sleep overtakes me . . . The more I think of it the more rejoiced I feel
that you did not get to London & would have been awful for you to
have been amongst strangers. I . . . never have felt happy . . . Good
night my darling, I will write again soon . . . Ever your own, Gus.*

We picked our way through every sentence. Every surviving
word. The letter was tender and affectionate, romantic and
sometimes even sensual. Clever too. Gus wanted Annie to lay beside
him in the bunk, but then turned his sexual desire into something
nobler; one day, he promised, they would snuggle up in a cosy little
berth. Like most sailors, he claimed to be sick of the sea, largely
because it played well.

He also claimed to anticipate Annie's letters whenever the ship
docked and, for lack of anything else to say, told her about the crew
and the weather and the boredom on board. Whenever he could, he
slipped into something personal. He was relieved that Annie was not
going to London. She had been thinking about it, but had changed
her mind and finally, he closed with a whisper: *Good night my
darling*.

Annie kept the letter. Its envelope had fallen apart because she
had opened and closed it far too often. It was addressed to *Mrs.
Bowen, Holly Cottage, Haxby, York, England*. We wondered if those
'darlings' and 'pets' were genuine. Did he really care, or was he
simply toying with her? It was hard to tell. And we saw that Annie
must have harboured doubts herself. She could never know if he was
genuine. His declarations of love may have been false but they were
beautifully crafted. There was just enough love and tenderness to
please her, and we compared them with the letters he sent to Irish
Mary where, amidst the usual Gus charm, a frosty chill began to
grip.

Gus wrote to Annie the next day when the ship reached
Antwerp: *Sailors' Rest, Canal des Vieux Lions 37, Antwerp, My
darling, I feel just twice as well today as I have done since we left -
why? because I received your letter today. Yes, my word, you are*

lucky – about the house I mean.

Annie had evidently told him about letting her house in Gainford, and Gus was calculating how much money she might make. Gill giggled and shook her head. 'He's joking about her being lucky, and then he realizes, of course, that he's made a mistake. She's by herself and doesn't know if she can count on him.'

Yes my darling I know you must feel very lonely - I hope Mr. Marshall will come to see you - if it will give you any pleasure - why not? I have a faith in you that no one but yourself shall ever shake.

We checked the 1901 census to see if there was a Mr. Marshall living in Haxby, and found that he was the village schoolmaster. A married man with a family, but a respectable character who Annie could invite to tea.

Back to Gus. *There is a fellow waiting here for me & it worries me so I will finish this down at the ship. I must be alone when I am writing to you - then I kid myself that I am talking to you . . . At present it is impossible to say exactly how long we shall be away but I expect quite two months after we leave here, but as we have so many ports to call at you will hear from me frequently and the time will soon pass.*

Annie was anxious and wanted to know how long he would be away at sea, and Gus was trying to reassure her. *I thought Liebe and Ted were going to Cornwall, you say London - I am sorry the little one is so bad - also that I did not send you a kiss - but <u>such</u> are not good enough for <u>you</u>.*

I snapped my fingers and remembered a letter that Craufurd had written: *Ed. & Liebe have left the Spen. They are now at Holly Cottage, Haxby, York. Less pay (so they say) but easier and nicer work (Storekeeper for Railway Co). He hopes before long to get a much better post.*

I looked up. 'Annie's with Liebe and Ted, and that's why she's in Haxby.'

Another piece fell into place. But there was a huge part of the jig-saw that didn't fit. Agnes's role in the drama. Gus had been living with her in Liverpool. He had left Irish Mary and Beezie to be with this woman, and she seemed to be important to him. Yet at some point in 1898, he went to Bolam to see his family, and suddenly he decided to marry Annie. Agnes had turned up at the wedding, had scrawled her name across the certificate, then after all her fury had been vented, she went back to Liverpool and left them to enjoy their honeymoon. Quite frankly, it didn't make sense.

Ah, so they will be calling me Capt Bowen now eh - what a joke - I suppose you will have the front bedroom now - wish I was with you tonight. Liebe says she thinks of me every time she sees the sweet peas. Does that mean when they are done she'll think no more of me? Well, I must turn in - I shall be getting another letter soon from you I hope . . . In any case you will hear from me again before long. With much love my darling, ever your own, Gus.

The next letter was sent on August 3. The ship was still in Antwerp, and Gus was delighted to have received a letter from Annie. By this point, he claimed to have written five, although we found only three.

And this new letter was damaged. In a piece of unintentional origami, Annie had folded it over twice and torn a piece from a corner, leaving two gaping holes at the middle, so only fragments remained. *SS Aberfeldy, Antwerp, My darling, I recd your 2nd letter this afternoon. Should have had it before. Was beginning to think all sorts of things . . . is my 5th letter to you.*

The next sections were lost, but then his voice recovered, although still broken and faint. *Unfortunately, it is impossible to be back before the end of September at the earliest. I never expected to be here so long to . . . Do not expect to get away before . . . When this arrives & you will not feel so lonely. I do feel for you.* We kept squeezing the letter, hoping for more. Gus had been ill, but reckoned he was now on the mend. He added: *I guess they will miss Beezie when we take her away.*

Ever since Beezie had been separated from Irish Mary, she had lived with Craufurd and Hannah in Bolam vicarage. It had become her new home and both grandparents loved her. Here was Gus trailing a seductive fantasy, something that he knew would appeal to Annie. Once back, he and Annie would take Beezie away with them and live together, and they would be happy.

Two more letters arrived from Antwerp. *Wednesday, S.S. Aberfeldy, Antwerp, My own darling . . . We have just arrived here. From here we go to Constant to discharge part cargo from there to Tarantog and then I think Marinapul . . . It's useless to try and tell you how miserable I feel -* never *was so bad before - Thank God I shall not have to make many more voyages . . . With much love to all of you and kisses for ??? and ???, I am, my own darling, your loving husband, In great haste - I promise a long letter directly.*

Five days later, he kept his promise: *Monday, S.S. Aberfeldy, Antwerp, My darling, I am disappointed. Felt quite sure I should have had another letter from you at least, but no only two and I have sent you six. Well I must wait till we get to Constant now . . . I shall expect heaps of news.*

He was giving her his best attention. *I am not a bit in form for writing to night -* damn the sea *- I must and will have a job on shore after this.*

We both smiled.

Well dear I wonder how you are by this - at any rate you are a fortnight nearer the event and I trust keeping a good heart . . . Well love to everybody and tons for your dear self, I am my darling, your loving husband, Gus Bowen.

Chapter 22: Constantinople

By August 25th, the ship reached Constantinople.

My Darling, You talk about luck - just fancy I have had two letters from you today . . . We got here this morn and leave again tomorrow.

By the sound of it, he had collected Annie's letters from the British Consul's Office or perhaps the British Post Office. *How delightful it must be*, his father wrote, as he imagined Gus in this exotic place, *running about among such lovely scenes and in the most enjoyable climate in the world.*

Constantinople occupied a special place in the Victorian imagination. 'The man who goes to visit Constantinople for the first time may be readily excused for entertaining romantic anticipations. He may conjure up to his mind's eye a seven-hilled city rising from the sea, resplendent with glittering domes and graceful minarets, the white palaces of the Sultans, and stately residences of the pashas, all set in dark green masses of cypresses. He may picture to himself the shimmer of the Golden Horn, the beauty of the Bosphorus, and the Watteau-like landscapes in the Vale of Sweet Waters.'

Gus was filling his letters with so many 'darlings', that his charm seemed to rise from the page like body heat. *'Tis so nice to think that you care for my letters darling - if you only knew how I look for & how much I think of yours.*

The letters were well crafted, and quite possibly deceitful, and if ever there was a 'true' Gus behind them it was impossible to tell. Constantinople was much the same. A place of shimmering surfaces. Shortly after Imry Kiralfy closed 'Venice in London', his brother, Bolossy, projected an even greater extravaganza, and the Victorian public were treated to a new spectacle - 'Constantinople in London'. It would be bigger and better than anything that had gone before, and would treat Londoners to a day of 'Oriental skies and Oriental warmth'. Gus and Ted may have been part of the project because one of the key scenes centred on the harbour at Constantinople where ships lay at anchor.

Every defining feature of the Orient was brought to life. Visitors could saunter through streets of Byzantine, Saracenic, Greek and Turkish architecture, where latticed and shuttered fronts looked down from all sides. The agents of Kiralfy had been scouring Constantinople during the summer, taking plaster casts of architectural details so they could faithfully recreate the old Turkish houses and shops, with their venerable, worm-eaten timbers. There would be scenes from the Arabian Nights, plenty of minarets, mosaics, marbles and mosques, palace gardens, a tantalising glimpse of the Sultan's seraglio and a climb to the top of the Galata Tower. From here, visitors could admire the grand panorama that looked out over the Golden Horn.

Once the elaborate sets were complete, a small army of 'Arabs' was shipped in, 'direct from the Orient', to engage in carpet-weaving and cigarette-making, or anything that looked vaguely Arabic. Some of these men would operate the famous 'caiques' that scurried back and forth across the Bosphorus, and they would ferry visitors from one part of the show to another. The ferry rides included an atmospheric subterranean passage to the 'Hall of a Thousand Columns'.

The organisers delighted in revealing the elaborate preparations that went into the making of such a brilliant show. Here, after all, was a modern wonder. Journalists were invited to Olympia to see the illusory city rising up before their eyes. As they interviewed Kiralfy, plasterers and joiners would be banging away in the background, and there was a powerful smell of paint everywhere. Great play was made of the supreme artifice that was needed to make this vision authentic, and Gus would have grasped the point in a second. It took skill to fool people. Then again, so many people love to be fooled.

The real city was never quite what it promised. Once you got into the streets 'the illusion vanishes; its modern plague is dirt; the streets are unpaved and choked with refuse; on every rubbish heap rests a mangy cur.' The dogs of Constantinople were legendary. They slept throughout the day, lolling on pavements or stretched out in gutters, sometimes twenty or more in packs, and everyone took care to walk around them. At night, you could hear them howling as they protected their different districts. No one took responsibility.

In truth, the dogs were never a threat, but danger was everywhere. Throughout much of the 1890s, the city witnessed a series of frightening racial and religious riots, when hundreds of Armenians were butchered by Islamic crowds. Armenian struggles for independence were posing serious threats to the crumbling Ottoman Empire, and the Armenians in Constantinople were agitating for reform. Tensions were high. A steamer sailing from the Tyne in 1896 found itself caught up in the butchery. A mob of about thirty ransacked the ship and seized two Armenians who were killed in full view of the crew. Twenty other Armenians hid in the hold; the mob searched the ship from top to bottom, and the English crew looked on, helpless to intervene. Constantinople was a powder keg.

Annie wanted to know when Gus would come home. He tried to reassure her, calculating that it would be about six weeks. *Would to God it were tomorrow,* he said, and tried to convince her of his own misery. *However I am in good health and can weather it out.*

Then he turned to what he called her *trouble*: *I am afraid my darling you must make up your mind to go through your trouble without me. It is hard I know, darling, but you will keep a good heart for my sake. Remember my lips will be devoted to you and we will be happy darling in spite of it all. It is a rough way of expressing oneself but you understand.*

Annie was challenging him, and he was trying to placate her. Once he returned, he said, she would have his constant support. *I will make a point of disappointing those who thought that I was not to be relied upon.* We could see that Annie was beginning to complain. Conditions in Liebe and Ted's cottage were cramped and she was seriously thinking of moving. Most worryingly of all, Annie had been talking to his mother who had told her quite plainly that Gus would make her a poor husband. *I am sorry that my mother should think that I should make you a bad husband (But until I hear her say so myself I will not believe that she did say so) - Nance - you know that after you - my mother is my first consideration.*

He was overcome by emotion: *My heart is too full to write tonight lass - so you must forgive me. However I will let them see differently. I do believe you darling when you say that you will make me a true good wife.*

The ship moved on. After Constantinople it reached Tarantog, and then finally turned for home. It called at Constantinople a second time and Gus wrote on September 25th. *Well dear I think about you greatly just at this particular time - but trust by the time you get this - that the worst is over. Hope you will be very careful of yourself & be the same old Nance of long ago. You know what I mean darling.*

Gill looked up. 'I think Annie's pregnant. There was something about her *trouble*, and then this - *But trust by the time you get this - that the worst is over.*'

We read on. Gus expected to be in Constantinople for an hour before the ship sailed for Algiers, and then for Hamburg, and then for *Old England.* He had no news to give, and claimed that the only thing that was keeping him going was the thought of seeing her again. *Well good night my darling. Anxiously waiting for the morrow, I am, Yours for ever, Gus.*

Then, on October 1st, he sent a final letter: *S.S. Aberfeldy, My darling, I recd your welcome letter at Constant - You seem to have your share of knocking about since I left you - but I trust you eventually got a comfy and suitable place to make your nest in - You run things <u>too</u> fine for my peace of mind - should have been taking fits if I'd been with you - as I happen to know the folly of running things too close - however I presume that all is over now & trust you are going on all right Nance. Is the nurse nice. She will still be with you. Will not forget something for her from Algiers. Well my darling, how is that "Boy" getting on and what are we going to call him? Don't forget to save us a drop in the bottom of the bottle you know.*

Everything became suddenly clear. Emily's letter had been urging Annie to get out of Gainford before neighbours noticed her pregnancy. And here was a side to Annie's character that neither of us expected. I began working out the sums. If Gus expected the child to be born in September, or perhaps early October, it must have been conceived around Christmas. He had come home to visit his parents, he and Annie had rushed into an affair, and she had risked everything. Gill wondered if Gus might have seduced her, but it looked unlikely. Annie was no longer a young woman; she was in her mid-thirties and hardly an ingénue. Here was a woman who had made a choice.

Emily had written to Annie in the spring of 1899, a few months into this unwanted pregnancy, when Annie was sure of the signs. A time before anyone in the village could see the signs for themselves. She had arranged for Annie to stay with Liebe and Ted in Haxby, well away from prying eyes. A good place to hide. London had been another option but Annie had finally decided against it.

I paused for a moment, trying to assess the implications.

'There's a scandal looming.'

Chapter 23: Scandal

Over a thousand 'clerical scandals' appeared in our database of Victorian newspapers. During the first half of the century, most of them centred on religious or political controversies, but by the 1890s, sex had won out. Clergymen were easy targets, for here were high-minded men who were expected to live unblemished lives. Any fall from grace – especially sexual – would be met with withering ridicule. It was not just the sight of these spiritual leaders making fools of themselves that so delighted Victorian readers; clergyman were high-profile figures in the national and local community, and stood for the privileged power of the establishment, so they were legitimate targets. Victorian country parishes like Bolam might be peaceful enough in the green leafiness of their lanes, but this was an illusion. There were battles going on.

A Methodist Chapel stood across the way from Bolam vicarage, so whenever Craufurd opened his window, or peered over the top of his garden wall, it was there in his face, provoking him. Despite his modest talk of ministering 'quietly, humbly and diligently' to the needs of a retired village, he took a hard line against chapel people, and they took a hard line against him. From the early 1870s, the two sides struggled to control the village school. The Education Act of 1870 gave local ratepayers the chance to establish new schools, and

Nonconformist groups across the country had a golden opportunity to break the stranglehold of the Church of England. Craufurd dug in and fought a rear-guard action.

Bolam School was run on strict Church of England lines. Its children were taught to read and write, but were also drilled in the Church Catechism, and this offended Nonconformists. The school had pottered along in this fashion for many years under the shaky guidance of Miss Turnage, an impoverished spinster. She had no formal training and refused to admit government inspectors, and this marked her out as a perfect target for reform. The first challenge came in 1873 when a notice appeared in the village calling for a new school. Then, for reasons that have never been fully explained, the idea fizzled out. The storm passed, and Miss Turnage carried on. Almost incredibly, she survived for another twenty years, and might have lasted longer, but in December 1890, just before the start of the Christmas holidays, she set the children some homework, packed them off, went to fetch a pail of water from the schoolyard, and had a heart attack. Craufurd was asked to bury her on Christmas Day. He knew exactly what this meant. Her death would trigger a fresh round of conflict.

In point of fact, the school remained closed for another three years, and little was done to revive it, but a School Board was finally projected in 1893. Craufurd swung into action. He canvassed local landowners, urging them to keep it on Church of England lines. Lord Barnard was willing to loan the money, but advised Craufurd to sound out opinion, and this included Nonconformist opinion. A meeting was held, but ended in acrimony; Craufurd walked out and refused to work with people who he regarded as enemies. 'Lord Barnard's idea that Dissenters . . . should be on the management is wrong,' he told Edleston, 'Better to do without their help & their mischievous interference.'

'So,' I said, as I drove away from the archive, 'Craufurd makes enemies.' We had just finished a session in Durham Record Office, copying Craufurd's letters, and had gained a glimpse into the coming struggle. Contrary to Lord Barnard's advice, Craufurd refused to work with local Nonconformists, and was determined to keep the school under Church of England control. We saw the danger. If news of Annie's pregnancy leaked out, the ensuing scandal would ruin Craufurd. It would be used against him.

After thirty years in a rural parish where he and Hannah had lived contentedly, the thought of losing everything would have been unbearable. So Emily stepped in. The crisis had to be managed, and her father protected, and the first priority was to bundle Annie out of Gainford. It was not just the physical signs that were threatening. Annie might let something slip, or if Gus ran off, who could tell what she might do?

We could see how the Bowens would now lurch into panic mode. It was bound to happen. And if we could see it, so could Annie. She had given Emily the news, knowing full well what her letter would do. It would trigger alarm bells in the vicarage, and Emily would have to act. First, she would handle Annie and make sure she was discreet; no whisper of the pregnancy must ever leak out. Emily had done something like this ten years before when her own pregnancy was hidden. This would be the first priority, and Annie would fall into line as long as Emily did what Annie wanted her to do. For Emily would have to corner Gus and make sure he did the decent thing. He would have to marry Annie. No running away. So the female politics of friendship played out; Annie would use Emily to pressure Gus, whilst Emily did her best to protect the family.

'How easy would it be to keep a secret like this?' Gill asked, for we knew what a small community was like.

'At least they don't have a servant.'

The Bowens were never well off. They did their best to live in style, but behind their brittle show of gentility, they were always struggling to maintain appearances. For better or for worse, servants were beyond them. A young and relatively cheap domestic had been employed in the early 1870s, but had disappeared. As things turned out, it was probably best.

It was common knowledge that servants saw everything. Or failing that, they heard everything. And then they gossiped. An inquisitive servant in the Bowen household would have been a source of real danger. The family secret would have been impossible to hide, and sooner or later, it would have leaked out. Once that happened, the family would have been ruined. We knew this only too well because many of the 'clerical scandals' that appeared in the Victorian press were carried on the wings of servant gossip.

A housemaid carrying tea into the cosy, sunlit parlour of a country vicarage, caught the resident vicar *in flagrante delicto*. He was kissing a lady parishioner. The young lady lived in the cottage next door, and another servant saw how they contrived their meetings. Whenever the coast was clear, the young lady would whistle, and the vicar would jump over the hedge. Then a housemaid caught them in the fields, and soon afterwards, the cook saw them. 'I used to watch through the dairy window,' she said, 'and see Miss Burton coming constantly to the vicarage. She would come to the study and go out and no one knew she had been in the house.' Except of course, the cook. And then the servants. And then the world.

A domestic servant in another vicarage admitted that she eavesdropped on conversations. She obviously had her suspicions and caught the vicar one day fondling the breast of another servant. There was nothing untoward in this, he said, for he was simply sounding out the girl's heart after a bout of influenza. The servant and the governess were not persuaded, and were happy enough to give evidence against him in a formal hearing. Yet evidence of this kind was rarely needed. The real damage was done before. Parish gossip could be ruthless. In 1891, the wife of another clergyman begged a servant to refute rumours circulating in the village that her husband had made her pregnant. She talked of 'a fearful suspicion' that had taken hold and poisoned his prospects. The girl reassured her that the vicar was not the father, but it came too late; the village had decided.

And sometimes things became much worse. 'Saw a sight tonight I never saw in my life,' one Gainford man recorded in his diary. It was April 1897, two years before Gus and Annie's affair. 'Riding the Stang for Mr. Hitt and Mrs. Wheatley for illegal connections between them.' It was a traditional form of shaming. In truth, the custom was dying out in most parts of the country, but in Gainford it was still very much alive. Anyone suspected of breaking the codes of the community could be subjected to this kind of public humiliation, so here were two genteel lovers being exposed by their neighbours, their effigies burnt in public. It could easily happen to Annie and Gus.

In Cumbria, a young clergyman was suspected of having an affair with a village schoolteacher. He was ambushed by a gang of farm workers, tied to a five-bar gate, doused in disinfectant, and carried through the streets. Finally, they dumped him on the vicarage lawn. Might this happen to Craufurd? Perhaps not. But the scandal was enough. It would drive him out. Another report told of an impoverished curate in London who had taken in lodgers to supplement his income. His wife fell for one of the lodgers and began showing signs of infatuation. Before his arrival, she had been a late riser, but now she got up to have breakfast with him. It had been a source of deep regret to the curate that his wife never sang when he played the violin, but now, all was changed; she leaned enticingly on the piano, and sang to the lodger's tune. It was a peculiar form of Victorian infidelity. The affair blossomed, the marriage disintegrated and the curate was ruined. 'Matters became unpleasant in the parish.'

When Annie gave Emily the news of her pregnancy, the Bowens were plunged into crisis. Somehow or other, Emily would need to persuade Gus to face up to his responsibilities. It was the only way he could save the family. Everyone knew that Gus was a loafer. He was delightful and charming, but feckless. Emily would bring her influence to bear, but there was no guarantee she could pull it off. He might bolt. He and Agnes might disappear, and that would be that. They would settle in some distant part of the globe; a place where Annie could never reach them, and the Bowens would be left with the scandal.

Perhaps Emily's influence and power were greater than we thought? Perhaps she knew how to terrify Gus? Perhaps it was none of this? Perhaps he decided for himself? Whatever the reason, Gus stayed, and he married Annie. How much of this was love, and how much duty, was impossible to tell. *I will make a point of disappointing those who thought that I was not to be relied upon.*

Chapter 24: Taboo

'We seem to be threatened with a literature of pregnancy. This is intolerable.'

(Review of George Elliott's *Adam Bede,* 1859)

Pregnancy was a taboo subject in Victorian society. It was never mentioned in conversation, or described in novels, or (heaven forbid) in newspapers. Respectable women were advised to hold their tongues and cover their bodies, for this was the best way to negotiate a distressing condition. As the century wore on, the delicacy surrounding the subject seemed to become more extreme. A swollen belly signalled to the world that a woman was 'unchaste', so a number of corsets were designed 'to divert the eye from the condition of the wearer'.

How would Annie have known she was pregnant? Sexual knowledge was limited during the Victorian years but two popular books gave a practical insight. Chavasse's *Advice to a Wife on the Management of her Own Health* was published in the 1840s, and reprinted many times, so we could see it was read. 'The diffidence and ignorance of young wives, on matters appertaining to the management of themselves during the periods of pregnancy, labour, and suckling,' it began, 'call on medical men to use their utmost exertions to enlighten them on the above subjects, and in a mode the least likely to do violence to their feelings.'

Chavasse was at pains to justify his book, for there were fears that young women would read it out of curiosity. The book, he claimed, would not corrupt their morals but protect their health. Douglas Fox's, *The Signs, Disorders and Management of Pregnancy,* appeared in 1834, and ran into several editions, so it was obvious there was a well-established market for such material.

'How many women read them?' Gill wondered, 'Where would they get hold of a book like this?' It was another corner of Victorian life that was dimly lit. Fox reassured his readers that the book could be read by respectable women. It would help allay their anxieties, but he was treading a dangerous path.

Each book opened with a brief discussion of early signs – morning sickness, strange food cravings, shooting and lancing pains, enlargement of breasts. For his part, Fox was dangerously bold. 'Pregnancy in most instances,' he said, 'is first indicated by a cessation of the periodical discharge.' This was plain speaking that bordered on obscenity, and Chavasse was less open. 'The first sign that leads a female to suspect she is pregnant,' he explained, 'is her "ceasing to feel unwell"'.

Having found an appropriate form of language, Chavasse advised readers how they could set about calculating a likely date of delivery. A woman could estimate the date by counting the days, starting three days after 'ceasing to be unwell.' 'A good plan', he advised, 'is to make the reckoning after the following manner: Let forty weeks and a few days be marked on an almanac, from the time specified above, and a female will very seldom be far from her calculation. For instance, suppose the last day of her ceasing to feel unwell was on January the 15th, she may expect to be confined very near October 24th.'

Gill had a woman's understanding of this. 'Annie probably began to have her suspicions in January or even early February,' she said, 'but she might have kept it to herself. She couldn't really be certain, not at that point.'

Where was Gus? He may have been in Bolam, because he didn't sign up for another voyage until the 23rd February. A more likely scenario was that he was back with Agnes. We knew that he sailed from Cardiff on the 23rd February and stayed at sea until the 14th April, calling at Genoa and Sulina. By then, Annie would have known, and Gus would have returned to hear the news.

It was anybody's guess if Craufurd and Hannah were informed. Perhaps they were spared the worry, but Annie had been close to the Bowens and people might talk. Perhaps Gus and Annie had been seen together in the Christmas holidays? They could hardly have made love in Bolam vicarage itself, and there was little chance in the open air, not at least in December. But it happened somewhere. It was almost impossible to conceal affairs of this kind in a small village, where everyone kept a close eye on everyone else, and where gossip grew like grass.

'It has to be Annie's house,' I said, 'Her father's gone. Her mother's died. She's in the house by herself.' But this in itself raised even more shocking possibilities. 'Except, of course,' I added, 'if no one sees them going in and out of the house, once her pregnancy is discovered, they might suspect Craufurd?' Gill was appalled. How could I think such a thing?

But I could. We found a tiny souvenir in Annie's collection. It was a small token from Craufurd that seemed to be a wild flower. Annie labelled it - *The Rev. Bowen at Headlam Hall* - and marked the moment. A label had been cut out and attached to the flower, and kept all her life. It suggested that the two of them went walking, and that people might have noticed. Perfectly innocent walks, but walks that might have looked less innocent, once her pregnancy was discovered.

I looked out of the window on a glorious autumn day.

'Fancy a walk?'

We cut through the woods. Most of the trees were bare; their leaves fallen and bronzing the ground. The sweet smell of leaf mould hung in the air. An occasional breeze rippled through the trees, and the last leaves spiralled down. We walked in silence, one behind the other, down a narrow woodland path, seagulls gliding over us as they came in from the coast. I looked up and saw their bellies, plump and white against the blue sky. It was easy to imagine Craufurd and Annie enjoying days like this.

Gus had his faults; he knew them, and everyone knew them. His mother loved him, but saw quite clearly that he was a feckless man and did her best to warn Annie. We knew from the letters that Gus was always happy to admit his failings and that he liked to sport his rakishness. He would promise to mend his ways, and women liked it. People would see a difference, he said, just wait and see. He might be a loafer and a bit of a masher, but really he was just a decent chap who need a good woman to set him on the right tracks. It always worked.

We could never be sure if Gus ever loved Annie, but he married her. He did his best to look after her and be a father to her child, and there was something honourable in this. Instead of running away, he accepted a marriage that he didn't want and protected his family. Then we looked at Annie. She knew Gus's reputation and took a chance, playing fast and loose with a dangerous man. Emily joked about her being 'a good girl' but Annie wasn't. She flirted with danger and broke the rules.

'More interesting, when you come to think of it,' I said.

It was easy to see how things might play out if the scandal ever broke. The Bishop would send for Craufurd. A polite little note. Perhaps Craufurd would like to join him for tea? To begin with, the conversation would meander through different topics, both men sitting in their chairs, knowing exactly where the talk was going. Once the burning issue was raised, the bishop would offer advice. Craufurd had committed no offence himself, although one or two parishioners might have their doubts, but there was no denying the fact that his reputation had been damaged, and the Church's reputation too. There were really two choices. Craufurd could remain in post and weather the storm, but the prospect of him leading his congregation every Sunday, preaching to people who were discussing the scandal, was hardly a prospect that any pastor would relish? Perhaps, after all, there was only one choice? It would be best if he resigned the living and sought another. Things could be arranged.

Then there might be a pause. The brittle sound of cups on saucers. Soon, the bishop would have another idea, freshly minted. Might Craufurd consider retirement? After thirty years labouring in this small parish, he might welcome a period of well-earned rest?

Retirement was not an option. We knew from Annie's letters that the Bowens were not well off. They were borrowing money, and Hannah relied on a discreet clothing scheme to keep up appearances; aristocratic ladies would donate cast-off clothes to a magazine, which sold them on to Hannah and other readers at bargain prices. The crisis would be financial as well as social.

So, there was only one solution. Just one. Gus must do the decent thing and marry Annie. The marriage must be discreet. It would take place well away from Gainford where no one would know them. Emily had played the game herself and could arrange it. They would go to a large town like Middlesbrough. Once the ceremony was over, Annie would find a place to have her baby, probably with Liebe and Ted.

'Somewhere,' I added, 'where the Bowens can keep an eye on her.'

Chapter 25: Dilemma

Once Gus promised to marry Annie, there was another problem. His story of marrying Irish Mary had been accepted by everyone at home, including Annie herself.

'So I think he has a problem. I bet she says something like, "How can you marry me? You're already married!"'

His mythical wife in London had been a necessary deceit in the early 1890s, but now she was becoming a problem. Irish Mary had come back to haunt him. He could hardly admit that the marriage was a lie, because whatever credibility he still had would be destroyed at a stroke. So he had to kill her off. Irish Mary had always been kept at a safe distance, and the impression was that few of Gus's family knew her; only Liebe and Ted were privy to the secret. Fragmentary references suggest that she had suffered a breakdown and was now in York, so it was possible to give the story a new twist. He would tell Annie that Mary had died, and he was now a widower.

Yet there was another dilemma. Bigger still. He had come home to see his family at Christmas, and left Agnes in Liverpool or Manchester, or wherever they were living, and at some point, he would have to go back and give her the news. It was anyone's guess how he did this. An anxious ride back on the train followed by a scene of operatic proportions. We knew that Agnes had a temper, so the scene was bound to be stormy. Yet at the end of the storm, Gus managed to persuade her that she was the real woman in his life, which had the great merit of being true. Men were men and it was well known that they had their needs, for it was one of the great truisms of Victorian sexuality that men had carnal desires and women didn't; it was the way God made it; a law of nature. He was under pressure to save his family. He would have to marry Annie and avoid a scandal, but if Agnes would wait for him, he would find a way back to her. And almost incredibly, she agreed. On one condition: she would come to the wedding. She would have her day in church, and Annie would learn who the real woman in Gus's life was. And that was why we saw her signature exploding across the marriage register, full of feminine fury.

I emailed Pat and told her about these finds, and wondered what she made of them. Her main surprise was Agnes's age. Here was a woman who was thirty-four and not yet married, something that we had missed. In the context of the period, Agnes might think herself old, and the prospect of remaining single was hardly appealing. It was difficult for a single woman to support herself, and the older she got, the harder it became. The clock was ticking and Gus was asking her to wait, with no guarantee at all that he would return.

'It's changing,' I said. 'The story's changing.'

Once Gus persuaded Annie that he would do the decent thing, he rushed off to Liverpool to persuade Agnes that he would find a way back to her, and then he joined the *Fernlands*. The ship left Swansea and sailed to Venice on the 28th of April. There must have been times on that voyage when he was sorely tempted to jump ship. How difficult would it be to learn Italian? Why not disappear one night and sign up with another ship? Head off to Australia, or America or South Africa? Anywhere, as long as it wasn't England.

The *Fernlands* returned to Leith on July 3rd, and Gus was still on board. He hadn't bolted. It was Monday and things were tight. The wedding was scheduled for Saturday so he took the first train south. Everything had been arranged and a marriage license obtained; something quick and private that would require a minimum amount of fuss. A license would speed things up and avoid the need for Banns being read in Bolam. The prospect of poor Craufurd being called upon to do this for three successive Sundays on the trot was unthinkable. 'Why are they not marrying here?' people would ask as they shuffled out of church.

By the look of it, Annie was renting rooms in Middlesbrough and waiting expectantly. He was cutting it fine. He docked at Leith on Monday, and almost certainly went to see Agnes in Liverpool. He had a few days to be with her before they joined Annie. We tried to imagine how the scene might play out. Perhaps he arrived at Middlesborough with Agnes on his arm and introduced her to Annie? Perhaps he came on Friday and Agnes came on Saturday? Either way, there would be a tense meeting. Annie staring at Agnes, and Agnes staring at Annie. We knew that Agnes was on a mission. She arrived at church well-oiled with drink and hell-bent on settling things. This would be the moment when Annie would find out that Agnes was the real woman in Gus's life.

They married in St. Hilda's Church, Middlesbrough. We found several pictures of the building, most of them postcards from the 1890s and early 1900s, and could see how Gus might have sent one to Emily: 'Dear Em, Arrived last night. Married this afternoon. Weather poor. Annie well. Love to all.'

The church was on the corner of a market square. One parishioner admitted in the 1890s that the best that could be said of it, was that it looked 'sombre'. Like everything in this corner of Middlesbrough, it was covered in dirt. Iron and steel works were only a stone's throw away, and the orange dust thrown up by the works had settled on everything. The surrounding area had been part of the original nucleus of the town, but better-off citizens had long-since fled and taken refuge in the suburbs.

Local people would laugh and talk about going 'over the border', for this soon became a no-go area, and finally demolished.

We drove there one windy day and parked the car. Only the old Market House was still standing, a lost and lonely building in the barren emptiness of it all. Its windows and doors were boarded up and its walls covered in graffiti. A broken sign reported that the Community Centre had closed. I peered through the chain-link fencing and saw nothing. The place was desolate. Grass in the walls, grass in the gutters, grass in the pavements. Huge boulders had been dropped at strategic points to prevent boy-racers tearing the place up. Two hundred yards off, we caught signs of life; several workshops were operating, and we could see the distant flicker and flash of welding. But that was it. Ten or so cars were parked beside the Market House, but it was hard to tell who would leave them there.

We struggled to locate the church. It had long since gone. I fished out an old photograph, and tried to align it with what we were looking at, but it just flapped in the wind. There were two modern jerry-built houses a few yards off. They seemed to date from the 1980s and were part a reclamation project that had failed. One was boarded-up and deserted, the other was inhabited, a rusty car outside, some metal security grills bolted to the windows, and a massive wooden truss propping up its gable wall.

'I can think of more romantic places.'

Back in the centre of Middlesbrough, we had some coffee. I fished out a copy of the marriage certificate, and Gill peered at it.

'Is that what I think it is?' she said, pointing to a signature that had been pushed to the edge of the page by Agnes's wild handwriting. It was the signature of the officiating clergyman. At first glance, it seemed to be, 'The Rev. Bowen', and we wondered if Gus's father had performed the ceremony after all, but the curate who officiated had an odd style of handwriting, and his letter 'd' looked more like a 'b'. The signature was not 'Bowen' but 'Dormer'. The marriage had been kept secret, and Gus's parents knew nothing.

Chapter 26: Mystery

'Dearly beloved, we are gathered together here in the sight of God, and in the face of this company to join together this Man and this Woman in holy Matrimony; which is commended of Saint Paul to be honourable among all men; and therefore is not by any to be entered into unadvisedly or lightly; but reverently, discreetly, advisedly, soberly, and in the fear of God.'

A short pause as Dormer looked up and scanned the empty pews.

'Into this holy estate, these two persons present come now to be joined.'

We could easily picture the scene: Gus and Annie standing at the altar, the Rev. Dormer facing them, the Parish Clerk in attendance; behind them, an empty church, only Agnes sitting on Gus's side and an unknown witness on the other; the muffled sound of a Saturday market drifting in.

'If any man can show just cause why they may not lawfully be joined together, let him now speak, or else hereafter for ever hold his peace.'

We struggled to understand how Gus ever managed it. How on earth had he brought Annie and Agnes together on this momentous day? A shaking of hands and a kissing of cheeks? A tender scene at the railway station? Or did Agnes appear out of nowhere, like a ghost, sitting in the hollow emptiness of the church? Drunk by all accounts. The *vile woman*. The unwanted spectre at the feast. It looked as if she had filled the church with a woman's fury; a barely-suppressed rage that could lift the roof. At any moment, she could have stopped everything; told the curate that she and Gus were living in sin, that this marriage was a complete farce, but she held her tongue and went through with it, because Gus had promised that he would find a way back.

'I require and charge you both, as ye will answer at the dreadful day of judgment when the secrets of all hearts shall be disclosed, that if either of ye know any impediment, why ye may not be lawfully joined together in Matrimony, ye do now confess it: For be ye well assured, that if any persons are joined together otherwise than as God's word doth allow, their marriage is not lawful.'

A tense silence. The Rev Dormer turning to Gus, 'Wilt thou have this woman to thy wedded wife . . . '

'I will.'

'Wilt thou have this man to thy wedded Husband . . . Wilt thou obey him, and serve him, love, honour, and keep him . . .?'

Then the signing of the register. We looked again at our copy. Agnes's signature was there on the page, forever caught in its moment of detonation. And in that moment, Annie would have read the signs. If she had not read them before, she would read them now. There could be no doubt. This was a woman who was not just a casual acquaintance, someone who had been asked to attend as a convenient witness.

What happened after the ceremony is almost impossible to imagine, but we pictured them sitting in a murky bar, an uncomfortable threesome, sipping gin and cloves, trying to make polite conversation, a hollow ache spreading across Annie's chest. We knew that she set off next day to Haxby where she lodged with Liebe and Ted. This would be the place where she would see out the rest of her pregnancy. Gus probably accompanied her and Agnes returned to the station, catching her train to Liverpool, slumped in the corner of a carriage with a bottle of gin for company.

Two weeks later, Gus signed up for another voyage and set off for Constantinople. We read his letters and looked for clues. It was clear that Annie was complaining about the cramped conditions of the cottage, and finally moved. Right at the end of her pregnancy, she rented rooms in York, and even Gus was shocked.

Then we looked for a baby called Bowen that had been born in York in September 1899. Official indexes of births are divided into years and quarters. So we found the year, then the quarter, then the names. We went to the last quarter of 1899, clicked on 'B' and found the page listing all the Bowen children. There were a hundred and nineteen in all, mostly from Wales, some from London and Manchester, Birmingham and Birkenhead, one or two from Hull, Stockton, Sedgefield and Sunderland, but none from York.

So we started again. Ninety-eight Bowens appeared in the next quarter, most of them in Wales, and the rest sprinkled randomly across the country. We stared at the page for there was nothing in York. Over the next week, the silence grew. We found no mention of a child in Annie's letters, and there was nothing in the official records either, and you start to wonder. In a strange way, it's the kind of silence that speaks. Most of Annie's letters came from female friends who never asked her about a son or daughter, and this is the kind of thing that women always ask.

We had friends over for supper a week or so later, and I told them about this twist.

'We can find no trace of the child,' I said. 'I can only think she miscarried, or the child was stillborn. I don't think they recorded stillbirths at that time.'

'Was she really pregnant?'

It was the kind of question that comes out of the blue. For a moment, I was nonplussed. Why hadn't I thought of it? Over the next few months, I ran the question past anyone I could find, and whenever I gave a talk, I was particularly interested to see what other women thought.

'Before I finish,' I said, giving them a nervous smile, 'I wonder if I can conduct a straw-poll?'

The ladies looked up and smiled back.

'Do you think that a woman could ever fake a pregnancy to trap a man?'

I expected to be crucified, but it never happened. Many of them immediately nodded and began debating the pros and cons. They seemed to have no problem imagining the scenario. Some were less sure. Perhaps after all she did have a miscarriage? Gus was away at sea, and perhaps Annie had lost the baby and never told him because she was frightened of losing him? Others clung to the idea of Annie as victim. They didn't want to think of her as deceitful and scheming.

I already knew something about Victorian corsets that were designed to hide a woman's pregnancy. As one advert put it, they were specially created to 'divert the eye from the condition of the wearer'.

'And when you come to think of it,' I said, 'this makes it so much easier to fake it.'

So could Annie have fooled Gus? What about their wedding night in Middlesbrough? How could she have pulled it off? She was apparently six-month's pregnant, but there was no guarantee that they spent the night together. By the look of it, the wedding had been a tense affair, and Annie may have left Gus and Agnes to their own devices, quitting the pub and claiming to be unwell. Then there were the taboos surrounding sex and pregnancy. She could easily have spun a story about her delicate condition and Gus would have been kept at bay.

Annie's last-minute decision to leave Liebe and Ted's cottage looked suspicious. If she was faking the pregnancy, this was the moment when corsets and padding were no longer enough. So her complaints to Gus that the cottage was too cramped may have been a way of escaping. We were arguing and speculating over the deepest intimacies of Victorian life; the hardest places to explore.

If Annie was indeed faking her pregnancy, she would still have been having her periods, and homemade sanitary towels were hard to hide. How could she wash and dry them without Liebe noticing? Disposable towels were available in the late 1890s, and sometimes advertised in newspapers, so a woman could acquire them discreetly. Failing this, she could buy them from ladies' outfitters and chemists. It made the deception feasible.

But then there was a business card amongst the rest of Annie's belongings that seemed to solve the mystery once and for all:

Nurse L. Davies
Midwife and Dispenser
(Medical and Surgical Nurse – handwritten)
Certificated Obstetrical Society, London
And City of London Lying-in-Hospital
Qualified Dispenser, Apothecaries' Hall, London
4 High Petersgate
York

Nurse Davies's full name was Lydia Margaret Augusta Davies. A week or so later, we found two letters from Lydia to Annie, written a few years later, and saw that they were friends. It was possible that Annie had used Lydia to make the pregnancy believable. When Lydia arrived, Annie would tell her that she had miscarried. None of it true, but how was Lydia to know? She would tell her that she had concealed the loss of her baby because she was trying to buy time, terrified that her husband might abandon her. There was another woman in the wings. She had not told him yet about the loss. Would Lydia tell a little, white lie and say that the child was stillborn?

It was just possible. Midwives often helped women who were desperate. The most serious cases involved abortions. Sometimes, they might perform the abortion themselves, or pass on a discrete name, and there were plenty of reports of sympathetic midwives being charged with murder when the operations went wrong. Or sometimes they would lie to the authorities and say dead babies were stillborn, and this would help a woman avoid funeral costs. Here again, they were taking risks and might be punished. So what was to stop Lydia telling a lie like this? It was the easiest thing in the world. One women helping another.

When Gus got back, and Annie broke the news, it was just possible that Lydia was there, supporting her story.

'If Annie *did* fool him,' I sighed, realising the implications of what we were thinking, 'who was *the vile woman*?'

Chapter 27: Scam

According to the rather battered crew agreement that lay beside a bowl of bananas on our kitchen worktop, it was 24th of October 1899. Gus's three-month voyage to Constantinople was over, and he docked at Penarth near Cardiff. That first night on shore, he stayed with the Fergusons, old buddies from previous voyages. He knew several of the Ferguson men, all of them sailors. Whilst he was in the house, he struck up a friendship with Mrs. Ferguson. *My son was very fond of your husband*, she told Annie a few months later, *and we all thought such a lot of him, and he spoke so nice of you last October when he was here.*

Next day, he travelled north, almost certainly to see Agnes. Perhaps she was in Liverpool, perhaps elsewhere, for we had no idea of her movements; all we knew for certain was that she was moving. Gus would have written during the voyage, and she would have written back, and they would have contrived a meeting. For her part, Annie was waiting in York, ready to give him the news. Gus could delay his return, because Annie had no idea when his ship had berthed. A day and a night spent with Agnes would go unnoticed, but sooner or later, he would go to York.

And here we encountered the silence that ate away at the heart of the story. Apart from his letter to Annie about 'that Boy', written on board ship near Constantinople in October 1899, we could find no sentence in Gus's letters, and nothing in the others, that made any further reference to the child. All the anxiety and chatter about the baby gave way to silence.

'Perhaps she had the child adopted?' a lady suggested as I finished a talk one night. I nodded. It was a common arrangement.

'Women who gave birth to unwanted babies often had them adopted or fostered,' I said. 'Sympathetic doctors would sometimes arrange this. But why would Annie do it? The child was precious to her. It tied her to Gus, and Gus to her.'

By this stage, Annie had few illusions. Agnes's unexpected appearance at the wedding had brought the horror home, exactly as Agnes intended; a day to remember, and for all the wrong reasons. It was clear that the spectre of the 'vile woman' was beginning to haunt Annie, but she still clung to a hope that she might win him over. We often heard the sound of her voice in Gus's letters; the faint echo of her pleading - *I do believe you darling*, Gus wrote, *when you say that you will make me a true good wife* - and we saw how this tenuous hope kept the marriage afloat. The hope that one day he might come to love her.

Her agent in Darlington sent quarterly accounts. Annie kept them, and in the fullness of time they drifted up and settled in our attic. Little inconsequential pieces of paper that somehow survived; business accounts that were easy to make and easy to keep. It would have been harder to describe her troubles, to tease out the tangled sorrow that lay at the heart of her life. So the letters and diaries we always craved, the personal items that might have told us everything, were never written. Or if they were, they had long since gone. Here was a woman who stood at the centre of our story and remained stubbornly mute.

News of the child's death must have stunned Gus, for his letters show no sign that he saw it coming. He fully expected the 'Boy' to be there, waiting for him. Annie and Lydia may have pulled off their big tearful scene, but once Gus was able to gather his thoughts, a new day dawned. With no child to support, he was free. His obligations to Annie were over. But what was to stop her going back to Gainford and damaging his family, even now? He had to stick by her, at least for the moment. So they limped along as best they could, never really together, but never completely apart; Annie always hoping to draw him in; Gus looking for an easy way out.

There was an empty envelope addressed to: *C.A.A. Bowen Esq., 35, Hartoft Street, Fulford, York.* We parachuted into the street via Google Street View and began walking its length. It was a late-nineteenth century affair, typical of the time. Two rows facing one another, straight as a die. A perfectly respectable place, a little severe in tone, but pleasant enough. The census for 1901 reinforced the impression. It was made up of clerks, white-collar workers and skilled tradesmen. Gus and Annie stayed here for a short time in early 1900, but were gone when the census was taken the following year.

Strange to relate, Annie still had her house in Gainford. A letter from the North Eastern Railway was addressed to *Mrs. A. Bowen, North Road, Gainford*, and we wondered why she didn't go back. A fear of prying eyes was the obvious explanation; the thought of people asking questions.

'I guess the Bowens are probably telling people that they're enjoying a long honeymoon.'

But the honeymoon was over. And so too was the marriage. It lasted less than a year. By March 1900, Gus had drifted away and a new crisis loomed. Annie was abandoned and the Bowens were facing the same old scandal.

'There is a matter of <u>very</u> deep importance I want and must see you about,' Craufurd wrote in February 1900. He was sending a letter to his senior clergyman and friend, the Rev Edelston. 'My life may terminate suddenly at any time and I therefore want to be at peace with all men.' The next day, Craufurd wrote again. 'The doctor so strictly forbids all emotion . . . I often have to leave the room and go and sit <u>quite</u> alone. I do hope when I'm stronger you will both come and have a fine old ramble and make a long and happy day – but at present my very life depends upon quiet – When there are two persons talking together it is . . . well, I will explain all when we meet. I know you and Mrs. Edleston will perfectly understand. I dare not write more now – I gain strength daily.'

There was no stopping Gus. Not now. He persuaded Annie that he should take a job in Sheffield, even though she knew perfectly well he was living with Agnes. Towards the end of February, she wrote to him, asking for advice. Could he give her one or two ideas about financial matters? In truth, she knew more about these things than he ever did, but it was a way of keeping in touch, of letting him know she needed him. He wrote back in classic Gus style admitting his ignorance. *Yours for ever,* he lied.

Whilst in Sheffield, he wrote to Mrs. Ferguson in Cardiff. We didn't have the letter, but we knew his style. He would open with a line or two of flattery, saying how he often thought of her. Then he would come to the point. Could she do him a favour? He might send her a letter, every now and then. Nothing too complicated. Nothing to worry about. But inside, there would be another letter to "Mrs. Bowen". All he wanted her to do was pop the enclosed letter in a post box. Any box would do, as long as it was in Cardiff. That was all. He knew it sounded silly, but it would be a tremendous help. Eternal gratitude and all that.

When Charlotte Ferguson opened the letter, she remembered her sons. She knew how they sometimes got into trouble, because lads will be lads. Here was a woman of fifty being invited into a young man's world. A secret world. She had no idea what Gus's secrets were, but guessed he was writing to his mother. He was probably in some kind of bother. Sailors' wages didn't run to much and soon disappeared when the lads came ashore. She liked to think that he needed her because he was such a charming man. A little wild, perhaps but full of life. She would do her best.

The letter arrived and Mrs. Ferguson did exactly as he asked. When she opened it, she found another letter inside. It was addressed to "Mrs. Bowen". She had no idea what it actually contained, but she carried it to the nearest post box and popped it in, and Annie got it next day.

Dear Annie, You will see that I am in Cardiff - & sail on Thursday up the Meditn. for six weeks or two months . . . Now if you will send one £1 by return it will obviate the necessity of my taking any advance - in which case I can leave you half pay (i.e.) £3 per month - there are some things which I must have & failing four sovereigns I must take an advance which will prevent me leaving half pay - In haste - will give you full details when I hear from you. I sail on Thursday - Trusting you are well and not anxious about me. I am, yours ever, Gus

The Cardiff scam. He was living in Sheffield – almost certainly with Agnes - and trying to convince Annie that he was in Cardiff, lodging with the Fergusons. The same scam he had used in London to fool Irish Mary. He gave Annie his bogus address - *c/o Mrs. Ferguson, 7 Romilly Road, West Canton, Cardiff* - and told her that she could contact him there. This too was arranged. Any letter arriving at Romilly Road would be forwarded to Sheffield.

Annie was no fool. The scam, for all its elegance, was never elegant enough. Her suspicions were raised. Within a day, she telegraphed Mrs. Ferguson. Annie guessed that she was protecting Gus so she wrote again, telling her the full story. How she had married Gus, and how this *vile woman* had turned up on their wedding day, half drunk and full of fury. How Gus abandoned her and chose to live with Agnes. Finally, she asked for the contact details of the shipping office in Cardiff.

Mrs Ferguson was bewildered. Was Gus living in sin? Had he deserted his wife? She couldn't believe it. She 'fenced the question' and wrote to Gus warning him that Annie was on the warpath. She even forwarded Annie's letter. Then finally, on March 10th, she wrote to Annie: *Cardiff, Dear Mrs Bowen, Yours to hand in due time, I hope you will excuse my long delay in replying to you but I feel too shocked & grieved at what you have told me about Mr*

Bowen. I really don't know which way to write to you - but one thing, you can depend upon me, that he would not be allowed to bring any woman here unless it should be Mrs Bowen, that is yourself. . . My husband and son & the young men that Mr Bowen brought to the house last October has all sailed last week in the S.S. Fernlands the same boat that Mr Bowen was in when I seen him first - My son was very fond of your husband and we all thought such a lot of him, and he spoke so nice of you last October when he was here - but men are very changeable - I have had a little sorrow in that line myself but thank God not nearly so bad as yours - but trusting you have had good news before this time. With best wishes, I remain, Yours sincerely, Charlotte Ferguson. As I am an old woman of 50 years I hope you will excuse my scribble.

The game was up.

Chapter 28: Endgames

The Cardiff Shipping Office was down by the docks. This was the place where sailors signed up for new voyages. Annie contacted them via telegram and asked if there was any record of Gus sailing from Cardiff, and they confirmed her worst suspicions. Only one seaman called Bowen had shipped during the previous few weeks, and it was not Gus.

We turned to Mrs Ferguson's letter, the letter that had first drawn us into Annie's story. For years, we had struggled to work out what it meant, but here at last we knew. *Cardiff, Dear Mrs Bowen, Your kind grateful letter received last evening too late to answer. Well dear friend I note all you said about Mr Bowen and that vile woman. I am truly surprised at Mr Bowen lowering himself in such a manner and making so little of his lawful wife, but there are some women that would tempt the best men born with their fascinating ways, but you may depend he will tire of her before long, the vile drunken hag. Now Mrs Bowen I want you to forgive me for the part I have taken innocently enough although I am ashamed of it in the first place. Mr Bowen has not been here at all since last October – he wrote to me and enclosed your letter and posted from here to you, but remember I did not know it was to you. I thought it was to his mother and that perhaps he had got into debt and some* *trouble, so I was willing to shield him as I have sons of my own & I do not know what trouble they may get into. Yet even when your <u>wire</u> came I really did not know what to do for the best. I thought perhaps his mother was against you & would help him if you was not there – I even wrote and enclosed your letter to him and told him I would be his friend – but I cannot encourage & be a party knowingly to clandestine intercourse that would harm a good and dutiful wife. So of course when your letter came I did not know how to answer you. I fenced the question with you till I would get time to tell you the real facts as far as I know them, and believe me now it grieves me more than I can tell you by letter to be the bearer of bad news. If I could only tell you he was here & all right I should be so glad & happy. In fact he has placed me in a very unenviable position by writing to me at all but it may turn out for the best in the end. His letter came from 60 Howard Street, Sheffield. I suppose he will be very bitter with me for letting you know, but I will be able to stand all that, but could not have it on my conscience any longer. In fact I have been quite ill through it. So, dear friend, if I have wronged you in the least I hope you will forgive ????? and let me know how you are getting on and if you see him & all about it. I will be too anxious to hear from you & I trust you will be happy yet. I would like so much to see you and if you have some photo to spare I should be delighted with one. Wishing you to have all the happiness the world can give before long. I remain, Yours sincerely, Charlotte Ferguson*

I smiled and shook my head. Here was one woman writing to another, and blaming a third. The charming villain of the piece, the master forger of letters, the betrayer of Annie, was somehow forgiven. Gus was a hapless victim, just a poor man who had fallen under the wicked spell of an evil woman. Vamps and sirens haunted the Victorian imagination, especially at the end of the century: women who seduced men, women who corrupted them, women who destroyed them. Sometimes they took the form of tempting sirens who lured sailors onto rocks. Or sometimes they were water nymphs who pulled men underwater and drowned them in dark caverns.

Sometimes they were terrifying vampires sitting on the chests of sleeping men, lusting after their blood. Sometimes they danced like Salome and worked a potent kind of sexual magic.

So Gus was forgiven. How he cajoled Annie and won her over is anybody's guess, but he did. That autumn, they were together again. Annie had moved to Redcar where she was renting rooms, and Gus was staying with her, on and off. For the most part, he lived in Bolton, where he worked as a railway porter. We travelled to Bolton to see for ourselves. The archives were housed in a handsome crescent of civic buildings. Gus wrote to Annie from Bolton on November 1st, professing undying love and looking forward to a next meeting. *I am longing for Sunday week . . .* But then pleaded poverty and wanted money. *You know dear how badly off I am this week & next. Tomorrow is pay day & I have only one day's pay to draw. If you would send me ten shillings . . .* He knew that Annie was losing faith. *I know that I cannot expect you to place much confidence in me but I somehow think that you will this time.*

He ended the letter by promising that he would check train times. As soon as he worked them out, he would let Annie know, and she could meet him in Redcar. He also talked of being ill, and Annie saw her chance; she urged him to come home and offered to look after him. *It is of course out of the kindness of your heart that you suggest my coming to Redcar at once, but to do so (since I am a little better & able to go to work) would be to prove myself most ungrateful.*

He told her how the manager of the railway station in Bolton had treated him very kindly, letting him keep a job when other men were made redundant. His previous experience had taught him to hold onto one job until another one turned up. In another letter, he had asked for ten shillings, but she never sent it and he talked of the hardships he would have to face. *I suppose I shall get over the difficulty somehow.*

A telegram arrived the following week: *My dear Annie, Yours to hand yesterday. As you will see I have been chucked out of No. 1*

Fairfax street because I could not pay the rent and have not found another place yet. I have to get over this week without a single penny. If I am to come on Sunday I must ask for a P.T. not later than Wednesday – but must have the cash before asking. I think you might have sent the clothes when I asked you . . . In great haste, with much love, From your Gus.

It was the end of November and Annie was feeling unwell. She told him how she was toying with the idea of going to Bedford and wanted his advice. Gus knew she was forcing his hand and prevaricated. All he could do was suggest that she stay in Redcar until he found work there. Then he would join her and they would live together. *As to my coming to Redcar, unless I had work to go to, would be foolish. I think I told you most <u>emphatically</u> that I will not leave one job till I have another to go to. For you to come to Bolton (as I shall not be here long) would be madness and cost you a good deal more than the 15/- <u>your husband asked you to lend.</u>*

Prevarications. Suddenly, she saw it. The transparency of his lying. It chilled her and her mood tightened. She saw exactly what he was doing and wrote back angrily, accusing him of always keeping her at an impossible distance. Worse still, she knew that he was seeing Agnes and hiding his address. She told him of a conversation with his mother in which Hannah had talked of his affair. *What a very bad temper you must have been in when you commenced the letter*, he wrote back, trying to calm her, *& how differently you speak, to what you did when I <u>was</u> with you. Why this sudden change? What have I done?* Was it because of the money? Something as paltry as 15/-? *A stranger has done as much for me before this and more.* He tried to charm her. *I do <u>not</u> think that you begrudge anything you have done for me, & if it is in my power you never shall.*

But her suspicions were raised. He had to answer them. *If you read my last letter again, you will see that I <u>did not</u> say that you had not to come to me, but simply pointed out how very unadvisedly it would be to do so at present.* He dangled the promise of a new job in the North East, and then turned to Agnes. *As to Miss McWilliam, she had some money left when her uncle died – went to her relatives here & has since taken a situation. I have not heard anything of her since. I suppose a railway porter is not good enough for her.*

There was no point in denying it. Annie knew about Agnes, and knew about the bungled Cardiff scam. All he could do was try and convince her that the affair was over. Almost unbelievably, he was also seeking her sympathy; wasn't it awful that Agnes had rejected him because he was only a railway porter? As for his mother, he denied that he had ever discussed it with her. Then there was the issue of an address. Well, he said, it was easy to explain: his letters were addressed to the Post Office in Bolton because it was the safest and most convenient place. *I pass it daily & as I shall only be here a short time do not care to alter it.*

He ended by promising to use the money she sent to buy new clothes, and hoped they would be together very soon. She knew perfectly well that he was pulling away and spending time with Agnes. He often promised to visit on weekends, but rarely came. They were falling apart, and only his cadging seemed constant. *You know dear how badly off I am this week & next. Tomorrow is pay day and I have only one day's pay to draw. If you could send me ten shillings.*

For months, she had tried to convince him, and tried to convince herself, that their marriage might work, but now it was hopeless. All that remained were suspicions and recriminations. And Gus himself knew it was over. *Of course I know that I cannot expect you to place much confidence in me but I somehow think that you will this time. I shall find out about the trains tonight and tell you in my next what time I shall arrive in Redcar . . . I am, yours as ever, Gus Bowen.*

Annie must have stared in disbelief. There was no talk of 'your loving husband' or even 'Gus', and for months his letters had missed their 'darlings'. She could see the signs. At one time, he had done his best to fool her, but now he never bothered.

The last of his letters was written on December 10th 1900: *Dear*

Nance, I am afraid you will be in a great state about me & no doubt think me very unkind. I recd your letter with the enclosed 15/- also your wire on Sat night & was all prepared for going to Redcar on Sunday but unfortunately on Saturday night or rather early on Sunday morning, whilst loading up scenery from the theatre I had the misfortune to fall from the top of a truck & hurt my back. I have not been able to sit up & write till just now - I do seem to have some jolly bad luck.

Chapter 29: War

'I Charles Augustine Arthur Bowen do make Oath, that
I will be faithful and bear true Allegiance to Her
Majesty and Her Heirs and Successors, and that I will,
as in duty bound, honestly and faithfully defend Her
Majesty, Her Heirs and Successors . . . So help me God.'

1901: Bolton Town Hall; Wednesday February 13; two months
after Gus's final letter to Annie.

Sergeant-Major Kearney welcomed Gus and promised him a
grand adventure. Men were needed and the recruiting drive going
well; another forty volunteers on the books. The previous Sunday, a
parade of volunteers had assembled in Victoria Square and marched
through the streets to the Parish Church, a regimental band leading
the way. The route had been packed with cheering crowds. Inside
the church, every seat had been taken and the service filled with high
emotion. It started, strangely enough, with 'God of Love, O King of
Peace', but soon hit its stride with 'Fight the Good Fight'. As all the
hymnbooks closed, and everyone settled, the chaplain rose.

He was in reflective mood. Everyone, he said, had hoped that
they might welcome back the original volunteers sent out to South
Africa a year before, but a long and tedious war had bogged them

down. More men were needed. He remembered the mood a year earlier, when everyone was eager for a fight. He had sent off the lads in high spirits. But who in church today could doubt that the world had changed? The new recruits were facing an altogether graver reality. Reports from South Africa had been worrying, and quite frankly the past year had been disappointing. Indeed, the new recruits sitting before him should be commended, for they were coming forward in the sure knowledge that they were facing a life of danger and hardship. At the end of the service, each man was presented with a special version of the prayer book, complete with a bespoke inscription that read: 'He that keepeth thee will not sleep.'

Next morning, the men mustered in the Drill Yard, and then marched to the station. It was a bright day with a cold nip in the air. The Mayor addressed them on behalf of the Corporation and shook hands. The band played 'Goodbye Sweetheart', 'Soldiers of the King' and 'Auld Lang Syne'. Then as the smoke dissolved, and the train moved out, the band hurried through a quick rendition of the National Anthem. The war was going badly, but towns like Bolton could still put on a good show. Over the next few days, more recruits came forward, and one of them was Gus.

The discovery of gold deposits in the Boer Republics during the 1880s and 1890s led to mounting tensions. People talked of the British government annexing the Republics and gaining control of the gold. As the crisis deepened, an ugly mood of jingoism took over. By the beginning of October 1899, when Gus was writing from Constantinople and wondering how *that boy* was getting on, a wider drama was starting to unfold. British newspapers were full of war fever, and the country turning bellicose. One peaceful demonstration in London, organised as a protest against the coming conflict, was bullied and attacked. When a handful of speakers climbed the platform, a jingoistic element in the crowd started singing 'Rule Britannia' and 'God Save the Queen'. As one newspaper observed: 'It was a well-dressed crowd. The speakers and newspapermen who had the ill-luck to mount the platforms were, if anything, worse dressed than the average of the audience. One thing is clear – it was not the British workingman who made the proceedings impossible. "Traitors", "Robbers", "Dirty Skunks", "Aliens", were among the most chaste of the epithets and . . . the lovers of peace in the crowd were completely overpowered.' A knife was thrown and one speaker hit behind the ear. Thankfully, no lasting damage was done, but the assault was cheered.

War was declared in October 1899. The Boer army responded with a series of lightening raids, inflicting losses on several British positions, and the mood of the country darkened. The first batch of recruits sent to South Africa found it hard to adapt. Buller, the supreme commander, telegraphed for more: not just any men, he said, but men who could match the Boers in flexibility and speed. And this meant cavalry; the kind of troops who could hold their own on the wide-open terrain of the veldt. A reluctant War Office agreed, and volunteer units were organised across the country. The units would comprise men who could ride and shoot, and over ten thousand came forward. They were christened, 'The Imperial Yeomanry', because this was a fighting force made up of free citizens, proud to defend their empire. We found film footage of them riding back and forth over scrubby terrain. They dismounted and remounted, and were happy to play to the camera. Here was a glorious opportunity to shake off the dust of city life and teach the Boers a lesson. When the war dragged on for longer than expected, and the Boers turned out to be a more formidable foe than anyone imagined, a second draft was needed.

All the Bowen boys thirsted for adventure. Gus and Greg took to the sea and never came back to Bolam, except for brief visits. We saw them as free spirits, following their wandering stars, tasting the pleasures of a vagabond life. For many years, Bro was denied this freedom, and found himself pegged down by a family and job. Yet he too dreamed of action. He joined the Durham Light Infantry and spent his weekends soldiering.

I could see Gus propping up a crowded bar, or swaggering along a Bolton street, itching for action – a born jingoist. His middle-class Conservatism, and his rugged sailor's life, made him a perfect recruit, and what many denounced as jingoism, Gus saw as patriotism. 'Who does not remember with pride,' one volunteer recalled, 'the great outburst of patriotism which, like a volcanic eruption, swept every obstacle before it . . . ready to do and die for the honour of the Old Flag and in defence of the Empire?'

We were reading through contemporary accounts, and wondering why Gus had taken so long to wrap himself in the flag. The pay was good – five shillings a day, plus standard rations - and the thought of abandoning Annie must have been tempting. Each volunteer who became a member of the Imperial Yeomanry signed up for a year. Should the war last longer, he was expected to stick it out for the duration. If it ended sooner, he would be discharged and sent home, or given the opportunity to settle in South Africa. Recruits were aged between twenty and thirty-five, were good horsemen and excellent marksmen, and this invested them with an air of reckless bravura. We read through contemporary accounts and came across the devil-may-care language of 'rough riders' and 'sharpshooters'. This was an adventure.

Volunteers had to be men of 'good character', and this raised a smile. In theory, any man who committed a serious crime was rejected, and Gill wondered if we could get hold of Gus's criminal record – if he had one. I couldn't see it, and certainly couldn't see the Army ploughing through court records on the off chance of finding him.

In the midst of everything else, the Queen's health was giving cause for concern. Sympathetic telegrams flooded in, and the press reported daily on her condition. Everyone saw the prospect of her passing as a major turning point. After sixty-four years on the throne, the woman who had defined the Victorian Age was facing death, and when news of it finally broke the country was stunned. A contingent of Imperial Yeomanry left Southampton next day in complete silence.

We found a letter from Gus to Annie, much of it torn, and only fragments remaining: *Trooper Bowen, K Company Imperial Yeomanry, H Block, M(aida) Barracks, Aldershot.* We turned to Google and typed in 'Imperial Yeomanry' and 'Boer War'. There were scores of hits, but close to the top was an entry called 'Nominal Rolls'. It was hard to credit, but this was a complete listing of every man who had served in the Imperial Yeomanry. Collecting and recording the names had taken years. There were close to forty thousand, and nearly three thousand under 'B' alone. Gus was there, his name slightly misspelled, but unmistakably him: 'Bowen, Charles Argustini Arthur, 25556, L/Corporal, 66th Coy.,3rd Bn. I.Y.'

The website was run by Kevin Asplin, a military man. I emailed Kevin and asked if he could track Gus's army record, and sent a photo of a soldier from Annie's collection who I thought might be him. It was one of the many photos we found in the attic.

'I don't claim to be an expert on uniforms,' Kevin replied, 'and sadly I'm currently in Iraq and away from my library, but the uniform in question is that of a Sergeant Major, and with the badge on the sleeve, I'd be tempted to say it was from the RAMC. (Royal Army Medical Corps) The medal bar also seems to show more than one medal . . . and Gus would have had only one for his exploits in South Africa.'

So it wasn't him.

'Certainly his service papers would have survived,' Kevin said, 'and if you email me at the end of the month when I am back home, I might be able to take on the research for you.'

He was as good as his word. Once home, he sent Gus's Attestation Papers. They popped through the letterbox one morning and we immediately opened them. Inside were four pages. The first was filled with standard questions, matched by standard answers; Gus's name, his place of birth, nationality, age, occupation and marital status. On the next page, we saw his physical details. Almost exactly the same as those recorded ten years before when he tried unsuccessfully to join the Lancers.

His tattoos were still there, as prominent as ever; the heart and anchor on his right arm, and the Union Jack on his left.   I remembered how Charles Booth had watched men going off to war, and had noted how they all seemed different. They followed the flag for various reasons, some out of patriotism, some looking for adventure, some because they were running. One man might be running from a disastrous love affair, another from a broken home, a third from a dead-end job, and some like Gus might be running from everything.

During the forty-nine days of Sergeant-Major Kearney's campaign, there were 520 recruits in Bolton. We sat in Bolton Library combing through the old newspapers, tracking the men's progress. Most were rejected. Of the 234 who were tested, only 103 were competent riders. The riding examination took place on a Drill Ground close to the town centre, and turned out to be a wonderful piece of free entertainment. Large crowds gathered each day, most of them young men out of work. They giggled and guffawed as the raw recruits did their best to negotiate the hurdles. Of the 103 who made it through, only 47 were able to shoot. But the toughest test of all was the doctor's stethoscope. More than half of the men were rejected because they were chronically unfit, and this was repeated right across the country. The state of the nation's health suddenly became a topic of anxious debate, and added its own weight to the crisis. Was the Mother Country capable of producing the right kind of men? A hardy race of imperial warriors? The kind of men who had the heart and brains to run an empire?

For all that, the medical officer in Bolton thought Gus was a fine specimen, a man in tip-top condition. He was perfectly satisfied that he could see clearly, was able to move his limbs freely, and was not subject to fits. He had two fine lungs, and a wonderfully strong heart.

Chapter 30: Cavalier

The next day – Valentine's Day – he was handed a warrant card and told to report to the Cavalry Brigade Office at Aldershot. Gus went with a small group of men on the 2.45pm train. The Mayor of Bolton could not attend, so a minor official came instead, and wished them God-Speed and safe return. The crowds of the previous days had disappeared too, and the brass band was otherwise engaged, so it was left to Agnes and a small group of relations to wave their handkerchiefs. They cheered as the train pulled away, and the men leaned out of the windows. It was a low-key affair, but at least the army was happy to cover their travel costs.

Third class. First stop was the Yeomanry headquarters at Worsley, half way between Bolton and Manchester. It was here that Gus was required to complete his Attestation Papers. On the third page, he made a simple declaration: 'I hereby agree to allot to my wife at least one third of my pay', and duly signed it. On the last page, he was required to give details of the marriage, including the name of his wife, the place and date of the marriage, the name of the officiating minister, and two witnesses.

We imagined him shuffling the cards. The location of the marriage was easy. It was Middlesbrough. Then, for reasons best known to himself, he started to lie. He claimed that the ceremony had been performed by a seamen's chaplain, although we knew for a fact that it was the Rev Dormer. How close can you get to someone in the past? We knew that we would never have the chance to share a weekend with Gus, or buy him a pint, or register his facial tics, or catch his jokes - the little clues that would tell us everything. But this was enough. He was lying for the sake of it, concocting a silly fantasy. It was him.

Then came the decisive moment; another exquisite example of his forgery; almost instinctive in the way he fashioned it, but beautiful as ever. All that was required was a swift exchange of cards.

'Name of wife?' the clerk asked.

'Agnes McWilliam.'

We stared at the page and shook our heads.

The clerk entered the details, and Gus had a few seconds to gather his thoughts.

'Name of witness?'

It was irresistible. He had to do it. 'Annie Johnson,' he said.

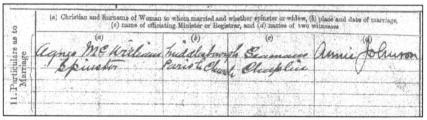

Gus's Attestation Papers: Agnes as wife and Annie as witness

We could see why he wanted Agnes as his wife. She must have his pay, otherwise, she would be penniless. But why did he name Annie as a witness? It was perverse.

Once in Aldershot, he was kitted out in uniform and given ten days training. Gus was billeted in H. Block at Maida Barracks, along with other men from Bolton. Glowing reports were sent back praising the men's conduct, and they were given extra furlough to visit family and friends.

'The number of khaki cavaliers who are now to be seen in the town,' one Bolton newspaper reported, 'testifies to the number visiting home'. For our part, we could see Gus strutting down Bolton High Street with Agnes on his arm. The perfect Khaki Cavalier.

'So he gets back to see Agnes,' Gill said 'and then what? Annie finds herself ditched?'

'Not quite,' I showed her a letter that had been sent from Aldershot on Tuesday 19th February, 1901. It was badly damaged. *Trooper Bowen, K Company Imperial Yeomanry, H Block, Maida Barracks, Aldershot. Dear Annie, Forgive me not writing before. I have left ??????????????????????????????????????as I shall not have sufficient money to draw I cannot come north. You receive my first pay one month from last Wednesday or 3 weeks tomorrow should ??????????????????????????????????????? in uniform & we might go to Skelton together if there was time. Trusting in any case to hear from you by return & please post early ....??????????????????????????????????????*

He was dangling the promise of a visit. One of Bro's journals caught the moment. It was February 25th, 1901: 'Gus turned up in the dress of the Yeomanry he has joined & now stationed at Aldershot expecting to sail next Sat. His wife was with him. They stayed at Bell's Queen's Head all night & went up to Bolam tomorrow.'

Gus and Annie remained in Gainford for two days, and then left by train. According to the army record, he embarked for South Africa on the 8th March 1901, but this in itself sparked another mystery. Annie had an envelope dated three weeks later, sent from London: *Soldier's Letter: C. Bowen, 23 Co. Imperial Yeomanry, Captain Commanding Imperial Yeomanry*

In point of fact, he enlisted as a private and rose during the war to be a lance corporal, but never came close to being a captain. Why worry? He could swagger on an envelope as easily as a street. Easier, if truth be told. He knew it would play well, for it would catch the eye of the local postmistress, and then the news would spread.

'That's Mrs Bowen,' people would say, as Annie walked proudly down Redcar High Street, 'the wife of an army captain.'

He had lied, and not just about his elevated rank. He had told Annie that she would receive his pay, knowing full well that it was going to Agnes. What did it matter? He would be in South Africa when Annie discovered the truth. The first instalment would reach her by mid-March, he promised, but when nothing arrived, she began asking questions. By May, Annie had followed the trail to an Army Paymaster in Ashton-under-Lyne, and was sending him her marriage certificate, just to prove that she was Gus's wife. She kept his reply: *Your marriage certificate is herewith returned. I am keeping all your correspondence as I intend if possible to prosecute the woman who has been receiving your money since February last. You will receive your payment early in June for that month in advance. Please be careful not to talk about this or this woman may escape.*

A grey morning in early February, birds singing in the trees; the ground still cold. We were gardening, and our hands growing numb. Finally, Gill straightened her back and rubbed her fingers.

'That's enough,' she said. 'Why are there no more letters from Gus?'

I knew what she meant. During his time in South Africa, nothing was sent to Annie. Once back in the kitchen, I fetched his Attestation Papers. According to the record, he arrived in South Africa on March 8th, 1901 and stayed until August the following year. He was there for a year and a half.

The Times had daily reports of the war, but never made any mention of Gus. By the look of it, he avoided a sniper's bullet and never went down with enteric fever, and in the context of the Boer War this was good-going. We went back to his Attestation Papers and found no mention of wounds, or 'special instances of gallant conduct.'

'Just an ordinary man's war,' I said, and knew as I said it how

silly it sounded. We were missing everything. Like the First World
War, so much of the horror was never talked about. All we had was
the number of Gus's Battalion, and the number of his Company -
'16th Battalion, 66th. (Yorkshire) Company.' In truth, I didn't even
know what a battalion was. We learned however that companies
were smaller than battalions, and sometimes moved from one
battalion to another. The 66th Company served for most of the war
in the 16th Battalion, but then switched to the 3rd Battalion.

The Times carried daily lists of casualties, and we found eight
from the 66th Company. First, there was Trooper Hartley, who was
ill with inflammation of the bowels at Springfontein in June 1901.
Then Sergeant Lister, who was killed in action near Philippolis on
June 20th. Corporal Bedford and Private Muller were wounded
during a skirmish at the junction of the Vaal and Varsch Rivers.
Three men fell dangerously ill in January 1902. The reports were
sketchy, but we were getting a taste of what Gus faced. Then Bro's
journal added its own news: 'Sunday June 2nd 1901: News of Gus.
Out of detachment of 20 which he went with, 3 were shot straight
off & he had his horse shot under him.'

We came across a batch of letters written by a young man who
served in the same company. Someone who had a boyish appetite
for adventure. Before the war, he worked as a bank clerk, and like
many men of his class, he felt hopelessly tied down.

'I shall try by hook or crook to get out to the front and see some
fun,' he said. 'I shall be awfully mad if anything happens to stop me
going to Africa. It will be a grand experience & I think would settle
me down & make me more contented.'

By the time Gus arrived in March 1901, the Boers were fighting
a guerrilla campaign, either striking at British supply lines or small
contingents of soldiers. The British claimed they were 'mopping
up', and a new kind of conflict was emerging. Lines of blockhouses
had been established to control enemy territory, Boer farms were
destroyed and Boer families herded into camps. It was a war that
still had its fair share of romantic skirmishes and battles, sieges and

sniping, but something mechanical was emerging.

We were looking at a photograph of an emaciated Boer child, sitting beside a ramshackle tent in one of the 'concentration camps'.

'Maybe some things are best not talked about.'

Chapter 31: Hiding

'Can you make it out?'

We were examining two crumpled bills issued by 'C. & A. Daniels', a shop that, according to John Betjeman, was a 'kind of Selfridges' somewhere up on the Kentish Town Road. The dates had been scribbled in pencil and were faded, so we angled them against the light. One of them was dated August 15, 1902. Gus returned from South Africa that August so it looked as if Annie was in London to meet him.

'Buying new clothes and hoping to dazzle.'

They came north and Bro's journal caught the moment: 'Saturday, August 30th, 1902: Brother Gus arrived by 7.20 am train. Spouse with him. He got home from S.A. Left Aldershot 26th. Kit left on platform. S.N. Dixon left it at Waterloo for him & wrote me. Had G(us) with me until midday train when he started with his wife for Marske.'

Annie knew that his pay has been directed to Agnes. She had chased the army and urged them to take action, but here she was, arm-in-arm with Gus, as if nothing had happened. They stayed a morning, but decided not to walk to Bolam to see Gus's parents.

Gus's mother wrote to Annie a week later: *September 8^{th,} Gainford. My dear Annie, I have had a letter from Emily this* *morning. I expect Gus will have turned up at Marske by this time. He left Gainford on Saturday by the train for Skelton to go to see Beezie. Whether he would ever arrive there or not I do not know. His money was sent on to Gainford - £26/10/3. He came to Gainford a week last Saturday, took £10, went to Manchester, telegraphed on Tuesday for £5 more to be sent by wire, arrived at Bolam late on Thursday night in a cab, came to Gainford on Saturday morning, got another £5. That is the last we know of him and if I were you I should do my worst to him. Don't think of anyone but yourself. I think his conduct disgraceful. You are quite at liberty to show him this. I have begged him to do differently and he knows it. I am just sending a line to Emily and it is nearly post time and I have to walk to Bolam. Yours affectionately, H E Bowen. PS. It is the wish of both Laura and Bro for Gus to do what is right and to live with his wife.*

It takes a lot for a mother to write a letter like this. She was denouncing Gus, and urging Annie to do her worst to him, and a new level of crisis was threatening. Their marriage was over. The truth was spilling out.

Against all expectations, Gus had come back after the war and spent time with Annie. On their first Saturday together, he had brought her to Gainford where he collected his army pay. They picked up the money and went back to Marske where Annie was now living. His decision not to visit his parents seemed a little odd, but gradually it made sense. Gus was looking for a way to see Agnes and this was part of the plan. Once he had pocketed the money and settled Annie in Marske, he would tell her that he was going to see his mother and father. Perhaps there was a private matter that he needed to discuss with them, but whatever the reason, he would need to go without her. There was no cause for her to worry. He would be away for a few days. Only a few days.

But instead of taking the train to Gainford, he went to Manchester. It must have been a belter of a weekend because the ten pounds he took was spent by the following Tuesday. That was when he telegraphed for more. By the look of it, he stayed with Agnes until Thursday and then travelled back. Annie was meant to believe he was still with his parents, but she soon found out. And this was why Gus's mother was denouncing him. The Bowens were living in dread that she would destroy them, and a scandal seemed closer than ever before. They did their best to reassure her, and Bro caught the moment: 'Tuesday September 18th. Walked up to Bolam with Bene (Bro's affectionate nickname for his wife) on Gus business. Found his wife there. Stayed dinner. Long jaw with Mrs G(us) re. Aldershot etc. Home 4.30.'

A Council of War. They invited Annie to Bolam to meet the family. Here was an urgent show of solidarity. Craufurd and Hannah, Bro and Laura, all standing behind her, and doing everything in their power to keep her on side. She had to recognise this. On the following Saturday there was a second meeting. Everyone knew that Annie was tracking Gus and, quite apart from anything else, was wanting her fair share of his army pay. If confirmation were needed, it came from the army: *Madam, Your husband's gratuity of £5 was included in the payment made to him when discharged and the amount owing to him was sent by cheque on the 26th or 27th of August.*

For three months between September and November 1902, she continued to chase him. On November 7, she contacted the police in Manchester and demanded action. By this point, it looked as if she had discovered Gus and Agnes's hideout and was accusing Agnes of stealing her money – Gus's last payment from the army.

One of the men in the Chief Constable's Office was given the job of replying: *Re Agnes McWilliam: Madam, I have to acknowledge the receipt of your letter of the 7th instant and to acquaint you in reply that you had better consult a solicitor on the subject. Yours faithfully, R. Corden, Superintendent*

In point of fact, Annie was driving Gus and Agnes to ground. Their hideout had been discovered, but only for a moment. Soon, they learned to keep their heads down, and this meant that we couldn't find them either. Every record was checked and rechecked, every possible bolthole explored, and nothing emerged.

'South Africa's a possibility,' I said, thinking they might have emigrated. The government gave soldiers the chance to take farming land in South Africa, and I wondered if Cindy could find them. But this was just one possibility. Gus's brother had settled in Calcutta and was doing well. Greg had risen through the ranks. According to one account, he was Harbour Master of Calcutta, and any man who could make himself Harbour Master of one of the busiest ports in the world was a man on the rise. So Gus and Agnes might have joined him. Gus was always promising to. Whenever Annie refused him money, he threatened to *go out East.*

I am very *glad you have hopes of going to Calcutta,* his father said in 1899, before the crisis happened, and enclosed a copy of Greg's address. We found several anonymous letters from India that seemed to strengthen the idea, but it was hard to be sure. Beyond that, there was nothing; no census records, no passenger lists, no sightings.

Then we thought of Liebe and Ted; two kindred spirits. They were in Annie's bad books. They had borrowed money from her and Annie was chasing them. Her agent wrote to her in June 1902: *Dear Madam, What have you done about Ed Davis (Ted)? Miss Hodgson called upon me to talk matters over and you will not get any more from her* - (scores of Hodgsons were in the census but none of them fitted. She drifted in and out of the story, a half-glimpsed figure at the window) - *& that being so, there appears little chance of anything more from Davis: I think it would be as well to take the £10 & give up all hope of getting the other.*

Then Cindy emailed. She began with bad news. Despite all her best efforts, there was no record of Gus and Agnes in South Africa.

'Okay,' she said, 'now for the new information. I must stress that I have not had the chance to look at it closely, but I immediately thought it might be him. I found a Charles 'Bowskn', who was born in England in 1868, who is living, according to the 1920 American census, in New Canaan, Fairfield, Connecticut. He has a new wife who was born in New York. They must have married in 1917 or 1918 because there are two children. I thought it might be a wonderful place for him to start a 'new life' because there are people there from all over the world - Russia, Italy, Germany, Ireland, Hungary, France. Perhaps I am wrong. I have not had chance to check, BUT I have attached an original image of the census. Let me know what you think.'

We analysed the page. He seemed to be the right age and was certainly from England, but apart from that there was no proof. It might be him, and if so, he had left Agnes.

Then a tantalising letter from Bro. He had written to Emily, and somehow the letter had found its way to Annie. It was sent in August 1903. Bro had left Gainford and was now carving out a new life for himself in the North West Territories of Canada: *Now it is very hot but all at once we will wake up to find everything one waste of white, then it will be difficult to find your way about as there are no roads or hedges; even now it is difficult as the trail or wheel marks is sometimes grown over in a couple of days. I got lost & was out all night with a pony . . . When the frost comes we will be shut up for six months & can do no outdoor work except feed the horses & cows. The country is simply one huge garden.*

He had built himself a log cabin and was giving Emily a description. The cabin was only one-storey high with thick sod walls lined with wood. A set of double doors had been added to keep the cold out, and he was hoping to persuade native Indians to thatch the roof. *We have none of us slept in a house since we left England or seen a coal fire, we have slept in tents or in the open, it's a beautiful climate, the air is so dry I haven't seen a spedy (trans. runny) nose or heard a cough since we came although we have slept on the ground even when buckets of water have been frozen in the tent & there has been two inches of snow on the ground.*

Nearly a hundred miles from the nearest railway, and thrown back on their own resources, they had learned to survive. A vegetable garden had been planted with lettuces, radishes, scallions, mustard, cress, peas and beans, and then some livestock acquired – four horses, a cow, a pony and two bullocks for driving, hauling and ploughing: *I should like to send a jolly long letter, but must put off such luxuries till the winter. We work from six in the morning till dark . . . to the accompaniment of the music of the axe, the hammer & the saw . . . This is the life to teach you what it is possible for you to do when you are thrown on your own resources.*

We could see how he was loving it, pitting himself against the elements. Bro had always hankered after adventure and this was his chance. And perhaps Gus and Agnes came too?

'The land beyond Annie.'

We contacted a librarian in Canada who was based in the small provincial town where Bro settled. We wondered if she might be able to find Gus. After a few days searching, she emailed back: 'After going through our sources, it appears that Bro and his family lived in the Lloydminster area for about twenty years, moving three times and ending at a location northeast of Lloydminster in the Greenwood district. According to Captain Bowen's obituary, published in our local paper in Feb.1944, he retired to Banff in 1922 and a few years after, moved to Penticton B.C. where he died. His wife, Laura passed away in Penticton in December 1940.' She gave a few more details and then added: 'There is no mention of Gus. I have tried other sources and he does indeed appear to have disappeared.'

Chapter 32: Photographs

We found over a hundred and thirty of Annie's photographs, but only two in frames; the faces that she kept on her mantelpiece. Gus's photo was one of them because she had written his name on the back. He was placed in a velvet-covered frame and put on display, and there it stood, patiently awaiting his return.

One day, I showed it to a friend. She came from an Italian family, and it reminded her of her grandmother who had lost her husband in the First World War. She never remarried. The old lady kept a photo of her young husband all her life, and it became one of the great stories in the family. Every night, before going to bed, she would take his photo from the mantelpiece and kiss the face, and when my friend visited Italy, she asked to see it. When it was put in her hands, the face terrified her, for there was nothing left. It had been kissed away.

I saw for the first time what Gus's photo had been telling us all along. It had stood for years in the dim light of Annie's rooms, and during that time it had faded, but the weak light filtering through her curtains was not to blame. His face had been lost by other means. We could see the fine details of his uniform, the brass buttons on his cuffs, the folds in his jacket. They were all crystal clear, but his face was gone. How many times had she lifted that photo and opened the back? How often had she touched and kissed that face, and found a way of keeping close? One day, there would be a knock at the door and he would be there again, larger than life, a sheepish smile on his face.

Most of her photographs had been stored in albums, but time had ripened their spines. Slowly and surely, the spines gave way and the faces were released; faces that meant something. I spread the photographs on the carpet, lining them up and trying to make connections. Most were *carte de visite* images that had first appeared in the 1860's and were a great sensation. People called it 'Cardomania', and everyone wanted them. A portrait would be taken in the nearest photographic studio and multiple copies ordered – twelve, twenty-four, perhaps even thirty-six. Over the following months, friends and relations would receive a copy, and they would send you theirs in return. Very soon, people were buying albums.

I found an article in a Victorian periodical that tried to make sense of the craze: 'It is a curious fact that the *carte de visite* have for the present entirely superseded all other sized photograph portraits. It enables everyone to possess a picture gallery of those he cares about, as well as those he does not. For we are convinced some people collect them for the mere vanity of showing, or pretending, they have a large acquaintance.'

We both laughed, for this was precisely the criticism levelled at social networking sites like Facebook; virtual friends who were not real friends at all. Without knowing it, we had stumbled across Annie's Facebook. We counted them. Annie had over a hundred and thirty 'friends', but two were obviously special. They had been taken from the leather-bound albums and placed on her mantelpiece, and there they stood, gazing at her.

We knew why Gus's face was there, but the other photograph was a mystery. It was housed in a brass frame that seemed to have a simple Christmas motif on its base; two robins were singing in a holly tree. We guessed it was a seasonal present from the late 1890s or the early 1900s. Once upon a time, the frame had boasted a glass front, but the glass had shattered and only tiny shard remained. Larger than a *carte-de-visite*, the back of this photograph was blank. There was no name.

Mystery Photograph: Face faded

An elderly gentleman posed for the camera. He seemed to be an easy-going and relaxed character, his legs apart, almost as if he was about to tell a story. A walking stick rested idly against one leg, and we could imagine him spinning it between his fingers. He was wearing a tweed suit and one hand was tucked into its belt. There was a white handkerchief in one breast pocket and a watch chain in the other. A patterned tie was held by a distinctive metal slide, and he looked to be a comfortable country gentleman who might enjoy a day's shooting. It was hard to see his face, for most of it had been kissed away. A halo enveloped his head. We could winkle out a few details but nothing more. He had a white moustache and several wispy strands of white hair and was probably balding, although it was hard to tell. Age and Annie's kissing had done their work. His double chin and fleshy neck suggested affluence.

I picked up the two frames and compared them. The two men in her life; the men on her mantelpiece; the faces that she never stopped touching and kissing. We wondered if this second photograph was her father, and something dawned.

'We've come all this way,' I said, 'and Annie sits at the centre of the story, and we don't know a single thing about her family.'

Chapter 33: Mother

Crawling beneath the roof eaves on that dark December night, I failed to see the thin sliver of danger that was waiting in the shadows. Somewhere in that crumpled bed of decomposing birds, mildewed straw, and rotting paper, there was a spike. I sometimes see them in restaurants, holding their own against electronic tills and computers; old-fashioned contraptions where waiters and waitresses come to impale receipts. I felt its sharpness against my leg, and realised it had missed me by a whisker.

When we came to look at the spike again, we began to see that part of Annie's life had been impaled and stratified. It carried the accumulated bills and receipts of her spending, layered in precisely the sequence she created. The slow sedimentation of her life: furniture being moved by a hackney-carriage proprietor; payments of rent; a jacket bought at a costumier's shop in the Tottenham Court Road; a gas bill from 1909; cleaning costs for a knitted counterpane; a doctor's bill; faded draper's and milliner's receipts; a grocery bill from 1904; a coat fashioned by a village tailor in 1899. Here too was a bill for funeral costs, added to the pile in 1898:

Horse Hearse from Gainford to West Cemetery - 1/0/0
Horse Coach from Gainford to W. Cemetery & Back - 1/12/0
Horse Carriage from Gainford to W. Cemetery & Back -1/10/0

We turned to Google Maps and called for directions. Stretched out before us, we saw the nine-mile journey that the funeral cortege must have taken through the Durham countryside. The road from Gainford to Darlington. I ran my finger over the screen, pausing to register the villages - Piercebridge, High Conniscliffe, Merrybent and Low Conniscliffe. It was easy to imagine the scene: hats being doffed, the funeral cortege lifting clouds of dust as it moved through the village streets, women coming to their doors, shielding their eyes against the sun; labourers in the fields straightening their backs and gazing over the hedge tops, as the black plumes of the horses passed by. Death moving slowly through a summer's day.

Two weeks later, we found a Form of Application for stocks and shares that was dated 1898, the same year as the funeral, and saw for the first time that we were looking at the death of Annie's mother. Scribbled on the back of the form were Annie's notes, capturing something of her mother's life. *Mr Naylor, mother's guardian lived at a house called Brookfoot. Large house. Dining room. Living-room. Library. Breakfast-room. An organ in the library. Brookfoot is about three and half miles from Halifax . . . Mrs Naylor was very rich.*

The Naylors lived in a place called Southowram, one of the many stone-built villages that you find dotted about the West Riding. Turning away from the lunacy of the M62, we drove along a road flanked by builders' merchants and car showrooms. Every now and then, we saw stone terraces on the hillsides, and the glint of water in the valley bottom. Finally, we turned uphill along Brookfoot Lane where the world was leafier and calmer. I wound down the window as we came into the village. It sat on a ridge overlooking the valley, where hay meadows and farmsteads were making the air sweet.

We had come in search of Annie's past. Samuel Naylor was a prosperous merchant who employed 'stone delvers' to work the quarries near his home. According to old trade directories, the 'delving' of stone was a major business in Southowram, with no less than thirteen stone merchants listed in the village in 1828. We drove around in circles looking for Brookfoot, the palatial house that Annie described in her notes. We could see it on the old maps, but there was nothing on the ground. The Naylors had lived in a house of some importance, but it was long gone.

Samuel became guardian to Annie's mother after her parents died in the 1830s. Before our trip, I contacted a librarian in Huddersfield and asked if she could help. She soon discovered that Annie's grandfather had been a prosperous tanner and currier in Cleckheaton. A brief notice of his death in one Yorkshire newspaper caught something of his social standing. 'The remains of the above gentleman were interred in the family vault in the body of White Chapel. Many gentlemen of the town attended to pay the last tribute of respect to their departed friend who was a man of sound judgement and liberal principles. He took an active part in the business of the town, and was much respected by all who knew him.'

Annie's mother was only fourteen when this happened. Her mother, a shadowy figure at best, had died a few years before. The family disbanded, and the fourteen-year-old girl was given over to the tender mercies of Samuel Naylor. She left no memories of her wealthy guardian, apart from a bare list of rooms in his magnificent house, and each room was lodged in her memory, like a jewel in a trinket box, there to be opened and treasured.

When her father died in 1837, Annie's mother was a boarder at a girls' school near Southowram. *Miss Paget's school was called Law Hill about 2 miles from South Owram where mother went to school. Miss Emily Bronte was a Governess there at that time.*

We drove over. There were several buildings, and the school itself stood closest to the road. A green plaque commemorated its link with the Brontes. We could catch a glimpse of the adjoining house, set back from the gate along a moss-covered path. Snowdrops were shivering in the breeze. We took photos, and stood for a moment, trying to imagine the scene in the 1830s. All around, there were green meadows and clear air. The smoke that had hung about the place in the Victorian years was gone, leaving the houses honey-coloured and soft.

Only the barest details remained. Annie's mother was called Anne Brooke. She left Law Hill around 1840, but there was no trace of her when the census was taken in 1841. She was not at Brookfoot and nowhere to be seen in the nearby area. The best sighting came in Dewsbury, ten miles away, where a fourteen-year-old girl called Anne Brooke was described as 'independent'. She was lodging in a boarding house run by a widowed shopkeeper. Then she simply disappeared.

We waited patiently for her to reappear, and finally it happened. According to a marriage certificate from October 1846, she was in a small village called Middleton-one-Row, more than eighty miles from Halifax.

Chapter 34: Seesaw

Another Victorian newspaper digitised; another dark corner of the past made bright. We typed 'Miss Brooke' into its eager search engine, and sure enough it found her. There was a brief announcement of her marriage. A sulphur spring had been discovered near Middleton-one-Row, about seven miles from Darlington, and a small spa opened. A new hotel was built, commodious new roads were constructed and people talked of the place being a 'Little Harrogate'. Less than a mile away, Lord Durham built an even grander hotel, and by the 1840s, the gentility of Middleton-one-Row was established. It stood on rising ground close to the Tees. There were fashionable horse races, weekly balls, shopping bazaars, billiard rooms and circulating libraries, and in one edition of the *Newcastle Courant*, we found an impressive list of visitors, some of them coming from aristocratic and gentry families, and some from the middling-ranks of Victorian society. Things were looking up. Middleton-one-Row was packed, and many of the visitors were single women, so local men with an eye to advancement could come here and do a little courting.

Annie's mother fell for one, and their romance was intriguing. She brought a thousand pounds to the marriage, came from a comfortable middle-class background, was well educated and blessed with social contacts, but for reasons best known to herself, she fell for a Darlington plumber, and in a society where class mattered, this was hardly playing by the rules.

There were no love-letters, no personal journals, no newspaper reports – nothing to flesh out their romance. Almost all the details were lost, buried beneath Annie's silence. Instead of talking about her parents' unusual courtship, she chose instead to list the rooms in Samuel Naylor's house, or talked in passing of her mother's schooling, or added one or two memories from her mother's early years. The rest was lost.

What brought them together? Love was the obvious reason. Why else would a middle-class woman risk everything by choosing a lower-class husband? Annie's father was called Thomas Johnson, and he came from a family of craftsmen who worked in Darlington and its surrounding area. Unlikely as it sounds, I found evidence of this in a biography of Lewis Carroll. In 1834, the Johnsons were contracted to do work at Croft Rectory, three miles from Darlington. Annie's father would have been fifteen at the time. Towards the end of the job, they etched their names on a windowpane without thinking it would be preserved and studied. A few years later, Lewis Carroll and family moved into the rectory and stayed there until 1868. The intense public interest that surrounded Carroll after the publication of the Alice stories meant that anything from his early life was conserved and analysed. Every nook and cranny of the rectory was searched and photographed. Etched names on a window pane might well contain vital clues to his imagination.

'I don't recall Alice ever bumping into anyone called Johnson,' Gill said.

'It was probably coded.'

Rabbit holes appear in the most unlikely of places, and they spin people into alien worlds. Annie's mother married her plumber and the world turned. She put money in his pocket, and spun him into dizzying orbit, cutting him off from everything that had gone before. A thousand pounds allowed him to break free from his father and to set up in business for himself, and soon he was acquiring workshops and showrooms of his own.

We tracked the young couple in the decades following their marriage. Shortly after their wedding, they moved to Northumberland Terrace, a handsome street in one of the more fashionable areas of Darlington, close to the villas of the great and good. We scouted the area. There were well-off widows living on comfortable investments, prosperous railway engineers and iron merchants, together with a range of professional men - clergymen, doctors and lawyers. The officer class of mid-Victorian society.

According to the 1851 census, the Johnsons had two sons, a servant, a handsome house, and were on the rise. Ten years later, they had somehow retreated to the centre of town and were living over the shop. All their servants had gone. Fast-forward another ten years, and they were back in suburbia again, reclaiming lost ground. It was a seesaw existence, and we saw for the first time how Annie's life had always been uncertain.

Maintaining an air of middle-class respectability was clearly a struggle. Each of the Johnson's children had to be educated privately, and we found evidence of this in Annie's papers. There were several battered class lists from a school in the West Riding called, 'Making Place Commercial College', where an elder brother of Annie was sent in the 1860s. We drove over to see it during our stay in Southowram. During the 1850s and 1860s, the school offered a progressive curriculum, with pupils being drawn from all over the country, including Herbert Asquith who studied here during the 1860s, although there was no mention of him in Annie's lists. The good years when the Johnsons could afford such things. The hopeful years. But the costs were high and their younger children were sent to less expensive schools in Darlington.

For her part Annie studied at Thornbeck House, a 'Collegiate School' for girls. According to the bills that she kept as mementoes, she was taught the classic accomplishments that a middle-class girl was expected to acquire, the feminine skills that best fitted her for society and marriage - music, French, German, drawing, dancing and singing - and interestingly, the bills were always sent to her mother.

Annie was the youngest of five. She was born in 1863, and for several years lived with three of her brothers and Lydia, her older sister. Then they disappeared. Lydia, died in 1870, after a severe bout of bronchitis. We looked at the card that Annie kept:

In Affectionate Remembrance of
Lydia Ann,
the beloved Daughter of Thomas and
Annie Johnson of Darlington,
Who died January 26th 1870, in the 18th year
of her age,
And was interred this day in the Darlington Cemetery.
"In life we are in death".
January 29th

We knew that Annie preserved a sampler that Lydia made in childhood, and kept it as a tender souvenir. Then her youngest brother, Harry, left in the late 1870s, and seemed anxious to escape: '*Dear Annie,*' he wrote: *I will leave you all my framed drawings to keep for my ???? Should I never return they are yours. Please God I hope ???? and Mr & Miss Hewitt will let you have them as soon as you want them. I remain, Your most affect. Brother, Harry.*

Most surprisingly of all, her two eldest brothers disappeared after working for many years with their father. By the time of the 1881 census, Annie was the only child left. At this point, her father had retired, and the family had traded down, moving to a less fashionable part of Darlington. Over the next few years, we spotted them occasionally as they moved from one house to another. Then, in the mid-1880s, they left Darlington altogether and moved to Saltburn, a seaside resort on the Yorkshire coast, only a mile from our house. It was here in the 1880s that Annie's mother made a will.

A little over a thousand pounds was left to Annie, and nothing to her other children. And just to make Annie's position doubly secure, her mother made her the sole executrix. We supposed it was Annie's reward for looking after her parents, particularly as they moved into old age. In another prescient clause, her mother insisted that Annie's property should remain hers and hers alone, free from the control of any husband.

Around 1890, they moved to Gainford where a trade directory listed her mother as a 'private resident'. No mention was made of her father. They lived at Stob Hill, a new part of the village, and their neighbours were retired gentlemen and gentlewomen, ageing civil engineers and merchants, who were turning the place into an agreeable middle-class retreat. Bro was not far away, living with his family in a pretty house overlooking the village green. Once settled, Annie and her mother could walk to the green and enjoy its tranquillity. We did exactly the same. It was a summer's day. Cottages and houses fringed the grass, most of them gentrified and desirable. Summer sunshine filtered through the trees and dappled the ground. A work-a-day village had been turned into a middle-class haven.

George Taylor lived in the village in the 1890s. He looked after his mother, and the two of them pegged along as best they could, never well off but always respectable. She was a dressmaker and he was a clockmaker. In 1896, he started a diary. We read through its pages, savouring the treasures. He gave us a seat on the village green, and we sat there, watching the Victorian year unfold. The world that Annie knew. Church bells ringing in the New Year. Excited day-trippers coming in by train on Whit Mondays. Local cricket matches. The first sound of the hunting horn. The gathering days of late summer and early autumn when villagers returned from the lanes, laden with elderberries, brambles and gooseberries. Wild geese flying overhead. Tar barrels blazing on Bonfire Night.

The souvenir programmes that Annie kept had their own story to tell too. She and her mother were part of the Gainford scene and loved its gaiety. Yet for some reason her father was invisible. Whenever we found directories, they listed Annie's mother, but never him. The programmes that Annie hoarded were addressed to her mother, but never to her poor father. We knew he was alive but somehow not there. When her mother came to make her will, she offered a clue. Annie was to take care of him: 'And I express my earnest wish that my said daughter will during the lifetime of her father (if he survives me) look after him, and take care that he does not lack such necessary support as she may be able to afford.'

Chapter 35: Father

We already knew something of Annie's father. He had been born in Darlington in 1817, the son of a plumber, and had worked alongside his father in the family business. Then his wife appeared on the scene. Her thousand pounds transformed him, lifting and propelling him into new worlds. Soon, he was setting up in trade for himself, competing with his father, breaking family ties and forging new links. We knew too that this transformation was fragile; sometimes Annie's parents were well off, sometimes struggling. Census records, parish registers and trade directories were all very well, but they gave us no more than the bare bones of the story, and we wanted more.

Would a provincial plumber from a small town in the north of England be important enough to find himself reported in newspapers? Scores of old papers were being digitised and their potential was just emerging. I typed in his name, and the search engine did its work. Where once it would have been an act of madness to trawl through newspapers looking for a man like Thomas Johnson, casting a tiny net into an endless sea of words, hoping against hope to catch a miniscule fish, now everything was possible. We could search for a plumber in a tweed suit across forty metropolitan and provincial newspapers, scoop through a hundred years of print, and make it all happen in seconds. Up from the depths he came.

The first thing we noticed was that he was on the rise. Annie's father had acquired showrooms in one of the best locations in Darlington and was winning major new contracts. By the early 1870s, he was advertising for more workers and promising full employment. In 1874, a public house was acquired in the centre of town and immediately demolished. In place of the pub, he built bigger and better showrooms and expanded his empire, and nothing it seemed was beyond him. In 1876, he made donations to Darlington Hospital and made sure the press was informed, so here was a man with ambition who like to promote a civic image.

Yet there was a darker side too. He could be abrasive. In 1876, when Annie was ten, he fell out with his landlord and ended up in a protracted legal battle. It emerged that Thomas was leasing showrooms, but when the lease expired he refused to leave. He had commissioned new showrooms but they were not yet ready, so when his landlord gave notice to quit, he simply refused to go. A tense standoff ensued and lasted for months. Finally, his landlord lost patience and hauled him to court. Thomas claimed that he had acted reasonably throughout but no one was convinced. Nor were we.

Then in June 1877, he instructed a Darlington auctioneer to sell all of his plumbing business. Newspaper advertisements appeared and handbills were distributed. All those years of prosperity and cutthroat dealing were brought to an end, and our first thought was that he had made a fortune. But the auction failed and more adverts appeared. Finally, his sister came forward and saved the day. Unlikely as it sounded, she took over the business and began running it herself, and in a male-dominated world, this was a brave thing to do.

A sleepy Tuesday. Late October. Another case for Stockton County Court to untangle; one of the complex little dramas that fill provincial newspapers with the intimate details of day-to-day living. The fine-particle dust of broken lives. We were working our way through newspapers, hunting for Annie's father, and came across her mother instead. She was contesting a maintenance order that had been made against her by one of her daughters-in-law, and the solicitor handling her case was telling the court that Annie's parents married in 1846. He went on to say that her mother had brought £1000 to the marriage. The marriage lasted until 1875 or 1876, when 'Mrs Johnson commenced proceedings in the Divorce Court for a judicial separation.'

It hit us like a thunderbolt. A Victorian woman would only think of this in the most extreme circumstances. Rules governing divorce had always been weighted in favour of men. Before 1857, a husband who suspected his wife of adultery would bring a charge of Criminal Conversation. The charge, in point of fact, was levelled against her lover, and if the husband happened to win, the lover would be fined. This was a breach of male honour because one man had stolen the property of another. If the husband was so inclined, he could then go to the Ecclesiastical Courts to gain a separation from his wife, and if his purse allowed, to the House of Lords where he might in the fullness of time obtain a divorce by promoting a private act of parliament. The whole thing was time-consuming and ruinously expensive and, needless to say, women had no equivalent rights.

In the 1850s, the system was finally reformed. Divorce was now covered by civil rather than ecclesiastical courts, and women were given new powers. The double standard still prevailed; a man might divorce his wife if he could prove her adultery, but a woman could only divorce her husband if she could prove his adultery, together with evidence of either incest, bigamy, desertion or cruelty.

'The Divorce Court has astonished everyone,' one paper reported, 'No one believed that there was such a mass of festering matrimonial misery floating under the surface of apparent social happiness.' An alarming surge in cases had taken place in the wake of the new legislation, and everyone was shocked. Where would it all end? People debated the issue anxiously. It seemed that a hidden reservoir of misery had built up, and the new legislation had inadvertently thrown open the floodgates. People should wait. Things would settle down and the waters would recede.

Newspapers were quick to capitalise. Each week, shorthand reporters were sent to the Divorce Courts where sensational copy could be guaranteed. The headlines came thick and fast - 'Extraordinary Divorce Case', 'Singular Divorce Case', 'A Strange Divorce Case', 'Doings in the Divorce Court', 'Wholesale Divorce', and this frenzy of reporting was exactly the reason why respectable women were terrified. The prospect of giving your intimate details to the Divorce Court, and then having them publicised, was too hideous to contemplate. The whole process was mired in shame. So Annie's mother must have been desperate. There was no other explanation for it, and the old man in a tweed suit was beginning to look suspect.

This chance discovery of a provincial court case led us quite quickly to a bundle of papers at the bottom of a cardboard box in the National Archives. Right at the bottom, compressed under scores of other papers, we found the surviving evidence. We unrolled the parchments and spread them out, anchoring them down with weights. It felt like an autopsy. As we leaned over, we had to steel ourselves; this was going to be a deep cut: 'On the night of 25th June 1875 the said Thomas Johnson in violent and offensive language abused your Petitioner violently assaulted her and threatened to take her life . . . your Petitioner had to get her children out of bed and make her escape with them into the street at midnight.'

For the first time, we saw what had been hidden; a middle-class home that had been ruled by fear; the place where Annie lived. We moved from one bundle to another, photographing everything, mapping out an all-too familiar misery.

One of the moral panics that periodically convulsed Victorian society came in the 1840s and 1850s when Annie's parents married. Domestic abuse cases suddenly hit the headlines. Newspapers made a dramatic and terrible discovery. John Bull, the loveable rogue of British folklore, the doughty champion who had stood for all that was virile and sound about English manhood, was turning out to be a wife beater. For several weeks, no newspaper in search of a high circulation could do without a wife murder. It was essential copy. Attacks on women were becoming commonplace. Screams coming from a house were dismissed as nothing untoward. 'It's only a man beating his wife.' It was bad enough that these attacks were happening, but how on earth could they happen in Victorian Britain? They violated everything that the Victorians held dear, for this was a terrible blight that seemed to tarnish the reputation of 'the most favoured, the most moral, and the most domestic nation upon earth'.

Newspapers did their best to turn up the heat. It was not enough to report wife murders; they had to be discussed. Outraged letters appeared, editorials were written, debates generated, theories propounded. In the midst of this panic, a small number of brave souls tried to keep calm. 'Domestic ruffianism', they argued, was a 'retrograde movement', a temporary blemish on the face of modern society; it was undoubtedly alarming, and certainly deplorable, but it would pass. Others were less sure. Modern life, they said, was regressing. We were returning to the jungle. Some like the *Morning Chronicle* had an instant solution: 'Wife beating,' they said, 'is one of the blessings which we owe to the Celtic immigration of Irish labourers to London.' Get the Irish out, and things would improve. As the debate boiled, there were calls for harsher punishments. *Lloyds Weekly Newspaper* suggested 'the cat'. Wife beaters should be flogged and shamed. 'Not enough!' the *Chronicle* bellowed. Brutal husbands should be subjected to 'a sound and bloody scourging'. The offender should be 'knouted on the very spot of his crimes . . . the lash dripping with blood and the wholesome sight of a villain's back scored and flayed.' This was the best way to discourage violence.

The abuse in Annie's family must have rumbled on for years, and it was hard to believe that respectable neighbours had heard nothing. Thomas's brutality was matched by his wife's hysteria, or so he claimed. Annie's father defended himself by saying that his wife was a harridan, a scold, a woman who irritated and provoked him beyond endurance. Sometimes she flew into tempers that were simply ungovernable.

He was using a well-thumbed script. The moment Annie's parents walked into the offices of their solicitors, they were coached in the language of law. Wives talked of their husbands mistreating them with 'great unkindness and cruelty', and husbands talked of wives being 'unreasonable and provoking'. By the 1870s, this familiar script must have been sitting on the shelf of every solicitor in the country.

Yet behind the formula there was a depressing reality. The violence in Annie's family stretched over thirty years and almost consumed them. Annie's parents had eight children; four of them dying, four surviving. Annie was the youngest, and forced to experience the worst. What triggered their final descent into the Divorce Court is not clear, but Lydia's death in 1870 may have been the catalyst. When Annie's mother came to recite the worst of the violence, she went no further back than 1872. There were probably earlier incidents, but this marked the beginning of the end. On the thirteenth day of February, 1872, Thomas assaulted her and threw her out of the house.

His violence came after bouts of drinking. In December 1873, a ferocious attack forced her to take refuge in a Temperance Hotel, where she and her children remained a fortnight. They finally returned home, but only after he promised to mend his ways. A fragile peace was agreed, but then broke down. Less than two years later, Thomas threatened to kill his wife and she was forced to flee. This time she pulled Annie and Harry from their beds and ran into the street.

Then in July 1876, he came home in the early hours of the morning. Like the drunken husband of Victorian music-hall jokes, he was bent on beating his wife. If the door was open, he would beat her for not guarding the house. If it was bolted, he would beat her for locking him out. Either way, he would beat her. The door was locked. When Annie's mother opened it, he knocked her to the floor and dragged her along the passage, finally kicking her into the street. She sought refuge with a neighbour and never went back. A week later, she hid the bruises as best she could, and went to her solicitor.

She asked for a legal separation, citing her husband's violence. Thomas responded with counter claims, accusing her of hysteria. She bullied the children, he said. Two of his oldest sons had run off because of her crazy behaviour. Finally, they fought over Annie. If they separated, who would have her?

Each of them petitioned for a legal separation, and the case was scheduled for 1876. Petitions were met by counter petitions. One adjournment followed another, and the court gave them ample opportunity to gather evidence. It seemed to drag on forever. In the meantime, Thomas paid his wife £70 a year. Finally, the case was timetabled for July 1877.

At the last moment, Thomas capitulated. A compromise was hammered out and a thousand pounds handed over. It was the original money that Annie's mother had brought to the marriage. On top of the thousand pounds, Thomas agreed to pay her twenty pounds a year maintenance, and was therefore forced to sell everything. Annie and her mother moved to a new house in Darlington and Annie's brother, Harry, did his best to escape.

He left a short note and Annie kept it all her life: *I will leave you all my framed drawings to keep for my ???? Should I never return they are yours.* When Annie came to make her will, she remembered Harry. She left him everything. They had been close; the kind of closeness that comes from shared suffering. The two of them lived through a nightmare, and Annie knew the scars he carried.

Chapter 36: de Cuny

Three years passed. Annie's father sold everything - his showrooms, his foundry, his stock, even his life-assurance policies. None of it worked. Nothing saved him. Then one night in 1880, he reappeared in Annie's life, drunk and bedraggled, turned out of his lodgings, and nothing in his pocket. Not a single penny. This is what the successful businessman had come to: an out-and-out, hole-in-the-wall, down-in-the gutter drunk. Friends carried him through the streets, trying desperately to offload him. First, they came to Annie's mother and knocked on her door. Would she have him? Would she take him back? No, she said, she would never take him back.

So, they hauled him through the streets again, begging people to shelter him, but no one responded. People knew his reputation. So finally, there was nothing for it; Annie's mother would have to accept him. Reluctantly, she agreed, but only for the weekend. Come Monday, she shipped him off to new lodgings and paid his rent. For nine months, she kept doing that, but it was too much. There was only one solution, and it was almost unthinkable. She would take him back, and they would live together, but not as husband and wife. Thomas would become her lodger, and this is how they would live.

We went back to the 1881 census. The entry for the Johnsons was still there. In truth, we had hardly thought about it for more than a year. At first glance, it looked the same as ever, but nothing was the same. The bare facts were barer than ever. According to the census, the Johnsons were a lower middle-class family; a conventional Victorian household from a northern industrial town. They sat on the census page in perfect harmony; Thomas presiding over his kingdom, a man who was the 'head' of his household, the classic patriarch and *paterfamilias*. According to the census, he was sixty-three and 'retired'. Below him, his wife and daughter were his dependents. The Victorian family at home. A pleasing vignette of domesticity. And it was all a lie.

Filling out a form must have been easy. Living the lie, a little harder. Almost everyone in Darlington would have heard of their troubles. The tale of their disastrous marriage would have gone the rounds, and the public spectacle of Thomas' final dissolution would have been told and retold. And if this were not enough, we came across another scandal. One of Annie's brothers parted from *his* wife, and Annie's father was obliged to help her. Then he was unable to keep up his payments, so she turned in desperation to Annie's mother. We were back in the County Court at Stockton, and the case that first opened a door onto their misery.

We tried to trace this abandoned daughter-in-law, but she disappeared. Strange to relate, her husband was easier to track, even though he was on the run. By 1881, he was living with another woman in Nottingham, and ten years later, he was dossing down in Goole Workhouse. The census was a bureaucratic machine of lumbering complexity, but sometimes it could capture life with the quickest of brush strokes; only two were needed to catch this man as he fell into the abyss. Another of Annie's brothers was found guilty of house breaking and sentenced to three months in prison, and it was clear the family had disintegrated.

In 1886, Annie and her parents moved to Saltburn. This new seaside resort had been pegged out on ground overlooking a picturesque bay. A delightful valley ran back from the sea, and the promoters turned it into a pleasure park, complete with leafy walks and bandstands, mineral springs and mock temples, croquet lawns and grottos, tearooms and gardens. New streets were laid out, a grand hotel was built, and an elegant pier constructed. Early visitors to Saltburn talked of its charm, but when a depression hit the area in the mid-1870s, houses fell vacant and shops were closed. By the time the Johnsons arrived, rooms were going cheaply.

One of the fragments that Annie preserved was a brief note that read: *With Love from Alice and Lucy de Cuny, Dec. 31ˢᵗ, 1891.* Their mother had originally been Margaret Gibson, the daughter of a tailor from Houghton-le-Spring in Durham, but after her father's death, she and her mother came to Saltburn. The new town boasted its fair share of mavericks, none of them more exotic than Viscomte Frederick William Louis de Cuny. Almost twenty years older than Margaret, he impressed her with his title and accent, and they married. Overnight, the daughter of a provincial tailor became 'Vicomtesse de Cuny' and it sounded impressive. In truth, Louis was penniless. He scraped by as best he could as a language teacher, and traded on his airs and graces.

Their marriage turned out to be fractious. Vicomtesse de Cuny often threw bread at her husband and threatened him with a poker, so you could say it was entertaining. He finally took her to court, and several local newspapers covered the story. What better copy than a French aristocrat being bullied by an English wife? It seems that the Johnsons lodged with the De Cuny's in Saltburn, and the thought of them sharing the same dinner table was intriguing.

The Victorians were genuinely outraged by domestic violence and wanted 'wife-beaters' punished, but they hardly ever talked about the hidden damage. Girls who witnessed this kind of thing were almost certainly damaged. They might end in disastrous relationships, living with dangerous men, repeating the cycle. There was nothing to suggest that Gus ever attacked Annie, but she allowed him to milk her of money, she tolerated his conduct, and she came back for more, drawn by his flame.

As for her father? Would she have kept his photograph? Would she have placed it in a frame, and squared it up, and kissed his face away? It was hard to believe. I slipped the photo in an envelope and filed it away. For a moment, I hesitated. How could I dismiss the chance that Annie loved him? I remembered the clause in her mother's will where she begged Annie to look after him. For all his violence, they still cared.

But on balance, it was hard to believe. Sometimes mysteries remain mysteries.

Chapter 37: Gussie

There was a sentence in one of Gus's letters that troubled us. *Much love to Gussie*, he wrote, *and the little man & heaps for yourself.* Here was Gus writing to Annie and talking about somebody called Gussie, and quite frankly it was baffling. We struggled to untangle the names, and it was only weeks later that we saw who Gussie really was.

She turned out to be one of Annie's best friends. Gussie was married to a newspaper editor called Tom Richardson who began his career at the *Northern Echo,* so there was every chance that he and Annie knew each other from their days in Darlington. In 1888, Tom was offered an editorial post in British Guiana and set off confidently for South America. The climate nearly killed him, so he retreated to New York where he worked for two years on the *New York Herald.* In September 1890, he came home, and it was then that Gussie met him. They married the following year and after a brief stint on a Brighton paper, Tom came north where he took up an editorial post in Hartlepool. The two of them stayed for eighteen months, and this seemed the most likely time when Gussie and Annie first met. As it turned out, it was the start of a life-long friendship.

By 1892, Tom was back in London where he launched a new

journalistic venture called the 'National Interviewing Association'. Celebrity interviews were the latest novelties in British journalism, so Tom would arrange interviews with well-known figures, ask lively questions, catch their responses and sell the interviews to London and provincial papers. For a while the scheme worked, and we found examples in various newspapers, but gradually they dried up and he moved on. Soon, he became London correspondent for the *New York Herald*.

Ever since his disastrous South American adventure, his constitution had been weakened. On his journey home from New York, he suffered a severe bout of rheumatic fever and this had damaged his heart. Friends urged him to rest but he brushed them aside. Gordon Bennett, owner of the *New York Herald,* suggested he take a holiday, but even this was ignored, and in the summer of 1897, his condition worsened. Tom died that September at the age of thirty-three. 'Mr. Richardson was possessed of a very high capacity as a journalist,' the *Northern Echo* recorded in a long and affectionate obituary. 'He was indeed a fellow of infinite wit, genial, cultured, with a rare literary taste and command of the niceties of language.'

We saw Tom's death as a catalyst. The friendship between Gussie and Annie deepened, as both learned to live with loss. Tom had died and Gus was disappearing, so the two friends shared a little melancholy. They could write and sometimes spend time together. We knew that Gussie was staying with Annie in November 1900, because this was when Gus wrote one of his last letters from Bolton - *Much love to Gussie and the little man & heaps for yourself.*

For a while, we thought this might be the mysterious *Boy* who Gus talked about in his letters. Annie and Gus's child. We never did find any record of his birth, but Gus rarely informed anybody of anything, not unless he could help it. But then we saw the truth. Buried deep in the chaos of Annie's papers there was an obituary. Someone called John H. Richardson had died in early 1934, and there was a lengthy appreciation of his life in *The Kentish Times.*

Annie copied the article and we saw that John Richardson had been an international banker who spent several years in Barcelona. This reminded me of a letter that Annie had kept, in which a correspondent said: *Gussie and John came to see me Xmas eve. John looked well and I thought him very nice. He will come and see me again if possible before leaving for Spain.*

We searched *The Times* and found a brief note of John's death. There was no mention of Gussie, or anyone else from Annie's letters, but a second entry in the paper mentioned that John Hannam Richardson was the son of 'Tom Richardson of Darlington', and this clinched it. He was Gussie's son. We fed his name into the 1911 census and found him working as a 'Bill Broker's Clerk' in London. He was living with his mother, Alice Augusta Maud Richardson, and this was Gussie herself. John would have been six in 1900, and he was *the little man* of Gus's letter.

A day or two later, we typed 'John Hannam Richardson' into Google and found him on a website devoted to a First World War prison camp in Germany. Most Englishmen caught in Germany during August 1914 were rounded up and held at a camp called Ruhleben, located on a racetrack outside Berlin. The website carried comprehensive listings of prisoners, including a substantial entry for John, who had been working in the Anglo-South American Bank in Hamburg. Much of the information had been supplied by his son, and our eyes lit up. We had always clung to the hope that one of Annie's correspondents might still have her letters. Gussie's grandson was called Bill Richardson, and we immediately set off to find him. Somewhere in the darkness of Bill's attic, there might be a pile of dog-eared letters.

Chapter 38: Frank

Chris Patton was the man behind the Ruhleben website. We asked if he could put us in touch with Bill, but several days passed without a response. Then a week. Then two. It looked to be a dead end. We also saw that Bill had deposited some of his father's papers in the University Library at Leeds, so I contacted them. Could they put me in touch with Bill? They promised to forward a letter, but warned that Bill had contacted them five years before and could easily have moved. I kept checking. Each morning I waited for the postman, and each morning there was nothing. Four months went by and things looked bleak. Our original discovery of the Ruhleben site had been in June, and we were drifting towards winter.

Then, out of the blue, Chris Patton replied. He was tidying the Ruhleben site and had just stumbled across our email. After apologising profusely, he offered Bill's address. Or did we have it? Well, in truth, we did. I told him about Leeds Library and our failed attempt to reach him. Never mind, he said, what about Bill's sister, Lady Cubbon, the wife of Sir Brian Cubbon, ex-Permanent Secretary to the Home Office?

Next morning, I drafted a letter to Lady Cubbon and told her about Annie's story. She replied quickly. Bill had indeed moved house and this was the reason our letter had not reached him. He was more than happy to talk, and two nights later, he rang.

'Hello, Tony, this is Bill Richardson.'

Bill remembered Gussie. She had been his 'Little Grannie', and the next day he sent a photo. It was a tiny print, so we blew it up as best we could. Bill was probably two or three when the photo was taken, and he was sitting on Gussie's knee. Both were posing for the camera and Bill's father was beside them wearing a dapper tweed suit, complete with waistcoat, plus fours and trilby hat. The photo had probably been taken by Bill's mother, and we could imagine the scene. 'Let me try and get you all in. Can everyone sit on the chair? John, try and squeeze up a little closer. And Gussie, can you hold Bill on your lap? Everyone look at the camera.'

Somehow or other, Gussie missed the moment. She was staring into the middle distance. Almost as if she had remembered something. We looked at her and thought we knew her face, so we immediately went through Annie's photos and tried to make a connection. She was there, resplendent in white fur, photographed on one of her visits to Annie.

Bill told me that Gussie's maiden name was Shortis. Apart from this, he knew little about her family background. Even more disappointingly, he had no letters from Annie. He suggested however that a cousin might help, so while he did his best to chase things at his end, we began searching records. Gussie was born in 1866 and was a little younger than Annie. When the census was taken in 1871, she was living with her family in a small village near Bristol. The entry looked routine, apart from one oddity; the kind of thing that makes you scratch your head. Apart from Gussie, the household was made up of her father, an elder sister and what appeared to be an aunt, but there was no sign of her mother.

Gussie

We noted that her father was married, so Gussie's mother was probably alive. The family employed one servant, and seemed to be well off, although not fabulously rich. Ten years later, we found them again; this time in a house called 'Parkfields', and the arrangement looked equally odd. Perhaps even odder. Parkfields was run by a feisty triumvirate of Gussie's aunts – Aunt Alice, Aunt Eliza and Aunt Lucinda. They were middle aged and Gussie was only fifteen. We could see that her childhood was comfortable; extremely comfortable by the look of it, but somehow fractured. Her father and relations were prosperous; they lived in villas with large gardens, they employed servants and drove carriages, and lived in a world that was warm and privileged, but somehow or other, her mother was always missing.

We began digging. Starting with her father. His full name was Francis John Shortis, but we soon cut him down to 'Frank'. He came from Bristol and was the son of a 'Provision Merchant'. In 1861 when the census was taken, he was living with his family, even though he was now in his mid-twenties. Instead of following his father into the family business, he had become a military officer, and was a lieutenant in the Lancashire militia.

Then Bill introduced us to Colin Shortis, his cousin. Colin was a retired Major General and Frank's grandson. A man well placed to tell more. We recounted the story of Annie and wondered if he had anything on Frank. He doubted it. Frank had never been a great letter writer, he said, but he promised to dig out what he could. A few nights later, he emailed: 'I've managed to find several bits and pieces,' he said, 'and bundled them together in a PDF file. It's not very interesting'

There were eight pages. The first was filled with notes. The second with a marriage certificate. Pages three and four carried announcements of Frank's military commissions. The fourth was a birth certificate. Page six had a family tree, and page seven a comprehensive listing of Frank's descendants. Which brought us to page eight, the last page, where a photograph was added.

We sat dumbfounded. Finally, I went to the filing cabinet and took out my keys. I unlocked it and peered inside. It was still there. After a moment's hesitation, I reached down, picked up the envelope, and let the mystery photograph slide out. The old man in a tweed suit.

'It's Frank,' I sighed, matching the photograph to the face on the screen. 'Gussie's father.'

For some reason, Annie had kept a photograph of Frank, and she had placed it on her mantelpiece. It stood beside Gus. And just like Gus, she had kissed his face away.

Chapter 39: Bluebeard

We soon learned that Frank had a troubled history, particularly when it came to women. It was hard to match the old man in the photograph with the stories that emerged, but Bill sent us a photograph that had been taken some years before when Frank was still in his pomp, sporting a dazzling white shirt and buttonhole, and we saw the man that Annie fell for.

Long before she appeared, he worked his way through three wives, and Gussie's mother was the first. He married her on the second of April 1861. We came across the marriage register and saw that her name was Mary Ann Puddy, the daughter of a farmer. Her signature was there on the page looking neat and tidy, and somehow vulnerable.

Marriage in the Victorian period was always a mercenary business. At the very least, people were expected to find partners from their own class, or better still, from somewhere above, so Frank's choice of a farmer's daughter was hardly inspired. He was the son of a wealthy merchant and this looked to be a case of marrying down. According to the register, he and his young wife were living in Portland Terrace, St. John's Wood, a notorious part of Victorian London.

The villas in St. John's Wood were populated by a strange mix of families, bohemian artists and high-class brothels. According to one artist who rented a fashionable studio here in the 1880s, the rural charm of the place was deceptive. The streets were tree-lined, the villas substantial, the gardens picturesque, but behind a tranquil, facade, St. John's Wood was one of the 'fastest' neighbourhoods in London. It occupied a patch of ground to the north of Regents Park. The terrace in which Frank and Mary lived had its own reputation. Four years after they were living there, a young French woman arrived. A wealthy gentleman paid her rent. He called on her every day but no one thought this the least bit odd, for this was precisely the kind of arrangement that was going on all over St. John's Wood. Suddenly, she died. Despite the coroner's best efforts to dispel the rumours that she died from a mismanaged abortion - 'Such things were done by doctors in Paris,' he stressed, 'but it could hardly be supposed that any respectable English practitioner would be a party to such proceedings' - the jury's verdict was unanimous. She was the victim of an illegal abortion. The mysterious gentleman who had paid her expenses was finally tracked down, and found to be an M.P., and this added its own spice to the prevailing assumption that St. John's Wood was 'fast'. The landlady of the house was called to give evidence and described herself as a dressmaker, but neighbours were convinced she was running a brothel.

Many of the best villas in St. John's Wood were occupied by women who lived under the protection of wealthy admirers. Large gardens and high walls hid them from the outside world, and who could tell what was going on inside? 'The doors in the garden walls of the villas were always jealously closed,' the artist remembered, 'and in many of them there was a small "Judas " through which the visitor could be scrutinized.' High-class *demi-mondaines* would admit their lovers but keep other busybodies at bay. Sometimes of course more sinister things were at work. When W. T. Stead published his famous exposé of child prostitution in the 1880s, he noted how these villas were often used by wealthy clients to deflower young girls: '"Here," said the keeper of a fashionable villa

. . . as she showed her visitor over the well-appointed rooms, "Here is a room where you can be perfectly secure. The house stands in its own grounds. The walls are thick, there is a double carpet on the floor. The only window which fronts upon the back garden is doubly secured, first with shutters and then with heavy curtains. You lock the door and then you can do as you please. The girl may scream blue murder, but not a sound will be heard."'

Most villas and apartments in St. John's Wood were rented rather than owned and so too was the furniture. As one couple broke up, another moved in. Frank and Mary were living in Portland Terrace when they married on April 2nd, but were no longer there when the census was taken five days later. Frank was in Bristol. We thought nothing of this until Kate Arscott joined the quest. Bill had enlisted Colin, and Colin had enlisted Kate, and soon we were sharing information. Kate was Frank's great-great granddaughter.

'Have you noticed the dates?' she said. 'Which of them comes first, the marriage or the census?'

She was right. Frank's marriage took place on April 2nd 1861, and five days later the census was taken. At some point, he had gone back to Bristol, presumably to give his parents the news. The census found him in the family home as his poor father filled out the form.

'Frank's not told him,' I laughed. His father had recorded Frank as unmarried. 'He's terrified. It's a clandestine affair. He's married a girl from the lower orders and he's terrified. He can't bring himself to tell them.'

We went back to the marriage register and saw that the wedding had all the hallmarks of secrecy; no relatives present, and only two witnesses who were probably dragged off the street. And now Frank had a problem. Whenever he broke the news he would be courting disaster. Meanwhile, his young wife was somewhere in London and we tried to find her. There was no trace of her in Portland Terrace, so we began exploring earlier censuses and discovered that she had grown up in a small village in Somerset. She moved to Bridgwater in the early 1850s where she worked as a dressmaker, and in 1851 was visiting an older dressmaker there. We gazed at the entry. A young girl of sixteen who was stepping out into the world. How on earth had she become Frank's mistress? We finally found her in the 1861 census. Like Frank she was keeping the marriage secret. According to the census, Mary Ann Puddy was working as a 'Court Dressmaker' in London, and we saw how the story must have played out.

In 1850, the *Morning Chronicle* carried Henry Mayhew's striking account of a court dressmaking establishment. He made great play of the stark contrasts that existed in these establishments between the sumptuous showrooms that wealthy customers saw and the sordid workshops above; the places where the dressmakers worked. A world of rags and riches. The front of the establishment projected an air of opulence. Wealthy ladies would step out of their carriages, the door would open, and a liveried footman would usher them into a splendid hall. They would climb a broad stone staircase, covered with an elegant Brussels carpet, and come to the first landing. Here, the mistress of the establishment would take over and she would direct them into 'the *premier magasin* or 'first show-room'. 'In every other panel there is a looking-glass from the floor to the ceiling, set in a handsome carved gilt frame. The floor is covered with a very expensive carpet of rich pattern, sometimes of a violet and amber colour. The window curtains are of rich dark green velvet. In different parts of the room there are counters of polished ebony, elegantly ornamented with gilding. The lady customer is then shown an assortment of magnificent silks and velvets.'

Hidden from view was a drabber world. The dressmakers occupied a room upstairs with a fireplace at either end. Functional deal tables filled every inch of space, and an ugly gas-pipe ran along the ceiling. The room was packed with chairs, and here the dressmakers sat for days on end, fashioning gowns. Two grades were employed: the 'worker bees' who were always confined to the garret, and the 'queen bees' who commanded the showrooms.

Queen bee or worker bee? People in the census were always listed in order of status, and Mary Ann Puddy was close to the top. She was one of the 'first-hands' who would front up the business; an attractive woman who would draw the eye of the customers. According to the language of the trade, Mary had come to London to be 'improved', but this was improvement on the grand scale. She would use her time to refine her skills, and then transform her fortune. A pretty dressmaker who would go to the top.

In 1863, the untimely death of a court dressmaker provoked public debate. A sensational letter went to *The Times* from her co-workers that claimed she died from exhaustion. The owners of the establishment were quick to defend themselves, but gradually the debate shifted. An initial concern over long hours turned into an exposé of the women's morals.

It turned out that court dressmakers had a saucy reputation. If you happened to be walking in Regent Street, you might see them on Sunday mornings as they swept by; young attractive women who knew how to dress. A little later, you might see them in Hyde Park, or catch them flirting in Cremorne Gardens, or dining out with young gentlemen in expensive restaurants. 'Every sixpence goes on their backs,' one woman complained, 'The fondness for dress and admiration in young girls in their class of life is a terrible temptation.'

When trade was slack, they stayed out late. '*Madame* did allow it for a time,' one older and steadier dressmaker recalled, 'but it became absolutely necessary to put a stop to it.' All manner of indiscretions were being committed. 'A further cause of misery is those terrible places known by the name of music halls. They are just the places for vain and dressy girls to be led away.' Next, a male employer gave vent to his feelings: 'They are all excessively foolish and ignorant, stupid and careless beyond belief. Dressmakers seem to be so even beyond all other women; but you cannot reason with any of them. Positively I think that most of them have no mind at all.'

There was no saving them. And even when you locked them up and kept them confined to the workshop, the dangers crept in: 'Letters come with coronets and elaborate monograms for the young ladies. Such things have but one meaning and commonly but one end . . . We have the greatest difficulty in enforcing the necessary rules for conducting an establishment like ours respectably.' The manager of a lodging house claimed that she had battled with this problem for years. 'I have unfortunately had to dismiss two or three girls; they were receiving notes from gentlemen, and making appointments to meet them.'

We could see how it played. Frank would come to the establishment with a female relation. As Mary showed the latest fabrics, there would be stolen glances. He would inquire after her name and wonder if she might favour him with an address. She would smile and pretend to doubt his intentions, but a day or two later, his letter would arrive. It would have an impressive monogram and she would giggle. Soon he would be taking her to the theatre, and then to a restaurant. The following Sunday, people would see them together, walking arm in arm, and note how fine they looked. He would invite her to his lodgings, and she would tell her employers that she was visiting relations. After the London season was over, she would move in with him, and begin to enjoy the cosy comforts of a little apartment in St. John's Wood. Then one day in April, there would be a secret marriage, and Cinderella would be a princess.

'Ever wondered what happened to Cinderella after she married the prince?' I asked one day. Gill looked at me and shook her head. I pointed to the computer screen. 'I've just found a newspaper report. Here it is: "Sudden Death of a Lady at Bourton". Frank's giving evidence on Mary's death.'

It was ten years later. They had moved out of London and settled near Bristol, where they rented a handsome house in a small village called Flax Bourton. According to the paper, Mary had been ill for months. She was suffering from sharp pains in her head, severe nausea and persistent coughing. Her doctors diagnosed erysipelas, an acute bacterial infection. 'It was during this illness,' they said, 'that she fell and injured her head. She had never recovered entirely from the effects of that blow and suffered from symptoms of brain disease. Her general health was extremely delicate.'

There were times when she seemed brighter. One night, she and Frank invited a guest to dinner. After he left, they sat together chatting and laughing in front of the kitchen fire. Frank remembered how happy they were. Suddenly, Mary fell forward. There was blood gushing from her nostrils but at least he managed to catch her before she hit the floor. Their female servant ran into the village for help and returned with a lady. Frank was still holding Mary in his arms, but there were bruises on her nose and forehead, and both women thought she had been hit. Soon, they began talking with other people and the news was out.

By the time the doctor arrived, Mary was dead. She was placed on a bed and examined. He noticed the bruises and described them as 'two slight contusions of recent infliction on the face'. If Frank's story was true, and he had caught Mary before she hit the floor, where had those bruises come from? He must have hit her. So, in the days following her death, he changed his story. During the inquest, he tried to persuade the coroner that he was confused by the speed of events that overtook him that night. He realized now that he never caught her at all, and that her bruises must have been caused when she hit the floor: 'He was under the impression that he caught her before she reached the ground, but he now thought he did not, as there was a mark on her face which was not there during the evening. The mark appeared to be a bruise and he was quite certain it was not there before.'

It was hardly convincing. Things were looking threatening and Frank was facing a murder charge, until two doctors stepped forward and saved the day. They performed a *post mortem* on Mary and found no bruises on her body, apart from her face. This in itself was odd. If she had fallen to the floor, as Frank claimed, there would have been bruises elsewhere, particularly on her arms and legs. In any case, the doctors had their own explanation. They reckoned that Mary died of "apoplexy caused by softening of the brain". Her death, they said, was a final seizure brought on by a much longer illness.

For all that, we noticed that one of them had doubts. 'She was suffering from concussion of the brain,' he said, as he remembered how Mary's illness first started. Apparently, she had fallen. Her condition had been 'caused by a severe blow to the head, which she explained to him was caused by a fall getting out of bed.' It was possible that she was lying. Frank may have been beating her.

Gussie was only four when her mother died. She was spared the worst of the gossip, but rumours surrounding her death would have reached the girl. It may have taken years, but someone would have taken her aside and whispered in her ear. Frank was beginning to look dangerous. Gussie's mother was the first of his victims, and a dark pattern emerged. He would court and charm his women and make them his mistresses. Children would come along. There would be a marriage and a period of happiness. Then Frank would tire of his latest wife, or she would lose her good looks, or he would grow jealous and insecure. Whatever the reason, he would destroy her.

In the mid-1860s, Anne Thackeray wrote a series of short stories offering modern versions of traditional fairy tales. In one, she told the story of Bluebeard, a sinister nobleman whose unfortunate wives kept disappearing. She chose an Italian marquis as her new anti-hero, a man with strange and magnetic eyes, a sarcastic smile and handsome face. It's safe to say that she never met Frank, yet if had, she might have chosen him instead. He fitted the profile perfectly.

Chapter 40: Frolics

Annie was drawn to dangerous men; this much was clear. Gus's mother warned her that Gus would make a poor husband, but she was drawn to him nonetheless. And perhaps, after all, she was drawn to his danger? Even now, she was keeping his photograph, and would take him back if he knocked on her door again. Gus was a loafer and Frank a swell, and she seemed to have a taste for such men. Frank could do terrible things to women and, by the time Annie knew him, his track record was well known, but for reasons best known to herself, she was smitten.

We thought of Bluebeard. A wealthy and powerful man with countless wives who all disappeared? Everyone knows there is something wrong, yet the heroine of the tale marries him. He gives her the keys to his castle. She has the run of the place and can enter any room. Only one room is forbidden. And this or course is the room she will enter. What strange perversity draws her in?

Back in the 1850s, Frank's father purchased a commission for him in the Militia, and we found several newspaper accounts of officers in his unit running wild. Some were hauled before magistrates on drunk and disorderly charges, others were caught fighting in the streets, and one villainous brute urged his terrier to destroy a lady's cat. Groups of officers strutted the town barging women off pavements. Young privileged men running wild.

Frank's world. We found no mention of him in the court cases that followed these offences, but he seemed to relish this sort of wildness. Take the case of the *Velindra*. In September 1865, Frank took a short trip with his wife and daughter on a steamship called the *Velindra*, rigged out with a special 'Ladies Cabin' and 'Retiring Room'. A place forbidden to men. Flouting the rules that were nailed on the door, Frank strolled into the cabin and stretched out on the sofa. Bit of a frolic in prospect. Soon, the ladies complained that they couldn't use the necessary convenience, so the manager was summoned. He tried to reason with Frank and persuade him to leave peacefully but Frank refused. Finally, the manager had no option but to eject him. They struggled, Frank blacked his eye, and the manager threw a punch back and, incredibly, Frank charged him with assault.

The case attracted attention, the court was packed, and the scene set. At one point, Frank gave evidence and found himself cross-examined by the manager's lawyer.

'Didn't the manager say that ladies were waiting outside,' the lawyer asked, 'and had been waiting to go in for a long time?'

Frank shook his head.

'Did he not ask you to go out?'

'No, he ordered me. I told him I should not go, and he took me by the collar.'

'And you resisted?'

'I did.'

'And when you had struggled to the door, you struck him?'

'Yes.'

But the lawyer knew something and posed a question. 'It was not such a violent blow as you generally strike, I think?'

''Tisn't likely that under such circumstances I should give a very tender blow.'

'You are in the habit of fighting people, aren't you? The beer house in Cumberland Street, for instance?'

The Chair of the Bench smiled. He knew about Cumberland Street. 'Mr Shortis is a very powerful man,' he winked, 'a blow from him is like a kick from a horse'.

A gentleman's joke. It seemed that the beer house in question staged organized fights. By the look of it, Frank was a fighter, a gentleman pugilist in the old tradition, a notable follower of 'The Fancy'. By the 1860s, bareknuckle fights were illegal, but plenty of gentlemen in Victorian England did their best to keep them alive. In a society that seemed increasingly effeminate and domesticated, fisticuffs were a glorious expression of a man's virility. What was wrong with a hearty Englishman testing his mettle in the ring? Better than tea-drinking! 'Kicking up a lark' was what they called it.

I reached for a tattered copy of an old book that had been sitting on my shelf for years; Pierce Egan's, *Tom and Jerry*. It was published in 1821 and caused a sensation. Thackeray thought it one of the best books he ever read as a boy. 'Tom knocking down the watchman at Temple Bar,' he laughed, 'Tom and Jerry dancing at Almack's, or flirting in the saloon at the theatre; at the night-houses after the play . . . singing a song; ambling gallantly in Rotten Row.' Two fashionable young bloods who were out to see LIFE. Two genuine 'Out-and-Outers' (Egan knew the patter), and their mission was to frolic.

Regency Bucks could stroll through life pursuing their pleasures with high and low. They were generous and impulsive and good with their fists. 'To look the character of a gentleman' – that was the trick. You had to acquire the style, but once you had it, you could strut through London doing whatever you pleased.

When Thackeray tried to buy a copy of the book in the early 1860s, he couldn't find one. Its day had come and gone. The Victorian Age had seen off the Age of Flash. Or so it seemed. Thackeray sighed, 'There is an enjoyment of life in these young bucks of 1823 which contrasts strangely with our feelings of 1860,' but in truth, Frank and Gus, and scores of other loafers and swells were keeping the flame alight.

In the 1860s, Frank was appointed guardian to a widow and her children. It was hard to imagine anyone trusting him with a job like this, but he set about doing it with his usual bravado. He found a cottage in Bristol that belonged to one of the wealthiest and most powerful families in the town – the Fripps – and set about installing his new charges. In point of fact, he had not consulted the Fripps, but had simply agreed matters with the sitting tenant, and the Fripps took offence. They sent an agent to threaten Frank with legal action, Frank rushed off a hot-headed letter accusing them of being moneylenders, and the scene was set.

A short time later, Frank and his brother were doing business in the Bristol Exchange. It was a Tuesday afternoon and several newspapers captured the moment: 'As the corn merchants of Bristol and neighbourhood were assembled in the Exchange, a scene occurred such as has been rarely witnessed there, and which excited no small commotion amongst the habitués of the market. A well-known citizen, Mr Stewart Fripp, entered the quadrangle and crossed to the stand at which Mr. Shortis was engaged, held out a letter, and in an angry and excited tone demanded if he was the writer of it.'

We guessed what was coming. 'Mr Shortis said that he was (the writer of the letter), upon which Mr Fripp said, 'In it you have insulted my father. Will you retract what you have said?' Mr Shortis replied that he had nothing to retract upon which Mr Fripp said, 'Then I demand an apology. I have here one written which I call upon you to sign.' Frank's reputation made it impossible for him to back down. 'Mr Shortis replied that he would do nothing of the kind, upon which Mr Fripp struck him a blow upon the face which cut his lip and drew blood. Mr Shortis who had contrived to keep his temper, said, 'I shall not defend myself', upon which Mr Fripp struck him other blows and kicked him on the side.'

It was only a matter of time before Frank charged Fripp with assault, and according to one Bristol newspaper the affair excited widespread attention. Opinion in Bristol was turning against him and Frank and his legal advisors wanted their case to be heard elsewhere. His barrister was anxious to get the facts before the public, for people 'had 'hitherto formed very incorrect conclusions'.

The swaggering military officer and prize-fighter was in trouble. Worrying rumours were abroad. The court congratulated Frank on not retaliating when he was attacked by Fripp, but Fripp's solicitor talked gleefully of his client giving Frank 'a good thrashing', and this was the version going the rounds.

Two years later, when Gussie's mother died in suspicious circumstances, many Bristol people looked at Frank and shook their heads.

Chapter 41: Danger

After Mary's death, we caught glimpses of Frank. Every now and then he surfaced in Bristol, making brief trips home, but Bristol was out of bounds. People were turning against him. Frank's second marriage was only three years after Mary's death, and we found ourselves standing on the wrong side of history again, looking on helplessly as another young woman signed her life away. The marriage register told us that she was called Sophia.

She appeared in the 1871 census and was described as a 'housekeeper', and if ever there was a need for inverted commas, this was it. She bore him a son and they married in Liverpool. What little we could gather about their lifestyle suggested a wandering existence. The clock was ticking. Sooner or later, Frank would tire of her, and then he would make his move. In the early 1880s they came to Greenwich, and it was here that he finally destroyed her. One night in July 1882, he sent for a doctor.

'On approaching her,' the doctor recorded, 'she ran away, crying out, "The Prince of Wales had told my husband no man must enter my house", and "The King of the Belgians is waiting outside to shoot you."' He completed the form that Frank wanted - 'Medical Certificate – Sched. (F) No. 3. In the small boxes provided, he set out the facts, as far he knew them: 'Her husband says she has frequently threatened to kill him and her neighbours as well – she is very violent at times & went about the house and garden all night long.'

A local magistrate committed her to a mental facility and she was taken to the Kent County Lunatic Asylum. 'Patient was admitted in a very noisy, excited state – shouting loudly and screaming – appears to have little idea of time or place – became very talkative after a little – speaking very fast in disjointed sentences & apparently addressing some invisible beings – answering imaginary questions. Memory is very poor – cannot converse at all. Physically she is a poorly nourished woman, expression anxious & vacant – pupils dilated.'

Significant numbers of women were locked away like this because they were driven mad by domestic trials and tribulations; the day-to-day blows that dented their minds. We read through the medical notes. In the beginning, the asylum doctors monitored Sophia on a daily basis, but soon the pace slackened. How could we blame them? Three of them had responsibility for one and half thousand patients. The next entry was seven weeks later, and then a month after that they saw one or two signs of improvement. 'Has improved slightly: more coherent than formerly, rather restless & excitable at times: health fair.' This was the time when Frank could have saved her, but there was no sign that he ever lifted a finger.

The moment passed. The following March, she was transferred to Ward XVII and classified as incurable. The gaps in the record grew longer. No one bothered to enter anything between March and June, and when they did, the entry was sparse: 'Nothing of much importance to note.' Entries dropped to five a year, then four, then three, and sometimes two. Early descriptions talked of her being 'restless and excitable', 'incoherent', 'rambling' and 'silly'. Over time, they gave way to 'weak-minded', 'dull and stupid-looking', 'childish', 'lethargic' and 'melancholy'. The word, 'demented' appeared and never went away. On several occasions, she was said to be totally 'blank', and we saw how she was disappearing.

Frank had found a new lady, a young actress called Emma Richardson. Emma was the daughter of a land agent who lived in Darlington. She became a professional actress and lived a little dangerously. The *Saturday Review* put it bluntly: 'Objections to the theatre are that actors and actresses are not virtuous characters, or rather, although modesty and prudery may forbid them saying so plainly, they do not much care about the men, but they think the women are bad.'

By the 1880s, these attitudes were changing. Actresses were not only acceptable now, but often celebrities. George Sims wrote extensively for the theatre and knew many of them. He may even have known Emma, for she was part of his world. A thoroughly modern type. The kind of woman who might sidle up to him on a railway platform, give him a playful squeeze, and ask if he could introduce her to the right people. *Without the Limelight: theatrical life as it is*, was Sims's attempt to capture the harsh reality behind the glitter. A world of advertising posters flapping listlessly on grubby walls; of endless struggles to find 'diggings'; of bizarre lodging houses in provincial towns that specialized in 'theatricals'; of bad weeks when audiences were thin and takings poor; of moments on the road when actor-managers abandoned their companies and left them penniless; of tedious Sundays on slow trains, and cold nights in railway stations; of hopeful visits to agents; crumpled song-sheets and botched auditions.

We could see how a woman like Emma, faced with a world like this, might turn to an old roué like Frank. He might promise her security. We found nothing to indicate that she ever played the London stage. Almost all her life was spent in provincial theatres, and her audiences were the people who sat in half-filled Theatre Royals that were dotted about the North of England and Scotland. How long could it last? How many flea-bitten lodgings could be endured? And what did the future hold? She could see how the best actresses struggled to find work as they grew older.

Then Frank appeared on the scene and presented himself as a man of the world, a retired army captain who had all the right contacts. They met in the summer of 1887, and a child was born the following spring. They called him Thomas Richardson Shortis, and in the fullness of time he became Colin's father. Finally, after an affair of three years, Frank married Emma. It was a bigamous marriage, because Sophia was still alive, but what did that matter? Frank was on the move again. He was fifty-two and Emma twenty-four.

Gussie now had a mother-in-law who was exactly her own age. In one of her letters to Annie, she made reference to this odd arrangement. She had come back from a bad-tempered meeting with Emma and told Annie how Emma had been *in a very nasty argumentative mood, the first time I have felt I couldn't get on with her since I have known her.* The two women did their best to be friends, and somehow pulled it off. Actually, they did more than that, because Emma's brother was none other than Tom Richardson, the journalist and editor who Gussie married.

It might be said that Emma's best performance was surviving Frank. She was the only one to escape him; a triumph in anyone's books. According to one report, she ran off in 1894 with another man and lived 'an improper life'. We both laughed; it would have gone against her principles to be 'proper'. But for all her feistiness and independence, Emma was frightened. It turned out that she suffered years of abuse at Frank's hands, and now he started stalking her. At one point, he demanded a meeting and she reluctantly agreed, but only in public. A place of relative safety. It was January 1895. Even here, he pulled a pistol and blacked her eye. She tried to hide her new addresses but he found them. On one occasion, he broke into her house and stole her jewellery. It was the last straw.

In May 1895, she took him to court. Several newspapers covered the story, and one of them described Frank as tall and well turned-out, a gentleman who appeared to be a retired army officer. Emma was described as 'a fashionably-dressed young lady' and certainly impressed the male reporters.

They had two children - Colin's father and a little girl called Vashti. Colin's father had been brought up by Emma's sister in Darlington, and Vashti had been taken away from Frank when Emma left him. Frank claimed that he had broken into Emma's home to rescue his daughter and wanted her back.

'Where did you sleep last night?' he asked, as he tried to shame Emma before the court.

'Three Blomefield-road.'

'Are you living in adultery with a man?'

She hesitated. 'I am. I joined him the day I left you.'

Yet for all his attempts to blacken her character, Frank was losing the battle. He had never shown the least interest in his children, and Emma could prove it. Sensing defeat, he handed the jewellery back and the case was dismissed. But here was the proof. Emma was the only one to survive him and to expose his brutality. Whatever lingering doubts we had about his hand in Mary's death, or Sophia's madness, were put to rest. Frank was dangerous.

It seemed incredible that Annie would turn to a man like this. We tracked Frank using the 1901 census, and found him sharing a house with one of his daughters. They had a female lodger. Perhaps Annie had lodged there too? We worked our way through Gussie's letters, and came across an envelope that was dated 1904. The letter was addressed to Annie, and then forwarded to Gussie's home in London, and we could see that Annie was staying there. Frank was nearby, and this may have been the time they met.

Then we made another discovery.

'Do you have any photos of your father when he was a boy?' I asked.

'Just one,' Colin said, 'Frank gave him a rocking horse on his birthday, and there's a photograph of him standing beside it.'

Annie had a copy too. We found several photos of this boy in her collection. He looked to be about three, and was sitting beside a girl with thick curly hair, almost certainly Vashti. Annie kept photographs and letters from Gus's family, and she kept mementos from Frank too. They were important to her.

We thought we knew her, but were constantly surprised. To begin with, we had seen her as an innocent young woman who had fallen for a raffish charmer like Gus; the naïve ingénue who was seduced and betrayed. Then she seemed to morph into a more calculated risk-taker who gambled on a dangerous affair. Next, she became a woman who faked a pregnancy. Soon, we were finding evidence of an avenging angel, hell-bent on destroying Agnes. And now there was this; a woman falling for a man like Frank. Taking yet another risk. There were hidden levels to Annie, but amidst all her complexities and surprises, one thing was clear - she was a woman who liked the company of dangerous men.

She survived Frank. He swept through her life and left no scars, just one or two telling photographs. Gus disappeared in 1902, and Frank died in 1908, so the affair must have happened in between, the years when Annie was making a new life for herself in London. She kept Frank's photo, just as she kept Gus's, and each of their faces were kissed away. There were no letters from Frank, and he never once appeared in her correspondence. It was a profound silence. Gussie never mentioned him at all. There was no sentence that started, 'I note all you said about my father . . .' Frank was a subject that remained off limits. The uncomfortable secret that both friends shared, and never voiced.

Chapter 42: London

We seemed to lose sight of everyone. Even Annie became a ghost. The flurry of letters that swept us through the 1890s and early 1900s fell away to nothing. Only fragments remained. Most of them were business-like and inconsequential and we piled them on the table: dividends on Annie's shares; pages from her bankbook; quarterly statements; a receipt for jewellery; a prospectus issued by the Kalgoorie Electric Power and Lighting Corporation, and a bill from a local steam laundry.

I often went walking that autumn. One rainy Saturday, I was on the moor. The day was blustery and wet, with a ferocious wind dragging clouds through my head. Sheep were scattered about in the earthy emptiness of it all; distant blobs in the darkening heather. Me, the rain, the sheep and the moor. Twenty yards to the right, there was a square of stone that looked to be an old sheepfold. A little piece of somewhere set down in the middle of nowhere. I stumbled inside, threw my rucksack on the ground, and rested against the wall. Sheltered and dry, I gazed up and saw the clouds, scudding by overhead. Then I started laughing. Earlier that day, I had learned that the 1911 census was suddenly available online, at least two years before its intended release, and it occurred to me that this would be our sheepfold. The place where the lost souls of the story would be gathered in.

We began with Annie and found that she was living in London in 1911. Frank had died some years before, but she was still there. Her new address was 35 Lichfield Grove, a suburban street in Finchley. She filled out the census in her own hand and described herself as a 'boarder'. The house was owned by someone called Ebenezer Hastings Farrow, a photo apparatus maker, and we found letters from Ebenezer and his wife that mostly dated from the 1920s and 1930s. They were obviously friends.

We knew from her letters that Annie was living in London in 1904, and had embarked on an affair with Frank. He had died in 1908 but she was still there two years later. *I am afraid I shall not be able to get to London this summer*, Emily told her in July 1910, *You seem to be having a nice time of it, and it is a jolly place to be in, and you seem to be in a nice part too.*

Middle-class women could now travel more freely. Job opportunities were improving, and the idea of the 'New Woman' was well-established, even if sometimes it was there to be mocked, so Annie's decision to make a new life for herself in London was understandable. She kept her own little hoard of souvenirs. We counted twenty-eight in all. In December 1904, her agent in Darlington wrote to her asking for a current address. On the back of his letter, she had written: *Mrs Nightbert, Langham Hotel*' and '*Mrs Best Oxford Street.*

The Langham was expensive. Too expensive for Annie. The idea of a magnificent hotel that could compete with the best in Paris or New York had been floated in 1862, and the original prospectus promised visitors 'a scale of comfort and magnificence hitherto unattained in London'. It catered for 'first-class families'. *Mrs Nightbert* must have stayed there, and Annie must have known her, but who she was remained a mystery.

We knew that Annie was in London in 1906 because she was seeking a job. She had drafted out an enquiry that she never sent: *33 Sutherland Avenue, Maida Vale, Oct 2nd 1906. Dear Sir, Have you any vacancy in your circularising department for a lady?* 'Circularising' was part of the new vocabulary of advertising. Several letters in late Victorian newspapers were already complaining that advertising companies were acquiring peoples' addresses and 'circularising' them with promotions – an early version of junk mail - but at the same time, several articles talked of the exciting opportunities that advertising offered women. 'America seems to be the land of promise,' one noted. More and more women were being employed in advertising so it was 'a calling which . . . many a bright, smart woman over here could very well carry on to a remunerative point'. Large retail stores were employing female copywriters and 'any woman of the necessary ability . . . may make an astonishing success in the field.' We later learned that Frank worked for a time as an advertising agent.

There was another note from 1906 that trailed a tenuous connection to Frank. *15 Mansell Street, 23/12/06, My dear Annie, Many thanks for yours. Glad to hear your "affair" has come off all right. Have no time for writing today but will do so next week. Fondest Xmas Greetings, Yours as ever, Jack (not Bill).* The tone was light and intimate, and Annie was close to whoever 'Jack' was. Frank's middle name was John, so it was just possible that he may have been nicknamed 'Jack', and his brother, Robert William Acheson Shortis, might well have been nicknamed 'Bill'.

Then we found a battered 1912 map of the London Underground system. No bigger than an A4 sheet, it carried its own x-ray of Edwardian London. Various railways had been running under the city since the 1860s, but they came together in 1908 to form, 'The Underground'. As a matter of interest, we tried to work out if Annie could reach Finchley from the West End. The 'Hampstead Railway' ran from Leicester Square to Highgate, then an electric tram took her to Finchley, so it was easy. Similar suburban lines were fanning out to places like Clapham, Wimbledon, Richmond, Golders Green and Finsbury Park. New suburban frontiers that offered modest families like the Farrows a patch of greenery.

'Events for June' were listed on the back of the map, including a Test Match between England and Australia. We scanned *The Times* and saw that Jack Hobbs and Wilfred Rhodes were opening the batting.

'There was an old man sitting in the player's pavilion at Scarborough in the late 1950s,' I said, suddenly remembering a face I had forgotten. 'I think I must have been about seven or eight at the time. "That's Wilfred Rhodes", my father said. I can remember him kneeling down and putting his arm round me. "There!" he said, "One of the greatest cricketers of all time," And I can remember staring at this wizened old chap, trying to make sense of him. He sat in the pavilion, right at the back. I can see him now, just sitting there. I think he was blind.' I stopped for a moment and looked at the map and newspaper report again. 'I can't believe it! He's opening the batting for England!'

Dear Mrs Bowen, I was pleased to have such a nice long letter – they are so very interesting about London – you will be staying for the coronation? A letter from one of her friends that had been sent in June 1911: *I wish I could have been at London for tomorrow. I am glad Mother and Corrie are with you.* Annie was catching the coronation of George V.

Then we found another souvenir. A faded programme that was folded in three, with one panel loose. We pieced it together. It was a programme for the Tivoli Music Hall. Annie had gone there on a Monday night in September 1910, and there were seventeen acts. Between a popular, light-operatic overture that opened the night, and some 'moving pictures' from Ruffell's Bioscope that closed it, we sampled the astonishing range of Victorian entertainment that was on offer.

'Ragtime!' I laughed, amazed to find Edwardian audiences getting their first taste of jazz. The 'Two Bobs' were a popular American duo who specialised in ragtime tunes. 'A pair of American singers, dancers and pianists,' *The Times* sighed with predictable disdain, 'who eclipse all their rivals in the hold that they have on the audience. It is not at all easy to follow what they are saying. A little more clearness of articulation would certainly add to the merit of their performance.'

There were other souvenirs. Little scraps of Edwardian London. One of them was a programme of Daily Organ Recitals that formed part of the Japan-British Exhibition of 1910, and this brought us face to face with an old friend - Imre Kiralfy. He was still there, working his magic. The great man was now specialising in diplomacy through spectacle. The Anglo-French Exhibition of 1908 had been staged to celebrate the *Entente Cordiale*, and the Japan-British Exhibition of 1910 did much the same, cementing economic and political relations with an emerging power in the East. Kiralfy was billed as its 'Commissioner-General'.

Then, in September 1913, Annie toyed with the idea of going to Paris. She seemed to be looking for a companion. *At the present time*, a friend said, *I know of no person going to Paris, but if I should hear of any one, will be pleased to let you know.* Time was running out. Two of her last souvenirs came from 1914. One was a ticket for an American audio-visual epic of God's creation. It was playing to packed houses. The second was a programme from Sadler's Wells. The old theatre had been turned into a cinema, and we could see Annie sitting in the stalls, watching the latest footage of a new war.

She never did see Paris.

Chapter 43: Strangeways

We spent the best part of a morning combing through the 1911 census looking for Gus. As ever, he was elusive. There was nothing to find, not at least under his full name – Charles Arthur Augustine Bowen – or indeed his age. We knew, of course, that he could lie about both. We tried something simpler and typed in 'Charles Bowen', and found sixteen hits. By adding his birthplace, we reduced them to one. A man called Charles Bowen who had been born in Skelton seemed to be living in an institution in Prestwich.

As the census page rippled into view on the computer screen, we tried to make sense of what we were seeing. It was a page made up exclusively of men: there was a fish hawker, several bricklayers, a chemist, one or two labourers, several miners, a fruit hawker, a pork butcher, a rag dealer, and even a jobbing gardener. Our first guess was that it might be the vagrant wing of a workhouse, but the truth came at the top of the page, tucked away in a corner.

It always seemed likely, and sometimes we joked about it, but it still came as a shock. Gus was in prison. Strangeways Prison. How he ended there was anybody's guess, but fraud was high on the list. Then bigamy. Soon we were thinking of bank robberies, crimes of passion and high-society heists. Whatever the crime, we were confident the prison records would tell us everything, which turned out to be silly, because a riot in Strangeways in 1990 had destroyed them all.

Serious offences were dealt with by Quarter Sessions or Assize Courts and each had their own special 'Calendar of Prisoners'. Each Calendar contained the names, ages, trades and previous convictions of offenders, together with brief descriptions of their offences. They were all housed in the National Archives in London, and a month later I ordered a batch. The discouraging news was that offences committed in one part of the country could lead to prison sentences elsewhere, so there was no guarantee that Gus had committed his crime in Lancashire. The fact that he was locked up in Manchester meant nothing. He might have been involved in a high-society fraud in Edinburgh, or a bank robbery in Cardiff, or a jewel heist in Mayfair. I had no time to plough through everything, so I made a shortlist. I would gamble on the crime being committed in Lancashire, Cheshire, Durham, Yorkshire or Northumberland.

I didn't know the length of the sentence. Was it a year? A month? Perhaps even life? I paused and took a deep breath. The odds against me finding him were forbidding. I didn't know where to look, or when to start. A glance at the Calendars soon revealed the wide range of offences that Gus might have committed. There was 'carnal knowledge'. He had plenty of that. Charges of 'forgery' or even 'embezzlement' were distinct possibilities. 'Concealment of a birth' or attempts 'to procure a miscarriage' were equally likely. During his many wild nights ashore, he could easily have 'exposed his person'. Annie could have entered the witness box and told the court how he was always 'demanding money by menaces', or 'sending threatening letters'. When all else failed, the police could nail him for being 'an incorrigible rogue'. It would have been a fair cop.

Two o'clock and the first day fizzling out. I had worked through the first batch of records and found nothing. I ticked them off and went back to 1910. The further I went back, the more likely it would be that he had committed a serious offence, but the less likely it would be that I would find him. There was nothing in 1910. By the end of the afternoon, I had reached the mid part of 1909. The truth of the matter was that I was losing heart. The next day, I carried on as best I could, and a final concerted effort took me back to 1905, but that was it. I wasn't going any further.

Two weeks later, we came across a tip-top website run by a man in Manchester who looked to be an expert on criminal history. I emailed him. 'We're researching the life and times of a character called Charles Arthur Augustine Bowen who appears to have been an inmate in Strangeways Prison when the census was taken in 1911.' I explained that we were looking for any details of his offence, but could not locate him in the National Archives. Did Strangeways have minor offenders? Yes, it did. The prison was used for short-term and long-term prisoners, and the good news was that magistrates' records were held in Manchester Central Library. None of them were indexed, so every bundle had to be searched. A week or so later, I sat down and prepared myself for a long session. Each separate conviction had its own certificate, and each certificate contained details of the court, the defendant, the offence committed, and the punishment meted out. Thousands of them. They had all been bundled together and crammed into leather-bound volumes that bulged like bibles.

After two dispiriting days in the National Archives, I seemed to be a man without hope. Yet who knows when things might change? Ten minutes into this search, I turned a page and there he was, standing in the dock, larger than life. The Court of Summary Jurisdiction in Minshell Street, Manchester. It was the 21st January, 1911, a Saturday, and Gus was pleading guilty to an offence committed the previous day. To use the language of the court, he had 'feloniously stolen, taken and carried away thirty pounds of bacon' valued at twenty shillings. The bacon had been lifted from a shop called 'Hunters The Teamen Limited', and Gus had evidently been caught red-handed.

Reality bled in. This was not a world of high-society heists and

Mayfair scams, but a bedraggled corner of Edwardian Manchester. A world of petty thefts and grey poverty. 'Hunters the Teamen Ltd.' were 'cash grocers', offering poorer customers a range of staple goods at knockdown prices. One of their many shops was located in Manchester and this was the place that Gus robbed. There was even a photo on the Web. The name of the firm was emblazoned across the front, its windows filled with tins of vegetables and cheap meat, all of them rising up in carefully-stacked pyramids. There were posters everywhere, most of them advertising cheap cocoas and teas. The hams hung in fleshy splendour above the door, and were far too high for anyone to reach. The more we looked at them, the more desperate the whole thing seemed. What on earth had possessed him to do such a thing?

Local newspapers gave us nothing. His attempt to steal a side of bacon from a grocery shop was too ordinary, too drab, too pathetic, to justify even a line of copy; Edwardian papers were looking for something more eye-catching and sensational. Even the certificate from the magistrate's court seemed to be clipped and impatient. Gus was found guilty of committing a petty offence and sentenced to three months hard labour. He was really nothing more than a nuisance.

During the 1890s, the Independent Labour Party staged meetings on a patch of ground in Manchester called 'The Clough'. These meetings were never very well attended, but when Manchester council decided to ban them, the ILP had a cause. Claiming they were defending the rights of every freeborn Englishman, the organisers flouted the ban, and the publicity surrounding the case soon led to larger crowds. Finally, the police moved in. Several arrests were made, and Henry Brocklehurst, the chair of this ILP branch, was fined five pounds. He refused to pay the fine and local magistrates had no option but to commit him to Strangeways. Brocklehurst remained in prison a month and his account of the experience – 'I was In Prison' – appeared in the *Manchester Evening News* in 1897.

'I am now in the "Black Maria" bound for Her Majesty's Prison in Strangeways,' Brocklehurst told his readers, capturing something of what it must have been like for Gus. They rattled along in this tin can, its iron-rimmed wheels clattering over the irregular cobble stones. A ride that almost deafened him. 'Keep your heart up,' the prisoners would say as they sat inside, 'it's not for ever.' Every now and then, the van would stop, and they would try and guess the location, but they know well enough when Strangeways was reached. The light faded as they drove beneath its arch.

We learned that Gus was herded like other prisoners into a reception room, stripped naked, weighed and measured. All his valuables were recorded and a prison uniform handed out. He might be lucky and get a clean one. Then a hot bath and a perfunctory medical. Next, he was lined up and handed bed sheets. The prison rules were read, and he was marched off.

There were well over a thousand cells in Strangeways, each the same size. Each with its regulation layout - seven feet wide, thirteen feet long, eight feet high. Four whitewashed walls. At one end of the cell, there was a barred window made of ground glass. At the other, a black door. A table stood to the right of the door and a four-legged stool in the centre. In one corner, a small shelf carried a slate, a pencil, a Prayer Book, and Hymn Book, several religious tracts and a Bible. There was a small brush and comb, a saltcellar, a bar of soap, a drinking can, and a wooden spoon. A blue *papier-mâché* jug and matching bowl sat on the floor. The prison regulations were hung from a peg.

Gus was fed a pint of meal porridge and given a loaf of bread, and that was it. No more treats. Left alone for the first time, he began to face the horror that would soon possess him. The hardest punishment of all. What they called the 'Separate System'. A system that was simple, deadly and designed to break a man's spirit. Prisoners would be isolated and cut off from the world. All forms of communication would stop, and they would be forced to reflect on their lives and come to a state of repentance.

Back in the 1840s, Dickens came across this kind of thing in America, and saw what it could do. The American prison operated on harsher lines than Strangeways, but worked on the same principle: the breaking of a man's spirit; the bruising of a man's mind. 'I am very glad to hear your time is nearly out,' Dickens said to an ex-sailor like Gus who had served eleven years in solitary confinement. There was no reply. The man stared at his hands. 'Does he never look men in the face,' Dickens asked.

You had to steel yourself to survive. Every night would be the same. At eight o'clock, Gus would lay down on a 'plank bed', a hard wooden frame with a wooden pillow, and for the first two months he would have nothing more than two sheets and a blanket. After that, he would be allowed a mattress, but even a minor infringement of the prison rules would lead to its withdrawal. The plank bed was as hard as a rock and designed to hurt. If Gus slept on his side, it would chafe his hips. If he slept on his stomach, it would bruise his knees. Lying on his back, it tore at his shoulders and heels. Sleep was never easy, but there was no escaping the bed; it offered its own form of punishment, and Gus would have to endure it every night. When he struggled to his feet in the morning, his whole body ached.

The bell rang at six. This was a sign to dress, to wash his face, roll his bedclothes and wait. When the door opened, he would place a tin can outside and this would be filled with water. All slops were taken away and the warder threw in a batch of oakum. Gus would start to unravel the fibres, sitting alone in his cell, picking away. A task that was meant to clear the mind and aid reflection. He would ponder his life, think about his past, repent his wrongdoings. If the system worked, he would turn into a better man. *I will endeavour to make amends for my past conduct.*

Day by day, the system unpicked him, just as surely as he unpicked the oakum. It slowly unravelled his character and loosened his will. For all the mind-numbing tedium of the work, it offered employment, a way of filling time. He would sit for hours, untying the knots, untwisting the rope, pulling out strands. Come Sunday, even this was denied, and the hard grip of an English Sabbath took hold.

Meals were served at 7.30, 12 and 6, but the food was poor and deliberately designed to weaken a man's body. After two days, Gus would feel its effects, and by the end of the first week, he would struggle to walk. Starvation diets led to illness, sometimes to death, and the sound of men coughing never stopped. Treatment by prison doctors was offhand, and men counted themselves lucky to survive. And then, having brought prisoners to the edge of physical collapse, the meals improved.

Each morning at 8.30, Gus would be marched to the chapel. An hour later, he went to the exercise yard and was ordered to run in circles. No word spoken. Throughout it all, he was watched by warders, and any attempt to talk would be severely punished. Around 11.15, he would face a daily 'Inspection'. The door would be flung open and he would stand to attention, an official would peer in and the door would shut.

All contact with the outside world was forbidden. The sound of Manchester drifted in, especially at night, but to all intents and purposes he was becoming 'a dead man in a dead universe'. It was Brocklehurst's phrase. Gus was allowed no letters, no visits or contacts with family and friends. Warders never talked to him but barked orders. Every fortnight, he was marched to the basement, armed with a thin towel and a bar of soap, and here he would squat in two inches of grey water.

Men found ways to survive. Messages were written on walls; clever signs were invented, and some of the older prisoners were skilled ventriloquists. Messages were tapped on pipes. In chapel, they talked as best they could under the cover of hymns. The most popular dodge was to scratch messages on metal plates. 'Cheer up!', 'Buck up!', 'It won't be forever!' 'The man that calls himself happy in this ******* place must be a ****** fool!'

His years at sea helped. Gus knew the meaning of hardship. But did anyone come out of this unscarred? Dickens doubted it. He had seen the damage on the face of every prisoner. 'I know not what to liken it to,' he said, 'It had something of that strained attention which we see upon the faces of the blind and deaf, mingled with a kind of horror, as though they had all been secretly terrified.' He asked one warder how the prisoners felt on their final day. 'They can't sign their names to the book,' the warder said, 'Sometimes can't even hold the pen . . . When they get outside the gate, they stop, and look first one way and then the other; not knowing which way to take. Sometimes they stagger as if they were drunk, and sometimes are forced to lean against the fence.'

On his last day, Gus was told to clean his cell. He rolled up his rug and blankets, towels and sheets, and marched to the Discharge Room. He swapped his prison boots for his shoes, and was then weighed. Then he was pushed into a cubicle and told to dress. A quick breakfast, the return of valuables, and the gates opened.

Chapter 44: 1911

Perhaps the old smile had gone. The old jauntiness. Now, there would be a corner of his life that was always dark; a place that Strangeways had hollowed out. We pictured him leaning against the prison wall, blinking in the daylight, trying to gather his thoughts. Then he would slip away.

Before Strangeways, our last sighting of Gus had been in 1902 when he came back to England after the Boer War. It was hard to reconcile the khaki cavalier of those days with the broken man now. Back in 1902, he had taken Annie to Gainford where Bro recorded their arrival. Piecing together the fragmentary clues, we saw that Gus had contrived a meeting with Agnes in Manchester, and that Annie had somehow found out. In an attempt to placate her and avoid scandal, Gus's family had taken her side, and Gus's mother had urged her to seek revenge – *if I was you, I would do my worst to him, I think his conduct disgraceful.*

Annie remained close to the Bowen family. She was particularly close to Emily, and we found Emily in 1911 working as the Matron in a miner's hospital at Skinningrove. Beezie was with her, working as a probationary nurse. Here were Gus's sister and daughter only half a mile from Annie, all of them good friends. *Dear Annie, Did you know I had Beezie as my probationer. It is so nice for us both, and she has grown such a nice useful girl . . . Bee makes one go out every day. We have just been in the woods getting honeysuckle.*

The letters chattered away. *Dear Annie, If you care to come down on Sunday I shall be very pleased to see you. Nurse W is going to be away for the weekend – so I thought we could have a good long chat.*

Dear Annie, For goodness sake get out of that smoke! If you don't come today come tomorrow and don't buy any plum puddings – I have a large one ready to boil up.

My dear Annie, I was sorry you did not get down on Sunday, although I know the weather was not promising. I had a nice hot tea ready for you – fish cakes – jelly and other things.

Miner's Hospital: Emily on back row with book; Beezie on far right

Out of the blue, we came across a photo of the miner's hospital with staff and patients outside. We had several photos of Beezie and one of the nurses was obviously her. I pointed to the matronly figure in the middle.

'This must be Emily.'

She was standing before us, a book tucked under her arm, and a pair of spectacles on her nose. A slim figure facing the camera and projecting all her matronly authority, taking care to maintain her guard, never letting it slip. The professional Emily. There was no trace of the young woman who had once lived wild. Nothing of the older woman who joked and gossiped. She had made a life for herself, and she was living it.

We had several photographs of the hospital. It sat in a deep valley. Hardly anything remained of the woods and primroses that had once been there, apart from a patchwork of allotment gardens where miners went on summer evenings to feed their hens and smoke pipes. Above them, the chimneys and towers of nearby ironworks dominated the skyline. This was the place where Annie and Emily stayed close, and met on rainy Sundays to eat their fish cakes and jelly.

When we came to look for Craufurd and Hannah in the 1911 census, we found Hannah in Skelton. She was back in the cottage that Craufurd painted fifty years before. A moment of genuine sadness. He had gone. By 1911, he would have been in his late seventies, and we remembered that his health had never been good. His letters to Robert Edleston in 1900 talked of dying, and later letters continued the story.

'Please kindly excuse the very large number of mistakes in my last letter,' he explained in March of 1908, when he was unwell. 'I am quite sure you would not wonder if you knew how bothered I was at the time – I wish I had waited until the fearful din was over. This is a fearful house. When I shut the <u>two</u> doors of the room I was writing in the noise of the wind nearly blew me off my chair, and it was blowing very big guns at the time. This and other things completely confounded me.'

There was another letter that had been written four weeks later. 'I hope shortly to write at length and tell you about our doings in this part of the world but I will not attempt it now as I had a very trying but very happy day yesterday in spite of a fit which threw me rather on my beam ends a few days ago but is gradually wearing off.'

There were more fits and Edleston sent for a doctor. 'I was greatly puzzled and could not the least conjecture the object of Dr Adams' call,' Craufurd told him, 'until he explained to me that he was a medical man . . . I have just had my forty winks and my midday cup of tea and my head now seems much clearer. I think I have taken all in now . . . Dr Adams has told me about many things of the utmost importance which I should never have known had he not called and seen me. What a charming man Dr Adams is! It does one good to have a chat with a man like him. I am now in great hopes that his advice which seems excellent may with God's Blessing produce a very considerable change for the better in my health which lately has been deplorably bad . . . The Summer will soon be over and dark gloomy 'indoor' days will be with us again.'

He never lasted the winter. We checked the records. Craufurd died only three months later and Hannah arranged the funeral. He was buried in Skelton. Friends and parishioners joined the cortege as it left Bolam and made its slow way to Gainford; the walk that Craufurd made his own. His body was taken by train to Skelton. Hannah copied a brief report of the funeral and sent it to her children. 'To be placed in your Bible,' she said. One copy reached Greg in Calcutta and was passed through the family until it came to Cindy. The report talked of Craufurd's early years in Norfolk, his theological training, his love of music and astronomy, his restoration of Bolam Church, and his 'quiet ministry'.

So Hannah came home. We found her in Pear Tree Cottage where she had lived as a girl, and the circle of life was complete. It was five minutes' drive from Brotton, and we stopped one day to gaze at the house. She must have kept Craufurd's watercolour. That night, we looked at it again. There was Craufurd standing on the frosty common, almost in a greeting. 'Come in!' he seemed to smile, 'You've had a long journey.'

The newspaper report that Hannah sent to her children listed the mourners at Craufurd's funeral, and Gus was not among them. At one point, we had archivists looking for him in every corner of the globe; some in India, some in Australia, some in America, and some in Canada. Cindy was doing her best to find him in South Africa. His absence at his father's funeral had only strengthened our conviction that he had emigrated, but now we knew the truth. Strangeways saw to that.

The prison was in Manchester and we recalled the memorandum sent to Annie from someone in the Chief Constable's Office there. Everything pointed that way. So we went back to the 1911 census, this time looking for Agnes. There was no one called Agnes McWilliam in Manchester, but amazingly we found her. She was staying with a married couple and calling herself Agnes Bowen. She and Gus had married, or so it seemed. We backtracked through the records and found no evidence of their marriage, so it was anybody's guess if the name was real. But married or not, they had two daughters: one called Stella and the other Frances. According to the census, a third child had died.

Stella had been born in 1902, shortly before Gus returned from the Boer War. We found her birth in the indexes and sent for a certificate. When it arrived, we saw that she was born on May 30th 1902, and this sent us back to Gus's army record. He served in South Africa from March 1901 to August 1902. The birth certificate named him as Stella's father, but it was manifestly impossible. Whilst he was away, Agnes had met another man, and a child had been conceived. Needless to say, her lover did not appear on the certificate.

We remembered how Gus's mother had given Annie an account of his movements. That fateful weekend when he went to Manchester and learned the truth: *His money was sent on to Gainford - £26/10/3. He came to Gainford a week last Saturday, took £10, went to Manchester, telegraphed on Tuesday for £5 more to be sent by wire.* Agnes's baby was four months old when Gus arrived in Manchester, and how he reacted is anyone's guess. Most men would have left her. A man's sexual desire was accepted - 'He is only sowing his wild oats' - and throughout life, Gus lived by this creed. A man was a man and that was that. But 'we never hear it carelessly or complacently asserted of a young woman,' one feminist laughed, 'that "she is only sowing her wild oats."' The double standard. Women were expected to live a purer life and were judged by stricter rules.

Against all odds, Gus never abandoned her. We could only speculate on how they faced one another, and how he reacted to her affair. They had exchanged letters whilst he was away in South Africa, so Agnes may have told him. We knew that he had tried to send her his pay, and Annie had stopped it. After that, Agnes would have struggled to survive, so living with another man was her way of getting by.

When Gus came back, he spent a few days with Annie, but devised a cunning plan to see Agnes. Perhaps he was hoping to keep things going as usual? Two women in his life, conveniently separated. Yet something happened that weekend. We had always sensed it, long before we knew anything about Agnes's affair, or indeed the baby. The elaborate charade that had been going for years was suddenly and inexplicably jettisoned. Gus stayed with Agnes, and this explained the consternation of his family and their need to support Annie. They could see that Gus had finally deserted them, and his mother urged Annie to take some revenge. *Do your worst to him*. He had abandoned them, and they were casting him off.

So he forgave Agnes and accepted the child. They called her Stella and no one in the family knew she was the daughter of another man. Their second daughter came along a few years later and was called Frances Augusta, the girl who, in the fullness of time, would become Pat and Grace's mother. Stella had been born in 'Rosamond Street East', one of the poorer streets in Manchester. Several photographs were taken in the 1950s, just a few years before it disappeared. There were maps too and street plans, several trade directories and census records, and we got a flavour. Agnes was living at the end of the street, so it was here that Gus must have joined her. Their house was a corner property, occupied by an Irish family who rented rooms to married couples. There was a separate apartment for a music teacher from Germany and we noticed that several European families were nearby. There was Isidor Liebermann, a watchmaker from Austria, and further down, Gustave von Ochlhaffen, a decorator and second-generation immigrant.

Many of the buildings were ordinary lodging houses, packed with people. It felt like a coral reef teeming with life, a place where a single woman like Agnes could survive. And she was not the only one. There was Ann Dentith, an artist's model, Minnie Howard, a confectioner's assistant, Harriett Scott, a tobacco-pouch maker, Emily Ogden, a mantle-maker, and Annie Graham, a shirt-maker. None of them seemed to stay long. I compared censuses and saw how they swam in and out. It was a good place to live, a good place to love, and a good place to hide. Gus and Agnes kept moving too, like the rest, swimming from one coral reef to another.

Their second child was born in Belmont Terrace, a tiny street that was tucked away behind one of Manchester's main thoroughfares. The street itself had long since disappeared, but we could see it on old maps. There were relatively large houses on one side and tiny houses on the other, and it came as no surprise to find that Gus and Agnes were on the poorer side. Their second daughter, Frances, was born here, and the local registrar was Emmeline Pankhurst. She signed their certificate. 'My district was in a working-class quarter,' she remembered, and 'it was touching to observe how glad the women were to have a woman registrar to go to. They used to tell me their stories, dreadful stories some of them, and all of them pathetic . . . I was shocked to be reminded over and over again of the little respect there was in the world for women and children.'

Gus and Agnes were here, hiding from Annie. She was asking friends and family to keep a lookout for them. Everyone knew that she craved information. *Auntie knows this street in Manchester very well,* someone said in 1906. Whenever a promising lead surfaced, she would contact local people and enlist their help. *Mrs Bowen I hasten to inform you as promised, that both are at No. 30, Sincerely yours, Cavin Stephens.*

Then, in 1906 she gave up. The year when she probably met Frank, and the year too when she made her will. At the beginning of the document, she described herself as 'the wife of Charles Augustine Arthur Bowen (Mariner)', and that was it. She never mentioned him again. In the event of her death, all her personal effects would go to Lydia Westwood, a spinster in Darlington, and whatever remained of her property and shares would go to Harry, her youngest brother. Harry had disappeared many years before, so her executors were told to place advertisements in newspapers and encourage him to come forward. If they failed, her estate would go to one of her nephews. Needless it to say, not a penny went to Gus.

He may not have known it, but he had been slapped.

Chapter 45: Soldier

One of the first photographs that Grace showed me turned out to be the last one we ever saw of Gus. Taken a few years after Strangeways, it showed him in uniform, quite obviously from the First World War. He was standing in a photographic studio, his hand resting gently on a frail table, his legs akimbo, almost as if some artistic sergeant major in the background has whispered, 'Stand easy!' We tried to see the details. There was a regimental badge on his cap, but Gus was too far away, and it was difficult to decipher. The image was familiar and universal. There he stood, ready for battle, like all the soldiers I had seen in history books, waving cheerily as they boarded trains, marching jauntily along French roads, and then staring back from the muddy horror of the trenches with the sullen look of dead men. He sported a moustache, all waxed and curled; the kind of thing much favoured by sergeant majors. And there he stood, his head held high, his neck stretched.

A proud, brittle man, his face half hidden beneath the peak of his cap. There was no doubt about it, he was getting older. His neck was looking scrawny and he seemed to be flexing himself for an ill-judged fight. We thought the uniform might even be fake. That Gus had popped into a photographic studio, donned a uniform and commissioned a picture, just to impress the ladies. A friend thought otherwise. It looked genuine, he said. The badge on Gus's cap was from the Royal Engineers and the uniform fitted. And he was right. It fitted like a glove. Nice and trim on the shoulders, sleeves the right length, trousers and leggings just so. We had giggled at the idea of a faked job, but we were wrong.

Gus in World War 1 Uniform

A large number of military records had been destroyed during the Second World War, so it was a matter of chance if we could find him. About two-thirds of pension and service records had been destroyed by the Luftwaffe. Our next step was to search medal records, but there was nothing there. Only one record seemed promising - an index card for a man called Charles A. Bowen, but it was sparse. The little information it offered was in some form of shorthand and stripped of meaning.

Google pointed us to 'The Great War Forum' run by an intrepid band of military historians who called themselves the 'Old Sweats'. I began telling them about Gus's history – his age, birthplace, service in the Boer War, years as a sailor, even his time in prison. Could they help? Perhaps the index card we found was really him? I attached his photo and next day one of them replied. 'Hi Tony, and welcome to the Forum! If you're looking at the "MIC of 237749, Spr Charles A Bowen", then I'm afraid his middle name was Alfred and he was born in Oxford c.1899.'

At least he had saved us months of searching. He tempered our disappointment with a new lead. There was another record for a 'Chas. Arthur Bowen of "G" Depot Coy, Royal Engineers' who had been awarded a Silver War Badge, and this suggested that he had been invalided out at some point during the war. It could be Gus.

Over the next few days, we kept watching the forum. Almost 140 members of the 'Old Sweats' had read our request and spent time looking at the photo, but no one was able to give us any information. So this left one possibility. Our next step would be to find the full Medal Roll of the Royal Engineers in the National Archive. If Sapper Charles Arthur Bowen turned out to be Gus, it might tell us something about his military unit. Once we had that, we could track his movements during the war, but the chances were slim. According to the guidebook, some Medal Rolls were more detailed than others, and the Royal Engineers had a reputation for being the worst. So hardly anything survives.

We already had press cuttings that Annie kept from the Boer War. She had snipped them from various newspapers and then stored them. None of them mentioned Gus in person, but it was obvious she was tracking him. She kept nothing from the Great War. The carnage on the Western Front was a distraction, and the closest hostilities ever came to her was a ghostly Zeppelin raid over Redcar. *Saw a Zeppelin on the 2nd May 1916 Tuesday evening 10.50 p.m. over the High Street, Redcar.* It passed overhead, she noted its transit, and that was it. She said nothing about her feelings, the excited talk of neighbours, or the response of local defence units.

We never found Gus's military record, apart from an enigmatic line that had been added to his Attestation Papers. It suggested he had been called up in 1917 – 'Called for under number 17605/17d/-4-6-17.' The uniform in the photograph certainly fitted, and we knew that he hankered after military life, so it was perfectly reasonable to assume he answered the call. The cap badge pointed to the Royal Engineers, but this was as far as we got. Perhaps he served in the trenches? Perhaps he remained in England? Or perhaps he won a medal?

Perhaps it was the war, but I began thinking about death. As long as Gus remained in England, we could still find him. His death would create a record. And once we found that, we might be able to track him further back, so we began moving through the death lists, year by year, quarter by quarter, and sometimes it felt unwholesome, as if we were lifting lids on coffins. I still have the notes. Each quarter of every year crossed off.

Chapter 46: Eccles Row

'I was never taken as a child,' Pat admitted.

I had rung her to pass on the news, and began by asking if she knew anything about Blackburn.

'I went to Blackburn as a teenager,' she said, 'But I might have told you this?'

'No, I don't think so.'

'Mom and I spent the summer in England. It was 1955. The trip was supposed to help Auntie Stella who was blind. Mom and Stella's relationship was always stormy.' She laughed and paused.

'Do you know where Gus and Agnes lived?' I asked.

'A cousin told me. Their house was near the canal. The street was called Eccles Row, and I think it was rough.'

There was a brief silence.

'Do you know how he died?' she asked. And, of course, I did

A few weeks before, Gill and I had gone to Blackburn. We parked the car, walked a few yards along a busy road, and came to a bridge over the canal. Standing beneath it, we could hear the roar and thunder of traffic overhead, but here in the shadow of the bridge the world was secret. Light was bouncing off the green water and shimmering on its underbelly.

Twenty yards off, we could see a man who seemed to be

exploring the place like us. He was checking a map and gazing around, obviously looking for clues. Suddenly, he folded the map, stuffed it in his rucksack, and quickly disappeared. Two joggers bounced by and nodded. A man who was obviously local watched his dog take a leisurely pee against an interpretative panel; the whole length of the Liverpool-Leeds Canal had been restored and turned into a heritage attraction.

'This is Brewery Bridge,' I said, pointing to a handsome structure that had been disfigured by graffiti. 'It led to Eccles Row on one side, and Primrose Row on the other.' We left the towpath and walked up. I leaned on the bridge's wall and looked out. The air was clear and bright, and we could see far beyond the town. There were hills and fields encircling Blackburn. 'One thing I remember my mother telling me,' Pat said in an email, 'was Gus's favourite Bible verse. It was, "I will lift mine eyes unto the hills from whence cometh my help."'

Eccles Row had gone, buried beneath a modern supermarket. And there was not much left of the surrounding area either; the world that Gus and Agnes had known in the 1920s. All of it rubbed out. Every single brick. Bulldozed away in the slum clearances of the 1970s. As chance would have it, I knew someone who worked in Blackburn library and enlisted her help. I told her about Gus and Agnes and how they moved to Blackburn during the 1920s. Could she track them? We thought they lived in Eccles Row. She knew perfectly well what sources to use, and a few days later got back to me. She had gone through the town's electoral registers and found them for ten successive years:

> In 1918: Gus and Agnes living at No. 31 Eccles Row.
> In 1919: the same.
> In 1920: the same.
> In 1921: only Agnes listed, but her name crossed out.
> In 1922: both of them listed.
> In 1923: both still there.

In 1924: both still there.

In 1925: both still listed, but Gus's name crossed out.

In 1926: both still listed, but Gus's name crossed out.

In 1927: only Agnes listed.

In 1928: only Agnes listed.

It was hard to know what it meant. Towards the end of the war, they had moved to Blackburn. They had rented a house in Eccles Row, less than fifty yards from where we were standing, but during that time, they were sometimes there and sometimes not. There was a map to accompany the electoral lists, and a rough star had been added to show the house. The map was dated 1931. They lived towards the end of Eccles Row. Across the street, there was a huge cotton mill that must have cast a heavy shadow. According to newspapers, Eccles Row had been built in the 1840s and was a primitive affair, with little in the way of running water and sanitation, at least in the early years. We pulled out another map from the 1970s and saw that it had gone.

Blackburn had a brief spell of prosperity after the First World War and for three contented years the cotton industry was back on its feet, ready to do business with the world. We wondered why Gus and Agnes came to the town, and here was the answer. Another possibility was that Gus was running. Landing jobs in Manchester would have been tricky after his spell in prison. Finding a house in Eccles Row that was cheap and affordable, and well hidden from people who knew him, made simple sense. What little money they had went on binges.

'Was there any mention of my grandmother's alcoholism?' Pat asked, quite out of the blue.

I was taken aback. 'Well, yes. We have a letter that talks of Agnes being drunk. Actually it says she was *a vile drunken hag*. But I always thought it was an insult.'

'No. My grandmother had a problem. My mother told me how she came back one day to Eccles Row. She saw a pile of rags in the street, but when she got closer, she realised it was Agnes, dead drunk in the gutter.' There was a brief silence, and I wondered if Pat was having doubts about telling me this. It was only momentary and she breezed on. 'Agnes hid her bottles everywhere. My brother told me everything. Actually, he liked her. She was jolly and good fun. She used to wait for the milkman and place illegal bets.'

I chuckled too.

'My mother rejected that. She refused to have a drop of liquor in the house.'

Frances

Stella was different. By all accounts, she was happy-go-lucky, warm-hearted and hospitable, earthy and never much bothered with notions of respectability. She smoked like a chimney and was as tough as old shoe-leather. Pat's mother, Frances, was different. Cut from finer cloth. She was Gus and Annie's second child, and she rejected their drinking and betting, their loose sexuality and poverty, their hand-to-mouth existence. Somewhere in the hungry belly of the 1920s, she walked away from Eccles Row and never came back.

Towards the end of the afternoon, Gill and I came across a coffee shop in Blackburn. The place was winding down, but we sat by the window as they mopped the floor. I pulled out a sheet of paper and pointed to a corner.

'It's exactly twenty years.'

It was 1922. Gus and Agnes had been together twenty years. When he returned from the Boer War in 1902, he found Agnes living with another man, but forgave her and accepted Stella as his own. He left Annie and moved in with Agnes and, crazy as it sounded, they were still together twenty years later. In 1922, they marked their anniversary by getting married. It was a bigamous marriage in Blackburn Registry Office, located in Cardwell Place. The street had little to offer. One or two buildings were left, surviving as best they could, but most were gone, including the Registry itself. A Victorian pub was still holding its head up, doing its best to survive ('Under New Management'), and across the way there was a taxi office, a fast food outlet and a newsagents. None of them looked prosperous.

Gus was fifty-four, Agnes fifty-seven. Ideal candidates for bigamy. Two people who were getting on in life and willing to take a chance. As Gus filled out the certificate, he described himself as a 'Fire Sprinkler Pipe Fitter (Journeyman)' and his days as a sailor were obviously over. He may have given up the sea, but he had not given up on Agnes. Against all the odds, he was still with her.

Well, almost. I pointed to 1921. It was the first year that Gus was missing, or at least not listed. Was he coming and going from Eccles Row, living there sometimes and sometimes not? A little later, he was crossed out altogether. *The Representation of the*

People Act, 1918, with Explanatory Notes was an exhaustive analysis of the electoral system at that time. It ran to 804 pages, and I did my best to wade through it. Women were now entitled to vote and this explained why Agnes was listed. The electoral registers were updated every year so we could track their movements. Lastly, the new qualification meant that any adult living in a constituency, for at least six months or more, was entitled to vote. So the years when Gus was missing, or indeed crossed out, probably meant that he had left.

Pat sent a parcel of documents. One of them was an official form that had been filled out by Agnes in 1919, allowing Frances to leave school and start work when she was fourteen. By 1921, Stella was nineteen and Frances sixteen, and both were working. These were the depression years. So, whilst Gus was forced to leave Blackburn and find work elsewhere, the girls and Agnes remained.

It fitted. 1921 heralded the start of the Depression. Gus was forced to leave the town as one cotton mill after another closed, and there was no longer a call for fire sprinklers. He hit the road. There was nothing particularly difficult in this for he had been hitting the road and turning corners all his life. The noble art of loafing.

'I was staying with my Dad just after Mom died,' Pat said, 'There was a narrow drawer beside my Mom's bed. Inside, there was a letter from Gus. It was June 1st, 1923, Mom's 18th. It was beautiful. He encouraged her to be a woman of good moral character.' We both held our breath, aware of the irony. 'I guess she felt it was very precious because she always kept it. It remained in her bedside drawer all those years, right until her death. I kept the letter for several years and thought it was in a suitcase, but I'm sorry to say, I can't find it.'

'Do you know where Gus was writing from?'

'Dewsbury. I found the house. I even took a photo, but only of the door. Why on earth I would take a photo of the door and not the house, I don't know. This might have been the trip when I was taking pictures of doors. He was staying at 5, Eightlands Rd, Dewsbury.'

So, there were times in the 1920s when Gus and Agnes were separated. There may have been arguments, sometimes even affairs, because they tested each other. Or perhaps it was just the hard knuckle of life, hitting them full in the face? In truth, it was impossible to tell. But one thing was certain – they were coming apart.

Chapter 47: Miracles

'Their hearts glowed with the expectation and conviction that this was destined to be the last revival before the coming of the Lord.'

Signs and wonders. A global manifestation of divine power. In the early years of the twentieth century, thousands of Christians found themselves newly 'baptised in the Holy Ghost'. Ecstatic converts experienced what they called an 'infilling of spirit', and talked of a fire falling from heaven, purifying and cleansing. Out of this fire came signs and wonders. Some talked in tongues, some had visions, some turned to prophesy, and some to healing. The Asuza-Street Mission in Los Angeles was one manifestation. The great Welsh Revival another. Remarkable demonstrations of divine power that were happening everywhere.

Particularly in Sunderland. The Rev. Alexander Boddy, vicar of All Saints Church in Monkwearmouth, hosted an annual convention that ran between 1908 and 1914. It became the focus for the newly emerging Pentecostal movement, and advertised itself as a spiritual holiday destination: 'Pentecost with Signs. To all in Sympathy: Six Days' Convention in Sunderland: June 6th to 11th. Whitsun Holidays. Cheap excursions.'

In July 1910, the *Newcastle Journal* found a newsletter from the Sunderland group and began poking gentle fun. Apparently, the Second Advent might happen at any moment: 'Possibly next year, but if the Lord tarries, we may have a large tent for the evening gatherings.' Followers were advised to book early: 'Many visitors now make their arrangements in advance for the following year as regards their rooms, subject always to the coming of the Lord before the next Whitsuntide Convention.' The apocalypse could not guarantee them refunds. In May 1913, the *Daily Mirror* weighed in with a full-page photograph, showing converts taking part in dramatic rituals of baptism. 'WOMAN FALLS PROSTRATE AFTER HER IMMERSION IN THE WATER. Extraordinary scenes at Roker, near Sunderland.'

The Sunderland Conventions continued until 1914, when the world ended, although not as most converts expected. That December, German warships bombarded Hartlepool only a few miles down the coast, and it was too dangerous to carry on. In the years that followed, the movement lost momentum, but in 1925 there was a second revival. George and Stephen Jeffreys stepped forward and established what they called the 'Elim Foursquare Gospel Alliance'.

'How did your Mam and Dad first meet?' I asked. We were sitting in Grace's living room. Pat was there too. Their mother, Frances, had married a charismatic evangelist in the Pentecostal movement, and it seemed incredible. We were struggling to understand how an earnest and dynamic young man called Hubert Entwisle, one of the rising stars of the Elim Church, had fallen for the daughter of a reprobate old couple like Gus and Agnes.

'He adored her,' Grace said, 'He was head over heels in love with her.'

It was as simple as that. Almost a year later, Dan Entwisle, the great-grandson of Gus, came across a box of tapes in his father's study, 'I don't know if you are interested,' he said, 'but one of them is a recording of Hubert when he was interviewed by my Dad in the

1980s.'

Hubert was talking about his early days with Frances.

'And the first time I went for Frances,' he said.

'To her house? In Eccles Row?' his son checked.

'Yeah, Easter Monday.'

I couldn't help but touch Gill's arm, for I knew what was coming.

'I remember knocking at the door and this tall man came . . .'

It was Gus.

'He said, "Good morning, young man, I think I know why you're here." She'd evidently tipped the old man off that I was probably coming! And he invited me in and said, "Would you like a cup of tea?" He was very nice.'

So here we were, after all the letters and censuses, the crew agreements and newspapers, listening to a man who talked with Gus.

'Then I heard the old girl coming down the stairs,' Hubert went on, 'Old Mother Gun, you know! Bumpety, bumpety. My heart began to thump! I could get on with the old man. He was great . . .'

But Agnes was different. She stormed into the room and berated him:

'"Well, what are you here for?"

"Well, I'm here for Frances."

"Where are you going?"

"We're going to a convention at Preston."'

He managed to pacify her, and she finally relented.

'I got on well with them from then onwards. But at first, she was a rather formidable-looking lady, I can tell you. I was scared to death of her.'

'Was she good looking?'

'Pretty much.'

'Putting on the Duchess' was how he described it. The way Agnes held her head up and swept through life. It impressed Hubert, but Frances rejected all that, and her rejection was not just the rebellious act of a young woman kicking against her parents, but the struggle of a lifetime. She locked her past away and never talked of it. It was a box that was never opened.

Her marriage to Hubert was her first step into a new world. Pat and Grace showed us a lovely photograph of their father. He was the son of a skilled worker in Blackburn and undeniably dashing. A little on the short side, but attractive and full of fun. And behind his handsome face, and thick curly hair, we saw a man with bright eyes. Someone who had an appetite for life. The Elim Church would be his rocket ship that would launch him into orbit. And we could see how the church welcomed him, and saw his potential. Here was a young man with a sharp intellect, a strong voice, a winning smile, a touch of charisma.

Hubert

Thomas Myerscough lived in Preston, five miles from

Blackburn, and spent his life organising Pentecostal missions to the Belgian Congo. Hubert's sister, Amy, was a recruit and left for Africa in 1926. Hubert was another *protégé*, but instead of going abroad, he joined the Elim Bible College in London, and by 1925, was pastor in a new church in Essex. Here, he proposed to Frances.

'So I said to her one day, "Look, Frances, why go home?" She wasn't too happy at home with her sister. Stella could be very awkward, very violent, and she could be very nice too. And I said, "There's no reason. Let's get married. Nothing to stop us!"'

Neither Gus nor Agnes attended the ceremony. Back in 1923, Gus had urged her to live a virtuous life, and she was doing it. The classic loafer and charmer had written from Dewsbury. A man living in lodgings, cut off from family and friends, and chasing dead-end jobs. He was doing his best to survive, and what Strangeways started in 1911, the depression years were finishing. He was becoming unpicked. Gus and Hubert liked one another, but this charismatic evangelist was taking his daughter away. More than that, he was everything that Gus could never be. There might have been a time, if the cards had fallen right, but the time had passed. Gus was scrabbling for work whilst Hubert was flying high; sitting in his rocket, going to the moon.

Hubert became a major figure in the front line of the Elim movement and worked alongside Stephen Jeffreys, its leader. Together, they swept through Essex. A journalist from the *Essex Chronicle* caught the fervour: 'The services are of a simple but striking nature. People are invited on to the large platform and . . . Pastor Jeffreys invites them to sit on a chair, over which he stands. Leaning over, he presses both his hands to the forehead of the person . . . All through the procedure, hymns of praise and devotion are sung.'

Miraculous cures followed. A deaf girl could suddenly hear; a man with a withered arm could lift a chair, an ulcerated leg was cleansed, a blind boy could see. 'God has sent me to Chelmsford,' Jeffreys proclaimed, 'to tell you of the coming of Jesus. He is coming, and you will soon know it . . . I stand for the full gospel, salvation, the baptism of the Holy Ghost, and the imminent return of the Lord.'

Then they swept north, first to Hull and Grimsby, and then to the Durham coalmining district:

THE EVANGELISTIC AND DIVINE HEALING CAMPAIGN
Conducted by Pastor Stephen Jeffreys
Is being transferred to
BISHOP AUCKLAND TOWN HALL
THE BLIND SEE, THE LAME WALK, THE DEAF HEAR, THE DUMB SPEAK
Come – Bring Your Suffering Ones
Jesus Christ, the same yesterday, today and forever. All Seats Free.

It was one of the great revivals of the age. 'The whole town, and villages for twenty miles around seemed to be gripped by the power of God. Some remarkable miracles of healing occurred. Congregations would queue up two hours beforehand, police having to control the crowds. . . As many as 1500 sometimes had to be turned away.'

The Bishop of Durham was horrified. His official palace was located in Bishop Auckland, and he could see what was happening. As his congregations dwindled, sensational movements like this flourished, and on March 19th, he wrote to *The Times:* 'Outside my gates, in the Town Hall of Bishop Auckland, a Faith-Healing Mission has been running through the familiar cycle – wide advertisement, waxing crowds, intense excitement, reported cures, rumours (steadily growing) of failures.' He contrasted this hysteria with the poverty and suffering of the area, and doubted it would do any good: 'In due course the missioner will betake himself elsewhere, the memory of his visit will fade, and the health statistics of the district will remain unaffected by his healing triumphs.' The world was plagued, he said, with 'the paradoxes of fanaticism', and a week later, he was dismayed to find that one of his domestic servants had been converted. If this was not enough, three more servants followed. 'A MAD WORLD!' one provincial newspaper screamed.

People were agitated. There would be weeks of intense emotion, thousands would flock to Jeffreys's meetings, reports of miraculous cures would spread like wildfire, and the whirlwind would sweep on. One prominent leader of the Pentecostal movement came to Bishop Auckland and found Hubert holding the fort: 'Those meetings were decidedly informal judged by the traditional standards of religious decorum,' he said. 'I dropped in one night a few months later, when Mr Hubert Entwisle was carrying on the good work, and received somewhat of a shock when the congregation clapped at the close of a serious Bible reading.'

By the end of 1927, Jeffreys was in Sunderland, the spiritual home of the movement, and during September and October a series of spectacular meetings were held in Victoria Hall. To begin with, the numbers were relatively small. Four hundred came to the first meeting, but soon there were immense crowds, and a contingent of mounted police had to be deployed. Three thousand people were packed into the hall each night, and three thousand left outside. 'An aged mother reclining on the flagstones was holding the place for a crippled son who could not spend the night in the open. A young woman resting on the pavement was ministering throughout the night to her sick husband.'

At the start of every meeting, fifty sick people would mount the platform.

'I only believe the Word of God,' Jeffreys told them, 'I never say I can heal anyone, but I say the Word of God stands. It is His Word that is taken, not mine. I take Him at His Word. I know I have been baptised with the Holy Ghost.'

When the sick were cured, and the congregation brought to fever pitch, Hubert stepped forward. 'Pastor Entwisle preceded his address by explaining the object of the gathering and the methods necessary to make it successful . . .' He faced a packed house. 'The greatest honour those present can pay to Pastor Jeffreys,' he said, 'is to re-consecrate yourselves to God tonight.' Everyone cheered. One local paper described the electric atmosphere as a strange mix of fervour and reverence. A number of converts were made, and Hubert worked his magic. 'I believe in faith,' he said, 'and Divine power to ensure our success, but I do not believe in fanaticism.'

When I talked with Grace and Pat, they were a little uncomfortable with this chapter in his life.

'He never liked that . . . ' Pat sighed and then hesitated, searching for the word.

'Fanaticism?'

'That's it.'

'It's the word he used.'

'Well, that's him,' she said, 'That's how I remember him. He preached and read from the Bible, but he never liked that stuff about speaking in tongues and miraculous healing.'

'I think he was riding the whirlwind. Your Mam too. But at least it took them both away from Gus and Agnes.'

Pat nodded and smiled, but I could see there was sadness. 'I don't think she ever got away, not really.'

Chapter 48: Worrying

At some point during the summer of 1928, Gus came back to Blackburn. He swallowed his pride and took a job as a door-to-door brush salesman. The family remembered his humiliation and the way he was breaking. He still trusted to his charm and hoped it would steer him through, but even his legendary charm was losing its power. Times were hard.

'That's why Agnes went to Sunderland,' Grace said, 'Gus couldn't put food on the table. She went there to eat.'

Agnes left him and lived with Frances and Hubert. Something was coming apart and everyone knew it. She was spending more and more time in Sunderland, and less and less with Gus. Her daughter was trying to make a new life for herself and Agnes – heavy drinker, occasional gambler, incorrigible flirt, the Duchess of Eccles Row – came along for the ride. Gus and Stella were left to fend for themselves.

'I've had a disastrous week,' Gus said, as he came home one Friday night. Stella wondered how the day had gone and he told her. The few orders he had managed to take the previous week had all been cancelled and he was bringing the brushes back. It was late September and the weather turning cold. A bad week. All his orders had been lost, and every day was as bad as the last. The long slog home, trudging past the gasometer on Grimshaw Road, the old wharf beside the canal, the Mission Room, and the deserted cotton mill.

'But what's the use of worrying?' he said, and slipped off his coat. That's how to do it. Make a joke of it and muddle through. The manly stoicism he learned as a sailor. And, who knows, it might still see him through? 'A man may be within an inch of losing his life, but he will not suffer himself to show it.'

The next day, he was in the house by himself. Stella was at work and the day becalmed. Gus was sixty. Sometimes there were pains in his arm. The weak heart that the army claimed to find all those years before was turning real. There had been several attacks. Nothing too serious, but enough to worry a man.

Then there were the deeper pains. The cold weather closing in; winter tightening its grip. Next week he would go out again, and try and make some sales, and then the week after that, and the week after that. Long days moving through the poverty-stricken streets; the hard faces of the housewives, their doors ajar, their eyes narrowing. The old charmer - 'We all thought so much of him'. Well, he couldn't work it anymore. Couldn't stop them from closing the doors. There was no need to look in a mirror. He could feel the sag in his body. He could see the way they looked at him. The way they turned away.

His father had been happy with a quiet life and the kind of pleasures that Gus never wanted. Not until now. Up on the mantelpiece he could see the photograph of Liebe, his favourite sister. She had slipped away, just like the rest. He had chosen a path, and the path had brought him here, to a lonely day in a silent house.

And the rest of his family? Greg and Emily? He didn't know. They had long since disappeared. He knew nothing of Greg's death: - 'Men do not die in Calcutta, they wither.' The city had finally claimed him. Emily was living with her married daughter and had finally retired from the miner's hospital, grabbing a few years of personal happiness. He knew of course that his mother was gone.

Nance - you know that after you - my mother is my first consideration. Yet even she had turned against him. *If I were you,* she told Annie, *I should do my worst to him. Don't think of anyone but yourself.*

Then there was Annie herself. He must have remembered the way she fussed. The care she took over her rented rooms. The same ritual everywhere: her little fireside rug, her bow-fronted chest of drawers, the photo of Gus on the mantelpiece. Her little stage set that travelled from place to place. And all he could do was stand there, leaning against the door, thinking of escape. *I see that you still think of Beezie?* Annie had wanted Beezie to live with them. And perhaps it might have worked? *She is a sweet dear good child and every one loves her.* Even Beezie had gone.

As the afternoon drew on, he lit the gas and made a meal. Eating was never easy, not alone. No sound of Agnes singing. The silence heavy. Everything running down. Not much of an appetite as it turned out. He put his knife and fork down, searched for a piece of paper and scribbled a note. Where was she now? Playing happy families in Sunderland? Saturday evening: the house bright and warm, laughter in the kitchen, Agnes singing, the smell of baking, Hubert writing his sermons. Coming out and joking with her? She would like that.

He searched for the coil and left the kitchen light on. The passage was dark. The stairs creaked. Once in the bedroom, he put the coil aside for the moment, took off his clothes, hung them all in the wardrobe, and climbed into his pyjamas. The view from the window was as dreary as ever; the idle mill across the way blocking out everything; no lights in the windows; no thrum of machinery; the world running down. He locked the window, tightened the catch, went to the door and closed it.

Stella saw the light burning in the kitchen and popped through to have a chat. There was no sign of Gus. Just an unwashed plate. At the bottom of the stairs, she called out, but there was no answer. At the top of the stairs, she tapped on his door. When she opened it, he lay on the bed, the rubber tube in his hand, and she could see that he had measured it. The coil was just long enough to reach the gas bracket. She held a handkerchief to her face, ran to the bracket, turned off the gas, and fumbled for the window. Their next-door neighbour came in and did his best. Doors and windows were thrown open and Gus carried out. But it was too late.

And at some point, Stella must have found his note and put it in her pocket. She didn't want the neighbours to see it, or the doctor. The message he had written. A telegram was sent to Sunderland; Agnes must come as soon as possible; Gus had killed himself. She must catch the earliest train. Both of them would be asked to give evidence the following Monday, and something had to be concocted.

By Monday, they were ready. Agnes told the Coroner about Gus's health. He had been ill for years, she said. There were sharp pains in his arm and he had suffered one or two worrying attacks. Sometimes he was low and depressed. Usually, she could lift him, but he had obviously hit a low point when she was away from home.

'On holiday with my daughter,' she explained.

For her part, Stella talked of the days leading up to his suicide. He hated that job. Gus had come home that Friday and talked of his awful week, and ended with a usual quip, 'What's the use of worrying?'

It offered a headline. The Coroner listened. He heard what they said and pronounced his verdict: 'Suicide by inhaling coal gas.' It was nothing less than the truth. But then added, 'There is no evidence to show the state of his mind'. It was Coroner-speak. He had listened to what Agnes and Stella had to say, and wondered if they were telling the truth, and he was right. They weren't.

When Agnes got back, Stella gave her the note. Even Pat and Grace knew nothing of it. Nor did we, but one day Dan phoned.

'Did you know,' he said, 'that he left a note?'

'What did it say?'

'My father told me. It was just a sentence.' He paused for a moment: "My darling doesn't love me anymore"'.

Chapter 49: Ghosts

His letters were full of *darlings.* We could step from one *darling* to the next and cover the whole saga. There he was, writing to Annie from his bunk on the ship - *I am just going to turn in & shall think of & pray for my darling until sleep overtakes me* – or rallying her spirits - *Yes my darling I know you must feel very lonely* - or saying how much he loved her letters - *Tis so nice to think that you care for my letters darling - if you only knew how I look for & how much I think of yours.* Or there were the good times that he promised - *I am afraid my darling you must make up your mind to go through your trouble without me. It is hard I know, darling, but you will keep a <u>good heart for my sake.</u> Remember <u>my lips will be devoted to you</u> and we will be happy darling in spite of it all. Well my darling, how is that "Boy" getting on and what are we going to call him?* Then there were his reassurances - *I <u>do</u> believe you darling when you say that you will make me a <u>true good wife -</u>* and the emptiness of his promises - *Never mind darling - if only you care for me a little. It shall be my life's duty to make you forget the past and be happy.* We always thought that he would come back to Annie, but it never happened. He stayed with Agnes. They tested each other, and when Agnes finally left him, he had a last *darling* to spend – *My darling doesn't love me anymore.*

Like the coroner, we could never fathom Gus. Not completely. We had his letters, and the letters of his family, some crew agreements, newspaper reports, photographs, census entries, birth, marriage and death certificates, but it never seemed enough. We always found ourselves wanting more.

We were not the only ones. Beezie mounted her own search. Ever since she was a girl, she had lost contact with her parents. In the 1890s, she had been taken from Irish Mary and left with her grandparents. We knew from the letters that there was a time in the early 1900s when Annie and Gus talked of Beezie. Could she not live with them? Annie would have her baby and then Beezie would join them? They would find a little cottage somewhere and be happy.

When Beezie was a girl and living in Bolam vicarage, she met Cecil Apter, the son of a clergyman. Cecil went off to India and became a tea planter but every now and then he came home to see her. 'Cecil is back again,' his father wrote in September 1920, 'he goes to Scotland tomorrow. On his return, he will spend a few days here, then to London and will then sail for India once more.' In May 1925, Cecil sent a telegram to say he would be arriving the following Saturday, and this time he would stay longer. He and Beezie would be married that summer. Beezie was given away by Robert Edleston because Gus had disappeared, so he missed his daughter's wedding, just as he had missed his father and mother's funerals.

After the wedding, they lived in India. We knew from Annie's letters that Beezie kept in touch and remained a friend. In January 1927, a year after her wedding, she wrote to Annie from India. *My dear Nance,* (her affectionate name for Annie) *I was delighted to have your letter . . . We had a very jolly Xmas, a friend of Cecil on his way to England stayed with us a few days with the aid of a goose and Xmas fare etc. and a few decorations we made Xmas as homey as possible. New Year's (Hogmanay) Eve they had a very swell affair fancy dress dance at the club - I went as a butterfly. Of course, nearly everybody on the district being Scotch - it was some night,*

*believe me? Champagne ad lib etc. We ended up by a leopard being
disrupted on to the ballroom floor. Some people left in their car and
just leaving the polo ground spotted 'Mr Spots', shot him, and
brought him back. How's that for a steady hand at 3 am after a frisky
night! . . . We are having delightful weather, snow on the Himalayas,
bitterly cold mornings and night fires, but just ok in the middle of
the day. I've got a dear little cat and a Belgian hare, great on boxing
. . . Au revoir for now.*

A few years later, her health failed. Perhaps it was this bout of
illness that prompted her to think about the past. Back in the 1890s,
she had been taken from her mother when she was only six, and her
father had disappeared when she was ten, so there were gaps in her
life. When she returned from India, she began searching. We don't
know if she ever found Irish Mary, but she looked for Gus.

By now, it was the early 1930s and Gus had killed himself in
1928, so she missed him by a few years. Still, she came to
Sunderland to see Agnes and Frances. Grace was a little girl at the
time and remembered the day as she opened a box of old photos.

'That's me,' she said, pointing to a little girl behind her
mother's skirt. 'That's Mam, and that's Beezie.'

The photograph showed Beezie and Frances holding hands and
smiling for the camera. Almost as if they were happy.

'Photographs!' Grace snorted, 'I can remember the tension. It
was like this.' She clenched her fists.

Beezie was still in touch with Annie. She knew of her marriage
to Gus, and this of course was dangerous. Here was someone who
not only knew about the marriage, but knew that Annie was still
alive. Agnes would have seen the danger. Her marriage to Gus was
bigamous and Beezie would have known it. She had to warn
Frances.

'And Mom realises that her parents were never properly
married and she's illegitimate!' Pat laughed, and for the first time
she saw how her mother had been haunted. We all looked at the
photograph. Frances and Beezie, holding hands. We could see that

Frances was making every effort to look happy. Agnes was in the background, less inclined to act the part. In the photo, she was skulking in the passage, and in another, she stood for the camera looking tense and belligerent.

'But nothing happened?' I asked. 'The scandal never broke?'

'It blew over.'

Beezie held her tongue. In the fullness of time, she and Cecil retired to Hastings, and she died there in the 1970s.

Frances and Beezie, with Grace looking on.

So the crisis blew over. Frances and Hubert remained in Sunderland. He broke with the Pentecostal Movement, established his own church, and became active in local politics. By the time war broke out, there were three children: Frank, Kirk and Grace. The plan was to evacuate them to Canada, and Frank and Kirk sailed to America in 1940. 'During world War Two,' Dan recounted: 'My Dad was evacuated to Canada to avoid the German bombs which fell in the UK during the Blitz. He never arrived at his destination. The ship he was in was torpedoed 300 miles off Ireland. He and his little brother were forced to abandon the liner as she rolled over and take to a lifeboat. They drifted in the dark night . . . A British destroyer thundered past them. It didn't stop but directed my father and the other children to a nearby oil tanker which at great risk had put its lights on to act as a beacon for the drifting lifeboats. Dad climbed up the side of the tanker on a rope ladder. He was helped aboard by a kindly British sailor, who told him everything would be OK. Dad knew how lucky he had been.'

Dan's father wrote an account of this dramatic night, and it signalled the start of a successful journalistic career. At the end of the war, he remained in Britain and became a well-known Fleet Street journalist, as well as a TV presenter. In the 1980s, he developed an interest in family history and interviewed Hubert. During his searches, he also found Aunt Stella in Blackburn.

'Stella went blind,' Grace said, 'Lost her marbles. She was different from Mom. Totally different. Whenever Mom came to see her, Stella would shout, "I'm not Pentecostal!"'

Stella and Frances remained at odds. Frances did her best to hide the past, to lock it away. Whenever her children asked her about Gus and Agnes, she spun them a fantasy.

'I always pictured Gus as tall and handsome, and dignified,' Pat said, 'Boy! Was I wrong! It would have been better if she could have let it all out, but she couldn't.'

Stella was less worried. She was more than happy to tell Frank every scandal. When they talked, the secrets that Frances was hiding came tumbling out.

'And Frank, your brother, rings your Mam?'

'He rang Mom that night. She had been sick a long time.'

'What happened?'

'He asked her if the stories were true. I don't blame him. I would have done the same.'

'And?'

'She took it badly. That night, she had a stroke. She was paralysed down one side. She never recovered.'

Chapter 50: Armour

The passage and middle room all newly papered. The bed is aired and clean and made up ready . . . Don't you think you could be happy? There is a new moon today and weather forecast on the improve . . . Do buck up and come . . . I shall look for you so don't disappoint and come prepared to stay. Your naughty but loving Peatums

Happiness. It never lasted long, but it came. And it often came in the form of Peatums. We were piecing together Annie's life in the years after Gus and Frank. Gus slipped from her bed in 1902, and Frank died in 1908, but there were forty years left. We wanted to know how she lived them. According to the letters, she took no other lover but contented herself with friends. We spent many happy days reading their letters, fleshing out their characters, letting them talk in our heads.

Peatums was a favourite. We thought it might be a literary reference but nothing confirmed it. A private joke by the look of it. Something that hinted at playfulness and deep affection, and possibly more. *I would like you to come as I need a friend most urgently. I hope to get my furniture over here on Saturday. I have a bed here now & Kitchen table . . . I still cherish a hope of you as a Sister, but you would have to be good to me. I was ill that day I should have visited you. So sorry to disappoint. However, there is plenty of room and affection here for you, whenever you care to come.*

Now Please be ready Tuesday morning, because I am coming Hail rain or snow. Your bed is aired, I have slept in it to ??? warm.

I miss you very much. It seems strange without you . . . Hope you will come for the Harvest Home tomorrow. We could hear the Broadcast of the Big Launch at 2.50 then we could go to the school for tea and concert. I really hope you will come to stay. Could you manage to stay all Winter?

Do please come. It is cosy here. We have a ham, a rabbit and a cake and the Coop have opened a shop at Castleton . . . Don't you think all this really ought to tempt you?

Will you please pack all your things and be ready and I will come for you . . . You can stay here permanently if you like . . . I really need a companion. It is so lonely . . . Boy Scouts Motto - Be Prepared. Now don't keep me waiting or else you will cop it by gum.

'The Nest'

She lived in a place called 'The Nest', somewhere in Danby, a pretty village on the North York Moors, about ten miles from where Annie was now renting rooms. One day, we came across a postcard that Peatums sent to Annie in the mid-1930s; it showed a thatched cottage with a man outside, his back to the wall. It turned out to be 'The Nest'. By the 1930s, thatched cottages like this were becoming tourist attractions, and several of Peatums' friends came to visit. She told Annie how they loved having *tea under a thatched roof*. Annie loved it too: its thatch and stone, its timbers and hollyhocks.

Peatums wanted Annie to stay. She would make up a bed in the kitchen. They would keep the house nice and warm, and they would live together, and soon they would banish loneliness. Annie flirted with the idea, but then worried about her independence. She was insistent on paying her own way, and everyone knew she was prickly. Not to worry, Peatums said, they could agree a rent. Annie said she would think about it.

We came across a newspaper article that Annie kept from 1935. It told the story of a local hero called Jack Mann. There was a photo of Jack, and another of his cottage: 'At Ainthorpe, near Danby, in a quaint old thatched cottage reputed to be 650 years old, built with genuine roof trees and containing an authentic witches' stick, there lives a man who helped make history in that epic of British gallantry at Rorke's Drift in the Zulu War of 1877. He would prefer to be known as No. 1376 of the 24th Foot, 25th Brigade.'

The article went on to recount how Jack joined the Army in the 1870s and served in the Zulu Wars. He loved horses and could handle them, so he acted as a scout. The British Army invaded Zululand in early January 1879, and by January 20th 1879 Jack's brigade came to Isandlwana. They pitched camp, but for reasons best known to themselves they failed to defend it. Two scouting parties were despatched. Jack's party reconnoitred ground, whilst the other party stumbled by chance on the Zulu army of 20,000 men. The Zulus attacked and every man in the brigade was slaughtered. When Jack returned, he surveyed the carnage. The Zulus went on to attack Rorke's Drift, but were repelled by a small garrison, and this became part of imperial folklore. Jack was involved in later campaigns, and at the end of the war was given a medal. According to the newspaper, he now lived in a charming old cottage, a hale and hearty veteran of seventy-eight.

Mr. Mann is out cutting Mr. Pollard's hedge, Peatums told Annie, *Mrs. Davidson paid him that day's work - that accounts for him being Blotto. That's what he does if I go away. So that is how my pleasure is spoilt. But I am determined to give up worrying about him, and I mean to have someone in the house living because it keeps him steadier. If you come in the winter I would not charge you anything for the room.*

In another letter, all her misery spilled out. *He won't come out of the garden or give up hammering about and if anyone tries to stop him then he sets off on tramp or has a round of the pubs. He really is an awful person . . . If I had any money I would go hundreds of miles away. I cannot stick much more of it.*

We thought Peatums and Mr Mann were brother and sister, but soon discovered they were man and wife. Her name was Fanny Caddick and she married Jack Mann in 1921 when they were both in West Yorkshire. Jack was sixty-three and a widower; Peatums thirty-six and a spinster. He worked as a labourer, and she as a nurse, and their marriage looked incongruous.

But Peatums was nothing if not resilient. Her nursing experience gave her a thoroughly jaundiced view of doctors. *I have had a bad attack in my knees,* she wrote, *and had to go to Lord Physic and let him see my legs.* It was one of her favourite jokes. *I have been really ill and Lord Physic honestly will not allow me out at night. Love Peatums.* Her ailments were legion – bad ankles, pleurisy, attacks of influenza, swollen legs and increasingly poor eyesight - *I now have glasses like young telescopes.* Throughout it all, she joked and joshed. *My lameness has kept wonderful & I have even got into Brown Wellington Boots. Some swank.*

We liked her. Her moods were mercurial, her ups and downs as unpredictable as the weather, but she was open and funny and genuinely touching. *The weather is lovely. Yesterday & today is like summer warm and sunny & no wind. Last week we thought we were at the North Pole. Please do come. I shall not lose my temper anymore.*

We saw how they sometimes fell out and stopped talking, but never for long. Tears and apologies followed, and they made up. *I want you to come back to Danby so that I can make amends to you. I shall never really be happy again till you come back. I promise you on my word of Honour. I have determined to pull up and try and regain my old self that people used to love. I shall never be able to thank you enough for helping me to realise where I was drifting . . . I have tried to be brave and keep on top . . . If you could only really believe how much I deeply love you in spite of all my faults.*

Towards the end, Annie seemed to drift like a ghost, wandering from one set of rented rooms to another. There were lots of temporary addresses on old envelopes, and the sheer number seemed to betray her restlessness. After London, she came north, but never settled. Sometimes she would live in Redcar, or talk of living in Redcar, then find cheaper rooms in nearby villages, but none of them pleased her. Finally, she came to Brotton and by now, it was the late 1920s. She rented a room in Days Terrace, better known as 'Piano Row'.

Annie lodged with Sam and Mary Payne. The couple were typical of the folks on 'Piano Row'; respectable types – mining officials, schoolteachers, clerks; people with social aspirations. The Paynes managed to make ends meet by taking in lodgers. Sometimes it might be the manageress of a local drapery, and sometimes a genteel widow like Annie. They did their best to make Annie welcome, but Peatums took against them. *That's why I don't like coming to Brotton,* she said, *there is always something catty. I detest insincere folk.* Yet for all her doubts, Annie stayed with the Paynes for years. We had the letters and postcards to prove it: *Dear Mrs Bowen,* Mrs Payne wrote on holiday, *we shall be at Brotton on Sunday about 2.30 or 3. Can you manage to get me 1pt. of milk on*

Sunday morning or Saturday night & light the fire if you are at home please. Annie's replied on envelope: *In the kitchen is tea laid for you both. I am asked out. Be in before chapel time.*

There came a point in Annie's life when she stopped being Annie and turned into 'Mrs Bowen'. As if she needed armour. Peatums's letters were full of jokes, but she never called Annie by her first name; she always addressed her as *Mrs Bowen*. Annie turned herself into the grieving widow, and people would have looked at Gus's photograph on the mantelpiece. At some point they would have asked about him, and we would have loved to hear her answer.

Mrs Currah was another friend. At one time, she managed a Hydro Establishment in Redcar, and then a reasonably successful restaurant. As late as the 1930s, she was still catering for visitors, but finding it increasingly difficult. People didn't want to stay in old houses anymore, she said. We found a postcard that Annie wrote to her in 1939. *I find that I only have a penny stamp so can't write a letter but want you to know that I have found your eyeglass case. You did rush away on Sunday . . . I had several things I wanted to tell you . . . I wonder if you would be so good as to call at Mrs Dales & ask her to come when able. I should be so much obliged.* Ladies of a certain age and class. Mrs Bowen, Mrs Dales and Mrs Currah. Friends who maintained an air of feminine formality. Walking through life in their armour.

Mrs Dales wrote to Mrs Bowen the next day: *Your friend called to see me last night and brought the postcard you had written to her for me to read.* Annie was looking for rooms. *I went to Newcomen Terrace to see some empty rooms this afternoon. They face the boating pool . . . There is a bathroom and lavatory inside for your use, and there are some people in the next flat below, quiet elderly people.*

None of it mattered. Annie had got wind of something new. Mr and Mrs Patton had bought our house and were looking for a lodger. We found a note written in pencil that seemed to confirm it. The last move that Annie made. The note that brought her here: *Tell Mrs Bowen - Yes she can have the rooms and if she will let me know when she wishes to come I will get them all ready for her. Mrs Patton.*

We were standing in the attic and wondering where Annie slept. It had been a rented flat, and several lodgers had lived here over the years. The wind was getting up and branches tapping at the window.

We were coming to the very end. There was nothing in Annie's papers after 1939. A silence that could only mean one thing. We began searching for any record of her death, and found a woman called Annie Bowen who had died in our area in 1940. The death certificate arrived a few days later. She had died in Mrs Currah's house on the 14th June 1940.

Someone had tried to guess her age. 'About 85 years,' they said, but she was seventy-seven. She died from heart failure brought on by bronchitis, and we remembered her sister who had succumbed to bronchitis all those years before. Annie had suffered the same condition all her life, and there was even a newspaper clipping that she cut out, which advised readers how to suppress a cough in the cinema. The little things that tell you everything.

She died quite suddenly and an inquest was held, but the official records were still closed; another three years would have to elapse before we could see them. Local newspapers said nothing. An elderly lady dying in Redcar during the Second World war was hardly newsworthy.

And this is how it ends.

But at least we found her, and she had found us.

After Annie's death, Mrs Patton opened the door to Annie's bedroom and stood in the gloom. Facing the silence. The task of clearing her away. Everything to be swept from the mantelpiece. Everything to be lifted from the drawers. All trace of Annie removed. Her letters, souvenirs, photographs, all gathered up and bundled away. The room made ready.

She must have climbed the stairs, opened that little door in the attic, and pushed them through.

'They'll be safe there,' she probably said, wiping the dust from her apron, 'Somebody will collect them.'

Chapter 51: Annie

One Sunday there was a knock on our door. When I opened it, there were two men standing on the front steps, looking rather sheepish.

'I'm sorry to disturb you,' the older one said, 'but we were passing and my son thought I should call.'

I smiled and nodded.

'I didn't think we should descend on you like this,' he laughed, 'but he badgered me.' He pointed to his son. 'By the way, I'm Mr Patton,' and held out his hand. 'I used to live here, but I've never been back since I was a boy. I was wondering if we might look round, just for old time's sake? Would it be asking too much?'

Gill joined me. 'This is Mr Patton,' I said, accepting his handshake, 'He used to live here.'

All his childhood and teenage years had been spent in our house, but he had never returned after his parents left in the 1950s. We gave him a tour, and everywhere we went, he told us stories. On the first-floor, he pointed to a bedroom where he smuggled in girlfriends. When we finally reached the attic, he remembered constructing a full-size motorcycle there. 'I built it from scratch,' he said proudly, 'but couldn't get it down the stairs.'

At the end of the tour, we sat in the living room and carried on talking.

'So you were living here in 1939?' I said, making sure of my ground.

'Yes, when the war started. I used to climb the trees, out there in the front garden.' He pointed through the sash windows to the beech trees. 'Right up as far as I could go. They gave me a grandstand view of the raids.'

'Did your mother and father have lodgers?'

He turned and stared, his face blank. 'I'm sorry,' he said, 'I was miles away. Lodgers? Yes, we had a few.'

I took a deep breath, 'You don't by any chance remember an older woman coming here, just before the war?'

'Mrs Bowen? She used to have the room upstairs.' He looked at the ceiling above us and rolled his eyes, almost as if she was there.

'The church bedroom?' I laughed. 'It's our bedroom.'

'We gave her the best room.' He stopped for a moment and then leaned closer, 'And I'll tell you something. She used to cook her breakfast up there, and it was always bloody kippers!'

We began telling him about our discoveries, and then suggested he might like to look at Annie's photos.

'Hardly any of these have names,' I said, as I placed the old shoe box gently on my lap, 'but I wonder if you can recognise her?'

One by one, I lifted the photographs.

'No,' he said, 'that's not her.'

'This . . ?'

'No.'

'What about this?'

'No.'

All of them. The full set – a hundred and thirty, one after the other. None of them were her. He began to tire of the game and our hearts sank. If there was one man in God's creation who could point to Annie and say, 'That's her!', he was sitting in our living room on this Sunday afternoon, with the light fading.

'We'll have to be going,' his son said, looking at his watch.

At the bottom of the box there was a contact print. A woman was walking along a sunny street in the 1930s, and someone had printed 'Walking Pictures' on the back.

'I think this is one of those pictures from seaside promenades,' I said, and handed it over. 'They would take your photo . . .'

'That's her!' he laughed.

The clock stopped. Time seemed to lose its footing.

'It's her,' he said, 'It's her! She wore that fox-fur all the time!'

I glanced at his son. He was smiling. A quiet magic filling the room.

'Walking Pictures: Annie in Redcar, 1930s

'Walking Pictures'. A fast-exposure camera from the 1930s. A snapshot that seemed to catch Annie off guard. Later that night, we scanned the photo. She had spotted the photographer and was staring back. There was no smile. Just a frosty look. A last-minute glance. The day was obviously sunny, yet she was wearing her overcoat and fur collar, her black hat and leather gloves. Her favourite suit of armour.

We tried to match it with the other photographs. There was an attractive woman from the Edwardian years who seemed to fit. The years of Gus and Frank, of Craufurd and Hannah, Bro and Emily, Ted and Liebe. Whenever I gave a talk, I would show this photograph to my audience and say, 'If you have any doubts, keep them to yourselves. This is the Annie of my imagination.'

Annie as a young woman?

The 1930's photo had been taken in Redcar. We found other images that helped identify the spot. It turned out that Annie was passing Taylor's drapery in the High Street. A few feet on, she was coming to the Golden Lion Hotel, and here the photographer caught her.

A sunny day. Canvass blinds out. Across the street, a stylish young woman was glancing at a shop window. In the distance, small groups of people were sauntering along the pavement. A car was baking in the heat.

And here was Annie. Large as life. Coming towards us.

It took me a while to notice it, but once I did, I couldn't help but smile. For a few moments, I relished the detail without saying anything, but then I touched Gill's arm. 'Look,' I said, 'she's got a letter in her pocket.'

***

ABOUT TONY NICHOLSON

Formerly a history lecturer, Tony is now 'retired' and spends his time researching, writing and giving talks. (With a good deal of gardening, walking and pottering about thrown in for good measure). He still lives in the old house that is featured in this book.

You can follow him at - http://tonynicholsonbooks.com

Here, you'll find lots more about the story, including images and sources, as well as sections on its enduring mysteries.

ACKNOWLEDGMENTS

Many people helped in the making of this book.

The key players are featured in the story itself - Cindy Hatchett in South Africa; Pat Tibbs in America; Grace Zimmerman, Bill Richardson, Colin Shortis, Kate Arscott, Dan Entwisle and Mr Patton in England; Patti and Kim Bergh in Canada; Gill at home.

Thanks too to Christine Richardson, Alison Richardson and Evan Hadkins in Australia; Pat Pytcher and Lady Cubbon in England; Darcy Zimmerman in America.

Other people guided me through the key areas: Mick Stowe, Belinda and Bill Goyder, Jean and David Marsh were my trusted guides in Gainford and Bolam; Dave Day kept me afloat in Victorian swimming pools; his partner, Margaret, found Gus's army record; Allan Seaton provided Craufurd's watercolour of Pear Tree Cottage; Kevin Asplin found Gus's papers from the Boer War; Chris Patton runs the Ruhleben website and acted as an important go-between; 'The Great War Forum' did its best to track Gus in WW1; Peter Appleton offered insights into Gus's army photograph; Charles McNab, Sue Stahl and others chased information in Darlington; Tanya McDonald dug out endless crew agreements in Newfoundland; Diana Rushton helped in Blackburn; Barb Collins and Jean Henry in Canada; Robyn Drury in lots of ways.

Online sources have been invaluable. Particular thanks to The British Newspaper Archive; Periodicals Archive Online; British Periodicals Collection; Times Digital Archive; Ancestry; The Internet Archive, Bibliography of British and Irish History; House of Commons Parliamentary Papers; Illustrated London News Archive; Historical Texts.

The following libraries and archives were used – Teesside Archives; Durham County Record Office; North Riding Country Record Office; Darlington Centre for Local Studies; The National Archives; the Maritime Archives and Library at Merseyside Maritime Museum; the National Maritime Museum; The British Library; Wisbech & Fenland Museum; Stranraer Library; Bolton Library and Museum Services; Manchester Central Library; Leeds University Library.

Bob, my son, is a historian. He has provided me with many valuable ideas and helped bring the book to fruition. Working with him is a joy.

Finally, I would like to thank everyone who attended my 'Secrets of the Attic' talks over the years, and offered encouragement and insights.

Lightning Source UK Ltd.
Milton Keynes UK
UKHW02f1605141217
314459UK00007B/172/P